# POETS AND THEIR ART

## OTHER BOOKS BY THE AUTHOR

*Valeria and Other Poems*
*The Columbian Ode*
*John Wellborn Root: A Memoir*
*The Passing Show: Five Modern Plays in Verse*
*You and I*
*The Difference and Other Poems: Including the Columbian Ode*

# POETS & THEIR ART

## BY HARRIET MONROE

*New Edition, Revised
and Enlarged*

## THE MACMILLAN COMPANY

PUBLISHERS     -     NEW YORK

1932

PRINTED IN THE UNITED STATES OF AMERICA
BY THE CORNWALL PRESS, INC.

*To*
*Marion Strobel Mitchell—*
*poet, friend and fellow-editor*

FOIOA

# CONTENTS

[ vii ]

# Contents

FOR permission to use most of the rather brief essays in this volume the author hereby acknowledges her indebtedness to herself as the editor of *Poetry,* in which periodical they first appeared, sometimes in slightly different form; the two exceptions being *Contemporaneousness,* first printed in the *Atlantic,* and the final article on *The Free Verse Movement,* taken from a longer one in the *English Journal.* To the editors of these two magazines, much thanks from a fellow-editor.

*Poetry* having been the first and most persistent of the now numerous small American magazines devoted to the art, and having had the honor of introducing many poets now famous, it may be opportune to record here briefly the story of its origin, especially as a few inaccurate accounts have been printed during the past decade.

In 1911, after a vacation trip around the world, the author's chief occupation was serving as art critic on the Chicago *Tribune.* The constant recording of highly endowed exhibitions, prizes and scholarships in the arts of painting, sculpture and architecture, which were backed by powerful trustees and committees in all our larger cities, made her realize that poetry alone was left to shift for itself, and that its desperate situation at the time was largely due to this neglect. The art needed a friendly hand, and the author, casting about for some efficient protest, was hit in the head one sunny morning with the idea of starting a magazine which would serve as its organ.

Financing such an unheard-of experiment was the first obstacle, but a conversation with Mr. H. C. Chatfield-Taylor—novelist, historian and lover of the arts, who was always friendly to rash hopes—made a solution seem not impossible. Mr. Chatfield-Taylor agreed that the situation was deplorable and something should be done. He approved the author's idea of a magazine, and thought she could get an hundred venturesome spirits to pledge fifty dollars a year for five years toward the poets' organ. And he testified to his faith by offering to head the list.

During the following year the author devoted her spare time to this quest, and found it easier than she had expected. The men and women of might and millions whom she interviewed were usually friendly and rarely amused, and some of them gave her back her arguments more eloquently than she herself could state them. By midsummer of 1912 nearly six thousand a year had been pledged for five years, and it was time to begin the next chapter by summoning the poets.

It was almost a holiday game to go over the magazines of the previous five years, and concoct a circular to be sent to the more interesting of the poets there in evidence. The author sent these circulars, with letters, to—among others—Ezra Pound, whom Elkin Mathews had lauded to her two years before in London; to Vachel Lindsay, whose articles about trading rhymes for bread she had read in a summer magazine; to Amy Lowell, from whom a sonnet or two had appeared in the *Atlantic;* to Arthur Ficke and Witter Bynner, to John G. Neihardt and George Sterling and Allen Upward, to Agnes Lee and

Alice Meynell—to more than may here be mentioned. All these replied generously: Lindsay sent *General Booth,* Ficke sent the double sonnet on *Poetry* which led off the magazine's first number; and Ezra Pound, with a generous alacrity which the author will never forget, sent not only himself, but Tagore and the Imagists, offering moreover to keep the magazine "in touch with whatever is most dynamic in artistic thought" in London and even Paris.

A sentence or two from that first letter of Mr. Pound's may be quoted here as still pertinent:

> Can you teach the American poet that poetry *is* an *art,* an art with a technique, with media, an art that must be in constant flux—a constant change of manner —if it is to live? Can you teach him that it is not a pentametric echo of the sociological dogma printed in last year's magazines?

Thus far the editor had proceeded alone. But returning to town in early September after a month in the northern Wisconsin woods, she engaged an office in Cass Street, and asked Alice Corbin Henderson to serve as associate editor and be "first reader" of manuscripts which were already beginning to come in. And when Henry B. Fuller, Edith Wyatt and H. C. Chatfield-Taylor consented to act as an advisory committee, the editorial staff was complete.

The first weeks—indeed, the first year or two—were a continual excitement; and as the author looks over those early volumes of the magazine it is still interesting to note the names of many poets then unknown who are now famous, and to read the "first editions" of poems now quoted far and wide. *General Booth,* the *Gitanjali,*

[ xi ]

Joyce Kilmer's *Trees,* Rupert Brooke's war sonnets, Helen Hoyt's *Ellis Park,* Carl Sandburg's *Chicago,* Sara Teasdale's *Love Songs,* Edgar Lee Masters' *Silence,*— these are but a few of the poems now familiar on the lips of the world.

This book, while not a record of *Poetry's* adventures, necessarily reflects some aspects of its editor's experience. The experience has been illuminating in many unexpected ways. Writers of verse good, bad and indifferent, have called in person or by letter to the number of many thousands, convincing the editor, through countless comedies and tragedies of acceptance and rejection, that she was "dealing with naked souls." Although it is the function of poets to tell their secrets on the printed page, those who never get so far as print are perhaps the most confessional of all, and their letters, illuminating pitiful life-histories, are often extremely moving.

*Chicago: Feb. 1st, 1926.*


In the present edition of this book, a few new essays have been added in the first section, and others revised to cover work accomplished wholly or chiefly since 1925. But when the later work of a poet does not materially change the essayist's estimate of his general quality, or modify the symmetry of his career, the essay remains unaltered from the first edition.

In the third section, one essay has been added, *Memories of Vachel Lindsay.*

*Chicago: May 1st, 1932.*

## POETS OF TODAY

*Edwin Arlington Robinson*
*Ezra Pound*
*Vachel Lindsay*
*Carl Sandburg*
*Wallace Stevens*
*Edgar Lee Masters*
*Robert Frost*
*Edna St. Vincent Millay*
*Sara Teasdale*
*Amy Lowell*
*John Gould Fletcher*
*H. D.*
*T. S. Eliot*
*Elinor Wylie*
*Archibald MacLeish*
*Lew Sarett*
*Maxwell Bodenheim*
*Marjorie Allen Seiffert*
*Alfred Kreymborg*
*Voices of Women*

## EDWIN ARLINGTON ROBINSON

IT must have been about twenty years ago, one summer in Cornish, New Hampshire, that William Vaughn Moody introduced me to his friend Robinson. "He's a mighty good poet," Moody had told me beforehand; "very simple bare style—you must read *Captain Craig.*"

At that time I had never heard of Robinson, and the few words exchanged in our casual meeting did not reveal very much of a personality always singularly reticent. But I bought and read the *Captain Craig* volume and whatever else I could get hold of, and relished the nutty flavor of an original mind, the meaty richness of a poetic product sharply individual, and different from early or late Victorians, from the Celtic group, from the *fin-de-siècle* poets of the nineties, and even from the other two of the trio of intimate friends—Moody himself and Ridgeley Torrence.

Robinson had few readers in those days, but, few or many, he was ascetically vowed to the art. He is one of the few American poets who have accepted such meagre terms as the muse offered and made little further effort to earn a living. What this meant for twenty or thirty years no one has ever learned, or is ever likely to learn, from the poet himself. President Roosevelt, becoming aware of the man's work, tried to help him out financially through an appointment in the New York custom-house. But he struck a rock-ribbed obstinate character—Robin-

[ 1 ]

son did not like the routine, and he would not take the government's salary without doing its work. Neither sinecure nor desk-slavery for him, so he resigned after a brief trial, and persisted in the path he had chosen. And it took the laggard world a long time to come his way, in spite of the publicity attending the presidential pass-word.

In reading Robinson's *Collected Poems* in chronological order, one notes a gradual and sure development. It begins with *The Children of the Night*, poems of 1890-97. Here one finds no juvenilia—neither immature thinking nor faulty workmanship. To be sure, the poet tries ballades and villanelles, though hardly in the gay tempo of the Austin-Dobson fashion of the hour. And he offers many sonnets—a more enduring fashion, always with a firm touch on the form and with an eye for

> The perfect word that is the poet's wand.

With sonnet-like compactness he writes *Richard Cory,* one of the first, and still one of the best, of his numerous studies of tragic incongruities in human character. And in a number of poems he sounds the key-note of his austere philosophy; this *Credo* of his youth, for example, contains the germ of his later thinking, except that the assertion with which it closes would today be a question:

> I cannot find my way: there is no star
> In all the shrouded heavens anywhere;
> And there is not a whisper in the air
> Of any living voice, but one so far
> That I can hear it only as a bar
> Of lost imperial music, played when fair
> And angel fingers wove, and unaware,
> Dead leaves to garlands where no roses are.
>
> No, there is not a glimmer nor a call
> For one that welcomes, welcomes when he fears,

> The black and awful chaos of the night.
> For through it all—above, beyond it all—
> I know the far-sent message of the years,
> I feel the coming glory of the Light.

No facile faith could satisfy this poet—it is a stern spiritual discipline which he has accepted through the years, one not always relieved even by that remote vision of "the coming glory of the Light." But though the Puritan God of his fathers is never personally in evidence, we feel in Robinson's make-up something akin to him—an outreaching toward his implacable austerity and blinding majesty through orbit on orbit of modern discovery and thought.

In this keynote volume the memorable poems are all brief, and, except *Cory* and one or two others, are in sonnet form—*Cliff Klingenhagen, Amaryllis, Calvary* and *Verlaine,* besides the *Credo.* In these, and more emphatically in the long narratives of his second volume, it became evident that Robinson was chiefly interested in some of the less obvious aspects of human psychology—one might almost say the psychology of failure; and that he brought to bear upon this fascinating study a keenly sympathetic mind moved by wonder and awe, and lit by a somewhat acrid humor. The heart-motive was there also, but emotion was held in stern control—the intellect had to authenticate it. The long narrative *Captain Craig* was frankly an intimate study of a human derelict, one whose philosophy was staunch enough to win for his old age a dignified and self-respecting exit, and the blaring triumph of a brass-band funeral: the first entry—this poem—of a series of spiritual biographies whose latest magnificent number is *The Man Who Died Twice.*

If Robinson had been deflected from his purpose by the lack of response to his first two books, we should have had the imprint of an exceptional mind in a few memorable poems, but we should hardly have suspected the new poet's range and power. Between the *Captain Craig* volume and *The Town Down the River* he allowed himself eight years of maturing thought and developing art. The opening poem in this third venture, *The Master*, which is second only to Whitman's grand elegy among the numerous poems in praise of Lincoln, struck the strongest chord he had as yet sounded. A great soul is a more difficult subject than a small one, and this is a profoundly adequate study of the man who

> Was elemental when he died,
> As he was ancient at his birth.

Six years later, in 1916, Robinson put out *The Man Against the Sky,* in 1917 *Merlin,* in 1920 *Lancelot* and *The Three Taverns;* in 1921-24 the series of long narratives *Avon's Harvest* (this with shorter poems), *Roman Bartholow,* and *The Man Who Died Twice;* and in 1925 *Dionysus in Doubt.*

If the psychology of failure, or of that uncertain middle ground between spiritual success and failure, is Robinson's recurrent motive, it may be interesting to study his attitude and his methods in presenting that motive in art. It is heroic, not ignoble, struggle that engages him, or if not heroic, at least the struggle of highly strung sensitive souls to fulfil their manifest destiny; ending either in acceptance of compromise, or in tragic spiritual revolt that induces some kind of dark eclipse. The form is usually narrative, with the poet as the narrator, under some assumption of friendship or at least neighborliness;

but in the longer poems we have, as a rule, monologue and dialogue, the characters unfolding their perplexities, or recording their action upon each other, in long speeches which are not talk, as talk actually ever was or could be, but which are talk intensified into an extra-luminous self-revelation; as if an X-ray, turned into the suffering soul, made clear its hidden structural mysteries.

Robinson's method is thus akin to that of the psycho-analyst who encourages confessional monologue, or uses dialogue, as a probe to strike through the poison of lies and appearances and reveal the truth. When this poet has done with his characters—with Captain Craig, or Gabrielle Barthalow, or Avon, or "the man who died twice," or even Shakespeare—there is nothing to do but pass them on to the Angel with the Flaming Sword, for as far as earth has power to strip them bare they stand naked in tragic beauty before us.

Sometimes he uses his method with almost bitter brevity, as in *Richard Cory, John Gorham, Another Dark Lady, Lorraine, Clavering,* and certain sonnets of marital discord; but brevity which nearly always heightens the dramatic effect. Again he pushes it to the other extreme of too detailed analysis in speeches of too great length. The first long narrative, *Captain Craig,* would gain by compression; and one of the latest, *Roman Barthalow,* becomes prolix in the person of Penn Raven, who is allowed to absorb three hundred lines in five or six too explanatory and expository speeches, following the catastrophe and blurring its sharp agony with words.

Perhaps the temptation to excess is strongest in the two legendary poems *Merlin* and *Lancelot;* here it is emphasized by the academic traditions of conventionalized archaistic speech. Not that Robinson adopts an archaic style, or forswears all modern significance, in his use of the perpetually typical old tales; but to me at least his modern instinct and habit of mind seem out of place in Camelot, as if a tweed-suited and felt-hatted American were trying to possess the Vatican gardens and the Borgian suite of Pinturicchio-decorated chambers. I find him more at home in America, where the endless war between man and fate goes on as relentlessly as in mediaeval Camelot or ancient Thebes, and where his intuitive and searching mind finds no lack of subjects. Here his art is, beyond dispute, authentic and authoritative.

However, I would not exclude from my list of favorites at least two of this poet's eight or ten studies of famous men. Not *The Three Taverns*—I don't feel very close to Saint Paul in that; nor does Napoleon tell his secret in *The Island;* and even Roosevelt does not quite come alive in *The Revealer.* Rembrandt and John Brown both talk too explicitly to be quite in character, though the latter's last word is worth all the rest—that superb line,

I shall have more to say when I am dead.

But *The Master* is a masterpiece, and I am almost ready to say as much for Ben Jonson's monologue about his friend Shakespeare. At least I feel in this poem a close approach to the very man; not quite the whole story, perhaps, but a true hint toward the greatness and weakness of that enigmatic and fascinating character who told everybody's story but his own.

To return to the poet's neighbors: I have mentioned a few of the sonnets and other brief poems which portray some of them—sketches as powerful as a Zorn etching.

Somewhat more detailed are poems like *Flammonde,*
*Llewellyn and the Tree, Isaac and Archibald, Aunt Isa-*
*bel,* and the exquisitely tender and beautiful *Mr. Flood's*
*Party.* In all these—and certain others—one feels a
gleam of light into hidden places of living and individual
human souls.

In a few poems he studies his fellow-countrymen in
the mass, in a mood satirical, philosophical or even
prophetic. Cassandra utters a solemn warning:

> Are you to pay for what you have
> With all you are?

is a question which strikes to the heart of our too glib and
facile democracy. *Demos* gives the born aristocrat's
answer:

> The few shall save
> The many, or the many are to fall—
> Still to be wrangling in a noisy grave.

And in the recently published *Dionysus in Doubt,* the
satirical mood become almost banter as the "ivy-crowned"
god, whom prohibition would banish, questions the poet-
citizen

> Of an inflexible and hasty nation
> That sees already done
> Rather too much that has not yet begun.

As the poem goes on, the god's banter searches bitter
depths of our "herd-servitudes," lashes our "beneficent
severities" that try

> To moronize the million for the few.

We are reminded that

> An ultimate uniformity enthroned
> May trim your vision very well;
> And the poor cringing self, disowned,

> May call it freedom and efficiency.
> Others would somewhat rather call it hell.

In *The Town Down the River* we have a more solemnly portentous utterance: the poet's challenge to life, and life's indifference to his challenge, its persistence in its course. The young, the mature, the old, "plodding forward from afar," answer the scorn of the Watcher by the Way with protests against his efforts to stop them; until the Watcher himself is reconciled to the eternal movement of the race toward the mysterious city of hope:

> "Hark," said one; "I hear the River
> Calling always, night and day."
> "Forward then—the lights are shining,"
> Said the Watcher by the Way.

Of these few meditative poems—personal unfoldings of the poet's philosophy—*The Man Against the Sky* is the most important. The poem is a question, not an answer:

> Where was he going, this man against the sky?
> You know not, nor do I.

An "orient Word that will not be erased" is as far as Robinson can go toward hope. And it is not very far from despair:

> And all for what, the devil only knows!

he cries; and at last sums up man's protest in the bitter query,

> If after all that we have lived and thought,
> All comes to Naught—
> If there be nothing after Now,
> And we be nothing anyhow,
> And we know that—why live?

Robinson's more recent long narratives in blank verse, *Avon's Harvest* and *Roman Barthalow,* lead up to the

[ 8 ]

finest of all, *The Man Who Died Twice.* *Avon's Harvest* is a weird, almost pathological confession of a haunted soul, destroyed by over-sensitive brooding which leads to mania and death. *Roman Barthalow* involves three characters. Of these one, the titular hero and husband, comes alive after years of slow petrifaction and plucks what promises to be a new life out of the dead stump of the old. The second, the "resident saviour" who startles into sudden energy the two dead souls of husband and wife, carries his ineffable self away, none the worse, after the catastrophe and too many pages of dissertation. The third and most interesting, Gabrielle the wife, who has gone dead through pride, fear of life, intellectual aloofness and the shunning of emotion, cannot endure the sudden fierce revelation of her own spiritual demise, and drowns herself in order to die indeed: a marvellous study, this, of the over-protected and exacting woman whose too-beautiful mind and body demand the impossible and accept nothing short of the demand.

The latest of these soul-biographies, *The Man Who Died Twice,* seems to me Robinson's masterpiece in that kind. It is the record of a great soul, self-ruined and self-betrayed. Fernando Nash, born to be of the line of Bach and Beethoven, the man of genius who never fulfilled his genius, is a grand figure in his ruin, and in honor of his tragic agony the poet tolls deep bells and beats muffled drums. The solemn fall of the lines strikes on the heart like the slow march of a regiment passing with dirges to a hero's burial. It is quite wonderful what the poet has done with his simple instrument of blank verse, piling up splendid chords that seem to reverbrate through cathedral aisles as he records disaster.

The grim sardonic humor of the hero's fall—

> This foiled initiate who had seen and felt
> Meanwhile the living fire,

discovered beating a street brawl of salvation drums—
there is something modern and American and democrat-
ically grotesque about this kind of tragedy, as truth itself
is grotesque in its ruthless disregard of grace. But because the man does not lie to himself, he plucks a kind of
triumph out of failure:

> God was good
> To give my soul to me before I died
> Entirely, and He was no more than just
> In taking all the rest away from me;
> I had it, and I knew it, and I failed Him.
> I did not wait.

So he comes alive again before his final death:

> And a vast joy . . .
> Told him, in silence that was more than speech,
> That after passion, arrogance and ambition,
> Doubt, fear, defeat, sorrow and desperation,
> He had wrought out of martyrdom the peace
> That passeth understanding.

The poem is itself a symphony. Never has Robinson
rolled out such magnificent harmonies as in the superb
climax of this poem. His art, matured and disciplined,
has risen to a great universal theme—for there is no such
thing as success, and failure is the lot of all, the soul's
dignity being measured by the grandeur of its failure
rather than by the littleness of its achievement.

No doubt the poet, in spite of the hard battle he has
fought and the victory he has won, felt autobiographic

significance in certain lines. One may say of him, as he of his battered hero,

> There was in the man,
> With all his frailties and extravagances,
> The caste of an inviolate distinction
> That was to break and vanish only in fire
> When other fires that had so long consumed him
> Could find no more to burn. And there was in him
> A giant's privacy of lone communion
> With older giants who had made a music
> Whereof the world was not impossibly
> Not the last note. And there was in him always,
> Unqualified by guile, and unsubdued
> By failure and remorse or by redemption,
> The grim nostalgic passion of the great
> For glory all but theirs.

A few years ago we were all congratulating Mr. Robinson on his jubilee. The tribute of Edgar Lee Masters ended as follows:

> As a craftsman he is a master, as a thinker he is subtle and original, as an artist he has kept the faith. The poets of America look to him, now that he is at the meridian of his career, to fight on in the war of spiritualizing America, since he has inherited this day of hope after a beginning that did not bring adequate reward.

Somewhat shy and aloof, haughtily austere in thought and manner of life, imaginatively observant, impassioned like tempered steel, Mr. Robinson stands today, as in his more obscure yesterdays, adequate, uncompromising, a big man, a thorough and keen-visioned artist.

Someone has called him "the proudest figure in American letters." At least he led the modern procession for his countrymen; wilful and self-advised, he struck his own path, and found, no doubt with surprise, that he had blazed a trail for others.

THE name evokes memories. First, of being in London in 1910 on my way around the world to Peking; and of hearing about this young American from Elkin Mathews, his first publisher; and of carrying *Personae* away with me, and breathing the book's perfume on the long Siberian journey. Second, two years later, in the summer of 1912, memories of writing to this poet about my hazardous project for starting a magazine, a poets' own organ; and of his encouraging reply, his generous and enthusiastic promise of co-operation; and of the imagistic poems he sent, his own and others; and of the gay and peremptory and violent letters, the vivid and slashing articles, the loud praises and protests—of all the sharp flashes from that very live wire, our foreign correspondent. And then, early in 1914, came crimson-covered *Blast* across the sea, the eclipse of Imagism in Vorticism—*Blast,* the enormous magazine which cried out for "necessary blizzards," and was answered, with miraculous exactness, by the War. And after the War's near-eclipse of everything else through that tragic time, even of Ezra Pound's stormy energies, and after a few quieter separating years, there is that memory of our first meeting in Paris during the summer of 1923, when the fierce poet-revolutionist proved to be the mildest-mannered man who ever scuttled a Victorian ship, the very soul of courtesy and kindness. Indeed, so many and such personal memories are evoked that it is difficult to write about this poet with that ruthless detachment required by the high standards of impartial criticism.

At the time of that Siberian reading of *Personae* and *Exultations* I knew nothing of Mr. Pound's dynamic personality; so the impassioned beauty of his poems—their strange new insinuating rhythms, their half-interval cadences, their Debussy-like under-tones and over-tones— seemed to come out of the air, from some presence disembodied, impassioned, tense and sure.

> As bright white drops upon a leaden sea,
> Grant so my songs to this grey folk may be!

sang the poet in his opening *Grace before Song;* and the poems that followed had the crystal clarity and iridescent gleam of dew-drops in the morning sun. As Mr. Mathews had said, they were "pure poetry," with no dusty alloy of baser motive than the sheer command of the muse.

Re-reading those early poems now, after fifteen years of close attendance upon modern poets, I feel once more that old appeal of strangeness and beauty—"for there is no excellent beauty without strangeness." Later experimenters have not reiterated Pound's special magic, newer singers have not sung his tune. *La Fraisne,* with its quiet and perfect measures carrying the wistful wisdom of old age; *Night Litany,* weighted with the wonder of Venice; the slim whiteness of *N. Y.;* the swift speed of *The Return;* the splendid wave-pounding of *The Seafarer,* best translation ever made from Anglo-Saxon; and especially one of the noblest of all Christ poems, *The Ballad of the Goodly Fere*: all these keep their power and their surprise for me, as well as the haunting beauty of their music.

It was somewhat a twelfth-century revival, that music. Ezra Pound's early poems, after the rich orchestration of centuries of English poetry, sound to our inner ear like Palestrina after Wagner, Schubert, Beethoven. Their wayward cadences owe something, of course, to the Provençal poets whom he had so closely studied, something to Villon, something to Yeats. They recapture primitive simplicities and discard efficient regularities. They play with rhyme or not, they keep time with metrics or not, but always they follow their own wilful way and ride the changing winds of mood as lightly as a swallow.

The same wayward beauty inspires many of the songs in *Lustra*, published in London in 1916, most of which passed through my hands to the first printing. The motive here is more audacious, indeed often satiric; the music more emphatic for either gay or serious emotion, with less of the Provençal plaintiveness. To the early readers of *Poetry* these poems seemed to usher in an almost anarchistic revolution in the art; but today, after a surfeit of free and freer verse, of gymnastic experiment in poetic motive, rhythm, typography, we read them with as matter-of-course acceptance of their method as of Shelley's or Swinburne's. And in many of them we feel a surer, though often wilder, strain of the *Personae* harmonies. Such poems as *The Garret, The Choice, The Garden, Ortus, Preference, Fish and the Shadow,* the poignant third part of *Near Perigord,* the high-comedy-perfect *Villanelle: The Psychological Hour*—these and others are exquisitely wrought, with added assurance, in a method that rounds out and completes, sometimes with even keener beauty, the earlier experiments.

*Dance Figure,* for example, has the fragile loveliness of old Venetian glass:

Dark-eyed,
O woman of my dreams,
Ivory-sandaled,
There is none like thee among the dancers,
None with swift feet.

I have not found thee in the tents,
In the broken darkness.
I have not found thee at the well-head
Among the women with pitchers.
Thine arms are as a young sapling under the bark;
Thy face as a river with lights.

White as an almond are thy shoulders;
As new almonds stripped from the husk.

They guard thee not with eunuchs;
Not with bars of copper.
Gilt turquoise and silver are in the place of thy rest.
A brown robe, with threads of gold woven in patterns, hast
    thou gathered about thee,
O Nathat-Ikanaie, "Tree-at-the-river."

As a rillet among the sedge are thy hands upon me;
Thy fingers a frosted stream.

Thy maidens are white like pebbles;
Their music about thee—

There is none like thee among the dancers;
None with swift feet.

Other poems in this book were, of course, a deliberate satiric challenge. It began, for example, with *Tenzone:*

Will people accept them—
    (i. e., these songs)?
As a timorous wench from a centaur
    (or a centurion),
Already they flee, howling in terror.

[ 15 ]

Will they be touched with the verisimilitudes?
    Their virgin stupidity is untemptable.
I beg you, my friendly critics,
Do not set about to procure me an audience.

I mate with my free kind upon the crags.
    The hidden recesses
Have heard the echo of my heels,
    in the cool light,
      in the darkness.

    This challenge the poet repeated, sometimes even more impudently, in *Salutation, Further Instructions, Salvationists,* etc.; and with more confessional feeling in his *Pact* (with Walt Whitman), and in his consolatory advice to *The Rest:*

O helpless few in my country,
O remnant enslaved!

Artists broken against her,
Astray, lost in the villages,
Mistrusted, spoken-against;

Lovers of beauty, starved,
Thwarted with systems,
Helpless against the control;

You who cannot wear yourselves out
By persisting to successes,
You who can only speak,
Who cannot steel yourselves into reiteration;

You of the finer sense
Broken against false knowledge,
You who can know at first hand,
Hated, shut in, mistrusted:

Take thought—
I have weathered the storm,
I have beaten out my exile.

    The effect of the challenge, when it was first uttered in 1913, and re-enforced by other poets of the imagist group, was immediate and dynamic. It was due more to Ezra Pound than to any other person that "the revolution" or "the renaissance," or whatever one chooses to call the freer modern impulse in poetry, was on. Thus, without slurring the quality of his poetry, one may admit that most people who have watched the course of this impulse think of Ezra Pound first as a force. If, as Carl Sandburg said in a study of his work, "he has done most of living men to incite new impulses in poetry," the reason is not only the lithe impassioned *insouciance* of his verse, but still more the ardent professorial rage in him—the love of stirring up and leading forth other minds. There are many so-called educators in our over-instructed world, but few inspired teachers. Ezra Pound is one of the few, and that college in Indiana which once let him go from its faculty must have made the gods weep for its blunder.

Its blunder, but not ours. For the instinct of a great teacher was released from contact with undergraduates and applied to the vivifying of a sleeping art. His method has been fiercely destructive of rooted prejudices, but magically encouraging to every green shoot of new growth. His mind, being imaginatively creative, presented example as well as precept, offered beautiful poems to the world. But not all his work could be printed in books; he must make these books seed the future, he must found a school. So inevitably he gathered a group of poets around him, and reached out through them to ever widening areas of influence; until today there is no one writing the poetry of this age and the next who has not, consciously or not, felt the impact of his mind.

It is this sheer power which made him, to quote Sandburg again, "the best man writing poetry today"—the best man in the pugilistic sense of utter prowess, in not only writing poetry but making it effective and powerful by ramming it down people's throats. Today *Salutation, Further Instructions,* etc., having done their work, have lost some of their force; the modern undergraduate, probably, can hardly understand the excitement they aroused —the dust of ages, or at least of decades, which they shook into the startled air. But the modern undergraduate owes to them, for the clearer air he breathes, more than he will ever realize.

Part of Ezra Pound's passion of revolt against Victorian excesses came, as I have hinted, from his study of foreign poetry, especially the light-winged lyrics of mediaeval Provence. Thus translations—from Provençal, early Italian, Latin of the decadence, even Chinese (through Fenollosa et al.)—have gone hand in hand with his own work and have shared its personal and original tang. There be scholars, specialists in these various literatures, who question his competence as a translator; indeed, Professor Hale made out an extremely good case in a certain memorable controversy about the Propertius series. But although Mr. Pound seems proved an inexact Latinist, and for aught I know may be, to a less flagrant degree, inexact in the other languages, he does catch and pass on from those old poets something which usually escapes more careful scholars—he gives us an effluence, an atmosphere, a breath of perfume, more expressive of their feeling and environment than the most literal translation of their precise words. In short, he strives for, and sometimes attains to a rare degree, a poet's imaginative re-creation of another poet's feeling and rhythm; and this is the only kind of translation which can have any value as literature.

But there is danger in this preoccupation with old authors. Of late I have felt that Ezra Pound was sinking too deep in mental easy-chairs of the library, that he was paying the penalty of too much specialization, of isolation with literary groups, apart from the constructive forces which are making the next age. Super-sophistication is more desiccating than ignorance—the artist needs to refresh himself continually at the primal springs of life, by intercourse with simple people who plant and build and invent, and with powerful people who do these things mightily and direct the energies of the world. Prolonged exile from one's own place is always a dangerous experiment; and especially in the case of an artist who, like Ezra Pound, loves his country while he flays her. One seems to feel in his later work the effects of detachment from currents and growths essential to his full development, an inability to strike root richly into cultures unresponsive to certain secret needs of his soul. In a sense, he seems less at home in Europe than T. S. Eliot; he is less effectually transplanted. This may be one reason why his art of late, instead of broadening out and reaching up, has narrowed down to a merely literary inspiration, why it has lost its freshness and become secondary, deriving from books of the past instead of life of the present, and refining often to trivial excess. I cannot follow with sympathy his clever series of *Cantos,* and in the volume *Poems 1918-21* I find little of that swift keenness of emotional and musical motive which I have tried to analyze above. Apparently his inspiration has been intense rather than rich, a youthful fire rather than an enduring light; as with Coleridge, the critical and professorial habit may prove stronger than the poetic mood. And yet—and yet—no prognostication may serve us; at any moment this poet, or indeed any other, may surprise detraction with a masterpiece.

Indeed, there be critics of high degree who consider the *Cantos* his masterpiece, who find in its (to me) scent of the library, and its rhythms as rigorous as a Stravinsky suite, the very pulse-beat and blood-pressure of modern life. In a recent article we find Ford Madox Ford saying:

It must not be forgotten that Ezra is first and foremost his *Cantos*. At that immense and glorious work he toils noiseless and intent, . . . endowed with supreme genius, supreme patience, unceasing gusto for the Arts. . . . Browning and Ezra are the two great major poets of our and the immediately preceding age.

But *A Draft of XXX Cantos,* published in 1930, is only a beginning; already the poet has written other cantos, and there may be many more. So the critics will have time to debate their quarrel, and the world to decide whether songs or cantos shall prove the hardier growth. To the ultimate verdict it matters little, for already this poet's best work has the completeness of adequate beauty. As a leader, a revolutionist in the art, he will have a place in literary history; as a poet he will sing into the hearts and minds of all free-singing spirits in the next age—and perhaps in the ages beyond reach of our prophecy.

## VACHEL LINDSAY

A S I write, in March, 1924, it is ten years to a month
since Mr. Yeats, at POETRY's first banquet, saluted
an obscure young American and officially welcomed him
into the guild of bards. Ten years to a month since this
young poet of central Illinois, whose *General Booth* had
appeared in *Poetry* more than a year earlier, responded
to the elder man's compliment by reciting for the first
time a new poem then unpublished, *The Congo*.

Each of these two poems afterwards entitled a book,
and these two books were followed by *The Chinese Nightingale, The Golden Whales* and *Going to the Sun*—even,
more recently, by *Collected Poems*. And the obscure
aspirant of ten years ago has become probably the best and
farthest known of all our American poets of this vocal
decade. Surely it is time to pause and take account of
him, not piecemeal but as a unit; to find out what he has
done and whither he is going, and to question ourselves as
well in regard to our attitude toward his art.

Lindsay is his mother's son, but born under a moon of
magic that turned his horoscope the other way around.
Somehow her aggressive missionary spirit, which all her
life dominated the women's committees of her church and
sect, was glinted with romance in this ugly duckling of a
son, making him a mediaeval crusader in a world forget-
ful of chivalry. Of course she didn't know what to make
of her slow-developing, reluctant-minded youngling. De-

creeing Hiram College and a medical career to him as
autocratically as a pan-cake breakfast, she was flabber-
gasted when she encountered a will as firm as her own
and found him stubbornly preferring art.

It was a long formative period with this youth—fifteen
years of dogged persistence in his own course, against
bewilderment in his family and ridicule in his town, from
the time he entered Hiram in 1897 until in 1912 he
emerged as a poet with *General Booth.* They were years
of hard precarious fare, stubborn devotion, and no doubt
serious discouragement. For he did not make much headway as a student at the Art Institute of Chicago, and
under Chase and Henri in New York, where for five
years from 1900 he was aiming at the wrong art. Not
much headway as a painter, though the educational discipline of that service and of the lecture-period that followed—years of trying to draw, of earning money as
instructor-guide in museums, of plunging into Egyptian
art and other oriental lore—was inestimably valuable to
a crude boy out of a middle-western town; so that when
the Lindsays, in a lavish moment, took their incomprehen-
sible son abroad, they found him equipped for the trip
far beyond their own provincial standards.

Then Springfield once more, and that winter of 1909-
10, when the preacher-strain in him almost conquered and
we find him an itinerant lecturer for the Anti-Saloon
League—a winter illuminated by the dim dawning of a
consciousness that his own special art was poetry. At
last *The Village Magazine,* rounded out to picturesque
perfection by the demand it made upon all his arts—
typographic, limnal and literary, and upon his purse as
well. And finally his sturdy answer to the neighborhood

[ 22 ]

questioning of his muse's implacable call, an answer which started him on the road, penniless and afoot, to try out his vocation in the ancient way—as a beggar dependent upon nature and simple people, and exchanging rhymes for bread.

It was then—the early autumn of 1912—that I came across his vagabond tracks in some magazine article he had written describing his adventures. And it was inevitable that the editor of a new little poets' magazine should write requesting a look at some of those rhymes it told about. Not so inevitable, however, that the response should be *General William Booth Enters into Heaven,* a poem which had sung itself into his mind as he tramped along western trails. And by the time it appeared, in the New Year number of 1913, the poet—blond-haired, blue-eyed, beetle-browed; tramp, prohibitionist, campaigner for beauty—had added fuel to the fire of his poem by reading it to us with his own big voice.

From that time Lindsay's story is legible in seven or eight books of verse and prose, and especially in the *Collected Poems.* It is a consistent story; it has admirable unity. From the first this poet has been led by certain sacred and impassioned articles of faith—faith in beauty, in goodness (even human goodness, especially that of women), in the splendor of common things and common experiences; faith so sure, so living, that it has fed rapturously upon the present and never sought refuge in the past. These articles of faith may sound old-fashioned or eternal, according to one's temperament; at least they have upheld the banners of all the crusades ever fought, and will march proudly on, no doubt, till the end of time.

Indeed, Lindsay is a modern knight-errant, the Don Quixote of our so-called unbelieving, unromantic age. To say this is not scorn but praise, for Don Quixote's figure looms heroically tall in perspective, and his quests, however immediately futile, become triumphant in the final account. Lindsay's whimsical imagination, even as the madder fancy of Cervantes' hero, cuts the light into seven colors like a prism, so that facts become glamorous before our eyes. Booth strides, full-haloed, into a Salvation Army heaven; fat black bucks of South State Street dance along a mystical glorified Congo; motor-cars on a Kansas road are chariots from now to forever; Bryan "sketches a silver Zion"; Johnny Appleseed is a wandering god of the soil, as mythical as Ceres; our yellow neighbor the Chinese laundryman is a son of Confucius, and his nightingale utters deathless beauty. Lindsay links up the electric sign with the stars:

> The signs in the street and the signs in the skies
> Shall make a new Zodiac, guiding the wise.

And sometimes, not always, he does this so effectively that we believe him. For his art, at its best, is adequate; Rosinante becomes Pegasus and soars beyond the moon.

It is appropriate that the American sense of humor should be, in this poet's mind, the law of perspective which ensures sanity. Looking over a Sunday comic supplement the other day, I felt that it is in such laughter that hate dies among us. The neighborhood rages of Europe break into absurdity against it; if not the fire under the melting-pot, it is at least the crackling gas in the fuel. If Europe could only laugh as universally, as nonsensically, the heroic pose of war would become as

[ 24 ]

impossible among her quarreling nations as among our forty-eight widely differing states.

Lindsay's sense of humor is true to type in its extreme variety; a faint and wistful smile, yearning for elusive and everlasting beauty, in *The Chinese Nightingale,* it becomes a sly grin in *So Much the Worse for Boston,* a tenderly sympathetic laugh in *Bryan, Bryan,* a louder laugh in *The Santa Fe Trail* or *The Kallyope Yell,* and a real guffaw in *Samson.* But the laugh, whether whispered or loud, is always genial, is never a satiric cackle. Often there is a wistful pathos in it, the trace of those tears which spring from the same bubbling fountain of human sympathy. Like the Chinese philosopher squinting at the cataract, Lindsay feels the tragedy—he is aware of the littleness of man. And to know man's littleness is to know also his greatness, for the point of the cosmic joke lies in the contrast. One finds man's greatness implied throughout the four hundred pages of Mr. Lindsay's volume, and expressed without even the reservation of a smile in such triumphant or tragic poems as *General Booth, John Brown, Eagle Forgotten,* and *Abraham Lincoln Walks at Midnight.*

James Stephens, the Irish poet and teller of tales, praises *The Chinese Nightingale* as one of two masterpieces in the poetry of these prolific fifteen years—"a great poem on the one subject which poetry has any true concern with, the soul of man and its meaning and destiny." It is characteristic of Lindsay, poet that he is, that he states nothing in this poem, but disguises "the one subject" in imagery—in the quaint and almost humorous phantasy of oriental costume and magic.

The walls fell back, night was aflower,
The table gleamed in a moonlit bower,
While Chang, with a countenance carved of stone,
Ironed and ironed, all alone.
And thus she sang to the busy man Chang:
"Have you forgotten . . .
Deep in the ages, long, long ago,
I was your sweetheart, there on the sand—
Storm-worn beach of the Chinese land?
We sold our grain in the peacock town
Built on the edge of the sea-sands brown—
Built on the edge of the sea-sands brown. . . .

"When all the world was drinking blood
From the skulls of men and bulls,
And all the world had swords and clubs of stone,
We drank our tea in China beneath the sacred spice-trees,
And heard the curled waves of the harbor moan.
And this gray bird, in Love's first spring,
With a bright-bronze breast and a bronze-brown wing,
Captured the world with his carolling.
Do you remember, ages after,
At last the world we were born to own?
You were the heir of the yellow throne—
The world was the field of the Chinese man
And we were the pride of the sons of Han.
We copied deep books, and we carved in jade,
And wove blue silks in the mulberry shade." . . .

"I remember, I remember
That Spring came on forever,
That Spring came on forever,"
Said the Chinese nightingale.

The poem flows along like a river, iridescent with light,
melodious with sound, bearing its cargoes gaily to the
deep seas. There are lines which entrap the imagination
with their beauty:

"I had a silvery name, I had a silvery name,
I had a silvery name—do you remember
The name you cried beside the tumbling sea?"

Or:

> Deep, deep below the bay, the sea-weed and the spray,
> Embalmed in amber every pirate lies,
> Embalmed in amber every pirate lies.

And then the finale, fine and frail as a soap-bubble:

> "Man is a torch, then ashes soon;
> May and June, then dead December;
> Dead December, then again June.
> Who shall end my dream's confusion?
> Life is a loom, weaving illusion . . .
> I remember, I remember
> There were ghostly veils and laces . . .
> In the shadowy, bowery places . . .
> With lovers' ardent faces
> Bending to one another,
> Speaking each his part.
> They infinitely echo
> In the red cave of my heart.
> 'Sweetheart, sweetheart, sweetheart!'
> They said to one another.
> They spoke, I think, of perils past.
> They spoke, I think, of peace at last.
> One thing I remember:
> Spring came on forever,
> Spring came on forever,"
> Said the Chinese nightingale.

One would like to quote a number of poems to show forth Mr. Lindsay in his various moods: *The Righteous Kitten* for pure nonsense; *The Kallyope Yell* for utter flamboyance; *The Congo* or *Samson* for, not the Negro himself, but a sublimated expression of his meaning, his relation to our civilization; *The Leaden-eyed* for aphoristic wisdom; *Lincoln Walks at Midnight,* or *Eagle Forgotten* for tragic beauty. And still others, if one were to give a fair hint of his extraordinary range.

If this poet was born into a rather thin and bloodless

strain of puritan thought, his instinct for beauty led him early into richer regions. He has loved the mediaeval lily and the oriental lotus, even the scarlet African orchid; and has given us, if not their precise form and color, at least something of their several perfumes. Mr. Lindsay's mind, while child-like in certain aspects, is surprisingly sagacious in others. If one finds his thinking trivial at times, all of a sudden one may be astonished by such an evidence of searching critical insight as his article on Whitman in the *New Republic*. He is full of profound intuitions, and if he gropes among them sometimes, it is because his own awkward slow-moving self gets in his way and keeps him from turning on the light. But the light is there.

Lindsay imparts a new flare of whimsical and colorful beauty to this American scene, and presents its extraordinary variety of emotion and mood. It is a generous gift—it makes us aware of ourselves in the true tradition of authentic art the world over. And the gift is not likely to diminish seriously in value under the chemical tests of time.

IN this American melting-pot the English language becomes the mother tongue of the sons of Perse and Slav and Swede; and through that language, and the literature born in it, more and more as time goes on, must blow tropic and arctic airs, winds from East and West, perfumes of Araby and salt spray from the northern seas. No prophet can measure the ultimate enrichment of our art through this enrichment of our racial strain. Provincialism will hardly survive, and our democracy of precepts and precedents—an Anglo-Saxon inheritance, like our language, from the patterned and fenced-in past —will have to expand to the larger tests of cosmopolitanism and human brotherhood.

From certain of these newer Americans and their sons have come of late at once the harshest challenge and the most idealistic appreciation of this incomplete, but urgent and hopeful democracy which they find here. Such voices as Sandburg the second-generation Swede, Giovannitti the Italian, Rosenfeld the Yiddish Jew, are uttering at once the challenge and the aspiration with a passion rare among poets of the Anglo-Saxon stock. Of these latter at this moment only Edgar Lee Masters, and C. E. S. Wood of Oregon, occur to me as bent upon the same business, in the deepest sense a poet's business, of seeing our national life in the large—its beauty and glory, its baseness and shame.

[ 29 ]

In reviewing his first book, *Chicago Poems,* in 1916, I wrote:

"Carl Sandburg has the unassailable and immovable earthbound strength of a great granite rock which shows a weather-worn surface above the soil. Like such a rock, he has a tender and intimate love of all soft growing things—grasses, lichens, flowers, children, suffering human lives. One would no more question his sincerity than that of the wind and rain. His book, whether you like it or not, whether you call it poetry or not, is fundamental in the same majestic sense—it is a man speaking with his own voice, authoritatively like any other force of nature.

"I remember the emotion with which I first read many of these poems—in type-written sheets sent to *Poetry* early in 1914. That first conviction of beauty and power returns to me as I read them again. This is speech torn out of the heart because the loveliness of 'yellow dust on a bumble-bee's wing,' of 'worn wayfaring men,' of ships at night, of a fog coming 'on little cat feet'—the incommunicable loveliness of the earth, of life—is too keen to be borne; or because the pain of 'the poor, patient and toiling,' of children behind mill-doors, of soldiers bleeding in the trenches—all the unnecessary human anguish—is too bitter for any human being, poet or not, to endure in silence.

"Mr. Sandburg knows his Chicago, and the book as a whole gives us the city in a masterpiece of protraiture. The town—its streets and people, its parks and broad lake and the sand-dunes beyond—the whole half-formed metropolis—is painted in broad vital strokes and rich colors by the loving unflattering hand of an artist.

"The free-verse rhythms which this poet prefers are as personal as his slow speech or his massive gait; always a reverent beating-out of his subject. They are rugged enough at times—as when he salutes Chicago, 'stormy, husky, brawling,' and sets her high among cities, 'with lifted head singing, so proud to be alive and coarse and strong and cunning.' In some of the war poems his rhythms pound like guns booming, and when he talks back to the loud-mouthed Billy Sunday the swing of a smashing prose hammer is good enough. Or again, under softer inspiration, his touch becomes exquisitely delicate. Indeed, there is orchestral richness in his music; he plays divers instruments. Such lyrics as *The Great Hunt, Under, Beachy, At a Window, The Road and the End,* have a primal fundamental beauty, a sound and swing as of tides or bending grain.

"The spirit of the book is heroic, both its joy and its sorrow. It says, 'Keep away from the little deaths!' "

The years which have passed since this first tribute have brought much to emphasize its findings and nothing to contradict them. They have established the poet's fame, and for the most part silenced the cavillers who were so loud at first against his slangy diction and his disuse of rhyme and metrics; for the most part, though still one may hear a few rigid minds declaiming the inviolability of rules made by forgotten prosodists who, plotting out the trail of dead poets, decreed that poets living or unborn should follow no other route to Parnassus. These should be reminded of Debussy's aphorism: "No fixed rule should guide the creative artist—rules are made *by* works of art, not *for* works of art."

*Chicago Poems* is an urban book—the subjects are a

city and its people, including of course the author; also the War, which was killing men over-seas. *Cornhuskers* goes back to the western-Illinois country where the poet was born, and to the railroads he rode on, the taverns he stopped in, and the laborers and hoboes, the children, women, horses, he got acquainted with while earning a living at rough jobs. *Smoke and Steel* carries the tale into the shops and factories, taking for its special motive man-made machines and machine-made men. In a sense all three books are epic—that is, they give us the tale of the tribe in a strongly centralized locale. But the method is lyric rather than epic. The story is presented by flashes; it is revealed by strongly lit details, emotions, episodes, rather than told by chapters which knit together into a shaped and ordered whole. Even the two longest poems—*Prairie* in nine pages, and *Smoke and Steel* in seven—are series of lyrics following each other with a deliberate and effective irregularity, like a necklace of different-colored beads which harmonize because an artist strung them. And if *Prairie* is such a string, from it hangs a jewel of value, for the finale, with that marvellous line,

I tell you the past is a bucket of ashes,

is one of the imperishable poems of the world's new age.

One gets the very feel of the prairie in such poems—the planted prairie, flowing like a sea with corn; and bearing people of its own kind, simple, faithful to the soil, accustomed to wide horizons. Details fill out the landscape—*Laughing Corn, Fall Time, Prairie Waters by Night, River Roads;* and people it with human waifs and workers in such poems as *Illinois Farmer, Singing Nigger, Hits*

[ 32 ]

*and Runs, Potato Blossom Songs and Jigs. Smoke and Steel* stresses more strongly the gauntness of many human lives, their separation from their rightful human heritage, from all the richness and beauty of nature and art. If *Cornhuskers* dances out in the sun to a devil-may-care jazz tune, *Smoke and Steel* moves usually more slowly, asking bitter questions in queer harsh rhythms full of unexpected glides and dashes.

One feels in all these poems a true and deep emotion of love as the central controlling motive—love of the prairie country, the prairie towns and city, and the people who struggle through toilsome lives there. It is this which gives richness to Sandburg's music. In some of his finest lyrics the love becomes special and personal; his tributes to Nancy Hanks, Inez Milholland, "Chick Lorimer" (whoever she may have been), to Don Magregor, Adelaide Crapsey, Bill Reedy, Ossawatomie Brown, are remarkable for simplicity of style and nobility of mood. The emotion here, and in all his best lyrics, rings absolutely true in a strain of melody fit and beautiful; without a false note or a jarring word.

Granted the theme, and the emotional impulse beneath it, we have still to consider this poet's art: how far does he get the effects he aims at, and what means does he employ to produce them?

In my opinion, his finest lyrics rank, as artistic achievements, among the best in the language. The rhythm of most English lyrics, indeed of most European poetry of the last five hundred years, is an overlay, more or less adroit, of large cadences upon the iambic metrical pattern; as when large waves, swinging in toward the shore, bear the little parallel ripples along. Shakespeare's sonnets—

take the twenty-ninth or the seventy-first—show with what mastery he swung his large measures over the three-time iambic pattern of his verse. In a few songs he and other Elizabethans changed magically to a four-time ana-paestic pattern in each stanza—a trick used also by Byron in *There be none of beauty's daughters;* and Shelley, Swinburne and others used the anapaestic pattern throughout certain poems as the foundation on which they laid their larger cadences.

What Sandburg does is not, as some students seem to infer, the complete sweeping-away of the metrical pattern. There is an underlying three-time or four-time beat in each poem, his preference leaning, oftener than with most poets, to four-time, which admits that generous use of spondees—sometimes four long syllables in succession— from which he gets some of his most telling effects. But in his underlying pattern Sandburg permits himself more variety than the prosodic laws have allowed for, especially in the number of syllables to a bar, and in a free use of rests. In four-time especially he uses this freedom quite wonderfully, getting rhythms as different as in the quick-stepping *Gone* and the slow-moving *Our Prayer of Thanks;* while in *The Great Hunt,* which begins in a creeping four-time, he tries with magical effect the old but rarely used trick of changing the beat to three-time for the final stanza. And in two poems as different in movement as *Bringers* and *Four Preludes on Playthings of the Wind,* the underlying pattern is three-time and al-most straight iambic. On these patterns Sandburg, like all poets but more skilfully than most of them, swings the larger tides of his cadences.

[ 34 ]

Certain of these poems may be quoted here to show the intimate response of his method to his feeling:

### GONE

Everybody loved Chick Lorimer in our town.
　　　Far off
　　Everybody loved her.
So we all love a wild girl keeping a hold
　　On a dream she wants.
Nobody knows now where Chick Lorimer went.
Nobody knows why she packed her trunk . . . a few old things
And is gone,
　　Gone with her little chin
　　Thrust ahead of her,
　　And her soft hair blowing careless
　　From under a wide hat—
Dancer, singer, a laughing passionate lover.

Were there ten men or a hundred hunting Chick?
Were there five men or fifty with aching hearts?
　　Everybody loved Chick Lorimer.
　　　Nobody knows where she's gone.

### THE GREAT HUNT

　　I can not tell you now;
　　　When the wind's drive and whirl
　　　　Blow me along no longer,
　　　And the wind's a whisper at last—
　　Maybe I'll tell you then—
　　　　　　　some other time.

　　　When the rose's flash to the sunset
　　　Reels to the wrack and the twist,
　　　And the rose is a red bygone,
　　　When the face I love is going
　　　And the gate to the end shall clang,
　　　And it's no use to beckon or say, "So long"—
　　Maybe I'll tell you then—
　　　　　　　some other time.

[ 35 ]

I never knew any more beautiful than you:
I have hunted you under my thoughts,
I have broken down under the wind
And into the roses looking for you.
    I shall never find any
            greater than you.

### BRINGERS

Cover me over
In dusk and dust and dreams.

Cover me over
And leave me alone.

Cover me over,
You tireless, great.

Hear me and cover me,
Bringers of dusk and dust and dreams.

To say that there is less art in such manipulation of rhythms than in following accurately, for example, the exact metrics of a sonnet, is simply to show one's own limitations as a student of poetics. It makes no difference whether the art is conscious or instinctive. With Sandburg it is probably instinctive; he may not know a spondee from a kilowatt, but he has a marvellously sensitive ear—he listens for his rhythms over and over, and beats them out with elaborate care. None of the scholarly imagists, or other free-versifiers of the present period, has so greatly widened the rhythmic range of English poetry; and the prosodists of the future will have to study him in order to make new rules to enslave poets yet to come.

Another element of his art—his vocabulary—may call for comment. It is enough to say that any writer who can use the common speech of the people for beauty thereby enriches and revivifies the language. A static lan-

guage is half dead—the "well of English undefiled" will
dry up unless fresh waters out of the common earth continually fill it.

This use of so-called vulgar speech—of slang—is often
in the service of his rich and whimsical humor, a humor
rising with a grim smile out of dark fundamental incongruities: as in *Caboose Thoughts, Jabberers, Knucks,* or
this one, *Losers:*

If I should pass the tomb of Jonah
I would stop there and sit for awhile;
Because I was swallowed one time deep in the dark
And came out alive after all.

If I pass the burial spot of Nero
I shall say to the wind, "Well, well!"—
I who have fiddled in a world on fire,
I who have done so many stunts not worth doing.

I am looking for the grave of Sinbad too.
I want to shake his ghost-hand and say,
"Neither of us died very early, did we?"

And the last sleeping-place of Nebuchadnezzar—
When I arrive there I shall tell the wind:
"You ate grass; I have eaten crow—
Who is better off now or next year?"

Jack Cade, John Brown, Jesse James,
There too I could sit down and stop for awhile.
I think I could tell their headstones:
"God, let me remember all good losers."

I could ask people to throw ashes on their heads
In the name of that sergeant at Belleau Woods,
Walking into the drumfires, calling his men,
"Come on, you ——! Do you want to live forever?"

Sandburg's humor jokes with the earth, and with time
and fate, and other slow-moving obstinate obstacles.   And

again he takes off his hat to these enemies: some of his finest lyrics are salutations of death—*The Road and the End, Grass, Loam,* and especially *Cool Tombs,* which we cannot forbear from quoting:

> When Abraham Lincoln was shoveled into the tombs, he forgot the copperheads and the assassin . . . in the dust, in the cool tombs.
>
> And Ulysses Grant lost all thought of con men and Wall Street, cash and collateral turned ashes . . . in the dust, in the cool tombs.
>
> Pocahontas' body, lovely as a poplar, sweet as a red haw in November or a pawpaw in May—did she wonder? does she remember . . . in the dust, in the cool tombs?
>
> Take any streetful of people buying clothes and groceries, cheering a hero or throwing confetti and blowing tin horns . . . tell me if the lovers are losers . . . tell me if any get more than the lovers . . . in the dust . . . in the cool tombs.

A proper place to end, though *Cool Tombs* is no prophecy of death, but of immortality. Have I spoken of Sandburg's masterly use of refrain?—this poem is the supreme example. And if nothing else of his should survive, surely it is too beautiful to perish when the tides of time sweep away our pyramids and towers.

THE delight which one breathes like a perfume from the poetry of Wallace Stevens is the natural effluence of his own clear and untroubled and humorously philosophical delight in the beauty of things as they are. Others may criticize and complain, may long for more perfect worlds or search subliminal mysteries—for him it is enough to watch the iridescent fall of sunlight on blue sea-water and pink parasols, and meditate on the blessed incongruities which break into rainbow colors this earth of ours and the beings who people it. To him the whole grand spectacle is so amazing that no melodramatic upheaval of destiny could possibly increase his sense of awe and wonder, or disturb his philosophic calm. He is content to live profoundly in the beauty of a universe whose lightest, most transient phenomena are sufficient evidence, to a mind in tune with it, of harmonies magnificent to infinity.

For this reason his poems, even those which seem slight, become hints of this immutable perfection. Like a Japanese carver discovering a god in a bit of ivory, Wallace Stevens, in such a poem as the *Paltry Nude* or *Peter Quince at the Clavier* presents the ineffable serenity of beauty.

Man's interference with this serenity—an interference ineffectual in any ultimate sense—is the central theme of his longer poems. In the one-act play *Three Travellers*

*Watch a Sunrise,* a poem exquisite and deeply moving beyond analysis, this interference brings about tragedy; but even tragedy is shown as ineffectual to contradict beauty, whose processional march of splendor demands agony along with joy. In *The Comedian as the Letter C* the interference brings the more bewildering frustration of comedy; but even this falls whimsically into the scheme, for beauty invincible and immortal accepts frustration just as music accepts discord—and, lo and behold, the symphony moves on enriched. The hero of *Carlos Among the Candles* may be confused and amazed, but he goes on lighting the candles and illuminating with beams from the human imagination the inexhaustible beauty of the world.

It was during the fateful Autumn of 1914 that a few watchful readers first became aware of Wallace Stevens. The *War Number* of *Poetry* was in page proof when his series of *Phases* arrived, compelling the editors to squeeze an extra two pages into the make-up—a last-minute concession which sufficed for only four of the six or seven battle sketches in the group. To this day the others have never been published; indeed, *Fallen Winkle,* reprinted in *The New Poetry*, is the only poem of the series which the author has permitted to reappear.

For Mr. Stevens is the most abstemious of poets. It is the unwritten poem in his mind which interests him— the old ones, once they are registered in some magazine, may go fluttering down the wind like dead leaves. For nearly a decade his admirers pleaded in vain for a book, and at last, toward the end of 1923, they felt lucky to get one at all, even though they scanned it in vain for the poems in dramatic form above mentioned, and for many a briefer poem which any other poet would be proud to claim. The future collector of Mr. Stevens' complete works will have to pay a fancy price for certain back numbers of *Poetry* and *Others.* Meantime, one must be grateful for *Harmonium,* which brings together poems of high importance, whether old or new.

For one gets a stronger flavor of personality from a one-man show than from any mixed exhibition, and there was never a more flavorously original poetic personality than the author of this book. If one seeks sheer beauty of sound, phrase, rhythm, packed with prismatically colored ideas by a mind at once wise and whimsical, one should open one's eyes and ears, sharpen one's wits, widen one's sympathies to include rare and exquisite aspects of life, and then run for this volume of iridescent poems.

I should like to take my copy to some quiet sea-flung space in Florida, where a number of the poems were written. The sky, perhaps, is cobalt, with mauve-white clouds; the sea is sapphire, flicking into diamonds under the wind; the sand is a line of purplish rose, and there are gaudy bathers and loiterers on the beach. And here is a poet undaunted by all this splendor, a poet as sure of delight as nature herself, as serenely receptive of beauty. The bleak despairs of lesser men visit him not at all—his philosophy embraces the whole fantastic miracle of life, a miracle so wild and strange that man, confronting it, must feel the enormous humor of his lordly pose, and take refuge in

> The magnificent cause of being,
> The imagination, the one reality
> In this imagined world.

[ 41 ]

For the philosopher and the satirist temper the poet's rage in Wallace Stevens. Whether he ever writes his masterpiece or not—and that is always uncertain through the turmoil of conflicting claims which besets us all today —he is of the race of the great humorists, using the word in its most profound sense, the sense in which Cervantes, Shakespeare, Synge, Lincoln may be counted as great humorists. In such men agony sinks into depths dark, hidden and unconfessed. The hard black stone is there, but laughter washes over it, covers it up, conceals it. Tragedy is comedy with such men—they are aware of the laughter of the gods and the flaming splendor of man's fight against it. This poet is one of them; his work, however incomplete as yet, is haughty with their lineage.

Always, in his lightest play of whimsicalities as well as in his most splendid assertions of beauty, one feels this deeper note, this sense of ultimate vanities and ecstasies contending, in the human atom, against infinities that threaten it with doom. The play of whimsicalities may seem a mere banter of word-bubbles, as in *Ordinary Women;* the assertions of beauty may be as magical in pomp of color and sound as *Le Monocle de Mon Oncle,* which lifts to our thirsty lips

> This luscious and impeccable fruit of life—

or as *The Paltry Nude Starts on a Spring Voyage,* which we must pause to read:

> But not on a shell she starts,
> Archaic, for the sea;
> But on the first-found weed
> She scuds the glitters,
> Noiselessly, like one more wave.

She too is discontent
And would have purple stuff upon her arms,
Tired of the salty harbors,
Eager for the brine and bellowing
Of the high interiors of the sea.

The wind speeds her,
Blowing upon her hands
And watery back.
She touches the clouds, where she goes,
In the circle of her traverse of the sea.

Yet this is meagre play
In the scurry and water-shine,
As her heels foam—
Not as when the goldener nude
Of a later day

Will go, like the centre of sea-green pomp,
In an intenser calm,
Scullion of fate,
Across the spick torrent, ceaselessly,
Upon her irretrievable way.

But in either extreme of lovely or whimsical utterance
one feels the larger rhythms, one measures the poet's
sweep by spaces beyond our earthly inches.

Perhaps *The Comedian as the Letter C* is the most
complete assertion of cosmic humor which Mr. Stevens
has as yet confessed to the world. It is at least the pre-
sentment, probably more or less autobiographical, of the
predicament of man in general, or of highly sensitized
man—let us say the artist—in particular, as he tries to
live gloriously, and finds his soul caught in the meshes of
life's allurements. Many poets have made a tragedy of
this situation, shouting their agonies of rebellion and
despair in more or less effective verse. Mr. Stevens is
perhaps more keenly inspired in making of it a comedy

searching and profound, a comedy whose azure laughter ripples almost inaudibly over hushed and sombre depths.

His little human unit—this "Socrates of snails," this "wig of things," this "sovereign ghost,"

> This connoisseur of elemental fate,
> Aware of exquisite thought—

in short, this Crispin, who was "washed away by magnitude," is he not our modern exemplar of frustration, as Don Quixote was in his day?

> Against his pipping sounds a trumpet cried
> Celestial sneering boisterously.

And as he sails into the blue southern sea,

> How many poems he denied himself
> In his observant progress, lesser things
> Than the relentless contact he desired!

He is in search of "a sinewy nakedness"—this Crispin poet-man;

> He gripped more closely the essential prose,
> As being, in a world so falsified,
> The one integrity for him.

But alas, he finds himself settling down:

> Crispin dwelt in the land, and dwelling there,
> Slid from his continent by slow recess
> To things within his actual eye, alert
> To the difficulty of rebellious thought
> When the sky is blue.

And so he falls into "a nice shady home," into bewildering marital allegiances, into parental loyalties to four daughters, bluet-eyed,

> Leaving no room upon his cloudy knee,
> Prophetic joint, for its diviner young.

Thus enmeshed, what is a puzzled prophet to do?

> Should he lay by the personal, and make
> Of his own fate an instance of all fate?
> What is one man among so many men?
> What are so many men in such a world?
> Can one man think one thing and think it long?
> Can one man be one thing and be it long?

So the poet in Crispin comes to a bad end:

> So deep a sound fell down
> It was as if the solitude concealed
> And covered him and his congenial sleep.
> So deep a sound fell down it grew to be
> A long soothsaying silence down and down.

We must hope that the poem is not strictly auto-biographical, that Mr. Stevens, unlike his baffled hero, will get his story uttered—to such a degree at least, as may be within the reach of poor mortality. For this poet, like a super-sensitized plate, is aware of color-subtle-ties and sound-vibrations which most of us do not detect, and of happiness in fine degrees which most of us do not attain. He derives, so far as one may trace the less obvious origins, from no one; but like Napoleon he may say, *"Je suis ancêtre!"* for shoals of young poets derive from him. Quite free of literary allegiances to period or place, he distils into a pure essence the beauty of his own world. And beauty's imperishable perfection among shifting mortal shows is the incongruity at the heart of life which this poet accepts with the kind of serene laugh-ter that covers pain.

EDGAR LEE MASTERS, whatever else one may say of him, has size. He bulks large, and it may be that in that "next age," to which we accord the ultimate accounting, he will make a number of other figures now conspicuous look small. He has, not unnaturally, the faults that go with size—careless technique, uncritical sanctionings, indelicacies of emotional excess, far-sightedness which misses obvious imperfections of detail. The world will sift out and throw away many poems in his numerous books of verse; and much of his prose—not all —will go into the discard. But when hurrying time has done its worst, enough will remain to prove a giant's stature and other attributes of power in this Illinois lawyer-poet of a changing age.

A keen psychologist would find this man's character and development an interesting study. I wish I had known him during the festival summer of the Columbian Exposition, when, a young man just twenty-five, he was having a grand time while pretending to begin the practice of law. Youth must have been with him unusually exciting, for every experience was backed by tremendous vitality, physical, mental, emotional. For him the scale of life was enhanced by an imagination which carried ordinary adventures instantly to the $n$th power of fulfillment or frustration, bringing delights and agonies beyond the reach of lesser men.

Probably life was excitement enough at this time to satisfy the artist in Masters. When at last the instinct for literary self-expression began to function, the young lion's voice was about big enough for a mouse. *A Book of Verses,* published under the author's own name in 1898, was almost as mild an affair as Byron's *Hours of Idleness*—indeed, these two poets offer many proofs of kinship. But Masters developed more slowly; already thirty years old when this first book appeared, he had reached thirty-four, with his sense of humor still in abeyance, when he put out a solemn blank-verse tragedy on the subject of that be-whiskered busy-body of pitiable history, Maximilian, so-called emperor of Mexico.

Of course there was a drama in Mexico at that moment, but it did not follow academic lines. One would have expected a modern mind to find it, but Masters' theories of poetic art were intensely academic, and even eight years later, in 1912, when he issued *Songs and Sonnets* under the pseudonym of Webster Ford, we find him writing such things as an *Ode to Fame* in the most approved all-hail-to-thee style. This book also fell flat, of course; and its author, at forty-four a failure as a poet, was in danger of becoming embittered when even his friend Bill Reedy sent back his classic poems; for he could contrast the silence around him with the réclame which was beginning to salute the imagists and other free-versifiers during 1913.

One can almost see the satiric smile with which he said to himself, "If that's what they want, I'll give it to them!" But *Spoon River,* begun as a more or less satirical challenge to "the new movement," soon caught him up and carried him out to the depths. For the first time he

[ 47 ]

found a theme which drew upon his humor as well as his knowledge and fervor and sympathy; and a form which made him forget old-fashioned prejudices, and thereby freed his art. By the time the world found him he had found himself. And it was a big discovery.

It is hardly necessary to repeat certain things that were said of this book in the first flush of its success. It fulfilled the old time-honored principle: present a local group completely, in its heights and depths and averages, and you present the race as it is in every time and clime. *Spoon River*, with its humors and tragedies and commonplaces, its strange interweavings of destiny, is precisely central Illinois, the very heart of Middle-west America; yet Lucretius or Omar or Li Po would recognize its types and incidents, and probably the poets of the twenty-fifth century will still pronounce it true. And not only true but beautiful, for the form of those terse little epitaphs is not only a perfect fit but that triumphant completion and fulfillment which marks the masterpieces of all the arts.

*Spoon River* classed its author as essentially an epic poet—that is, a poet whose chief urge is to tell the tale of the tribe. And although Mr. Masters has written fine lyrics, most of his best poems emphasize the epic quality of his vision. There be critics who aver that he has done nothing since *Spoon River,* but such a myopic verdict can come only from minds groping for details and blind to mass effects. Since *Spoon River* the very titles of his books have spread a large canvas; he has travelled down the Mississippi in *The Great Valley, Toward the Gulf, Starved Rock* and *The Open Sea,* with *Domesday Book* crossing the Atlantic and accepting the immensities of the World War; and finally he has given us *The New Spoon River,* with its philosophical development of the earlier subject. And although each of these volumes needs weeding out, each of them, except perhaps *The Open Sea,* contains a few essential and memorable poems which help to symmetrize and complete this poet's record of our time and place.

Throughout one is swept along by the man's impassioned quest of truth. In this quest he is absolutely sincere and uncompromising; yet, though he admits humanity's crimes, and lashes our smug and faulty civilization with laughter or even fury, one feels always the warmth of a big-hearted wistful sympathy with all God's sorely tried and tempted creatures as they move about among illusions and are ignorantly stirred by appearances and dreams. He is the attorney for the defense before the bar of ultimate justice, admitting the strong case against his client but pleading the sadness and bitter irony of man's endless struggle between good and evil, between beauty and sordidness.

If he plies the whip on Thomas Rhodes and Editor Whedon, and stings with laughter Bryan and Mrs. Purkapile and the Reverend Percy Ferguson, he has a sympathetic smile for Daisy Frazer and Roscoe Purkapile and "dear old Dick," a wrench of the heart for Doc Hill and the pair at Perko's, and a splendid burning candle-flare of beauty for Anne Rutledge and Lucinda Matlock, for the husband and wife in *Christmas at Indian Point,* and a few other simple and loyal souls. And always one feels these more or less imperfect creatures cast into their true perspective by the poet's ever-present, clear-sighted sense of humor. It is a humor enormous, like

Swift's, in its satirical sweep and power, but more genial
than that of the Queen Anne cynic. It permeates all
his work, of course, and helps to make his portraits so
intensely and sympathetically alive. But his sense of
pity is just as keen, and the two in perfect unison sometimes combine to produce a masterpiece of portraiture
as incisive as Velasquez, like *Slip-shoe Lovey, Archibald
Higbie* or *Fiddler Jones*.

Indeed, the human tenderness of this often harsh poet,
in his handling of such a battered bit of flesh and blood
as Elinor Murray of the *Domesday Book,* cannot be too
highly praised: in spite of her manifest and numerous
slips and sins, he reveals her as nobody's slave—a free and
generous spirit capable of heights as well as depths, and
ecaping vulgarity by a certain inner flare of something
like a hidden and hunted love of truth. The poet turns
more lights on her than Browning on Pompilia in *The
Ring and the Book,* indulging too far his lawyer's love
of presenting the complete and voluminous testimony
of many witnesses. But, however over-laden, the book
is a powerful modern epic of democratic human averages;
an episode of the eternal struggle of the race to save its
soul, like Browning's and every other epic that ever was
written. To complain that much of it is prose mas-
querading as bad blank verse, and that even its best passages are guilty of excruciating banalities of style and
technique, is as idle as criticism of a mountain. The
mountain is there, imperfect in line, rough and craggy
in detail; but massive and mighty as it rests broadly on
the solid earth and lifts its brow into the clouds.

His capacity for fierce living and hard thinking is what
gives size and depth to this poet's work. One pictures

his imagination as a battle-ground of ecstasies and agonies —more completely than with most poets his puppets' feelings become his own. His philosophy therefore is built on human examples—abstract reasoning apart from life is impossible to him. It is an epicurean philosophy, no doubt, one which follows earthly paths and finds happiness a sufficient aim; but beyond this immediate goal lies the remote horizon of mystery. Mr. Masters may be a realist, but we are constantly reminded that his realism transcends mere fact, that the finite and the infinite are equally real to him and equally of the tenuous stuff of dreams. He makes *Elza Ramsey* say:

> Do you know what makes life a terror
> And a torture, Spoon River?
> It is due to the conflict between the little minds
> Who think life is real,
> And who therefore work, save, make laws,
> Prosecute and levy wars—
> Between these and the big minds
> Who know that life is a dream,
> And that much of the world's activity
> Is pure folly, and the chattering of idiots.

Again and again he chants the praise of life—this splendid garment of happiness which is offered so often in vain, and which most of us, at the best, wear so clumsily:

> O life, O unutterable beauty!—
> To leave you, knowing that you were never loved enough,
> Wishing to live you all over,
> With all the soul's wise will!

The desecration of life—that is the unpardonable sin which he lashes in countless poems. The magnificence of the opportunity and the insignificance of our response to it—that is the gods' food for laughter, and the poet's stuff of satire. Mr. Masters does not predict, though he does not deny, that some future life may give us another chance; in his mind that is irrevelant to the immediate and important issue—our unworthy and inadequate use of the life we have.

And of course our efforts at religion are the chief of our inadequacies. His *Sarah Dewitt,* receiving her husband as a gift of God and then finding him "just a thief," says:

> Friends, it is folly to prison God
> In any house that is built with hands,
> In man or woman, in passionate hopes,
> In the love of Truth, or the Rock of Ages. . . .
> For God is Proteus, and flies like magic
> From earth to heaven, from hope to hope.
> You never can catch Him, and this is the reason:
> The game of the soul is never to find,
> The game of the soul is to follow.

Indeed, it is the narrow and self-righteous patterns of respectibility whom Masters whips with his sharpest satire, the static immovable human clods who obstruct the path of the adventurers, of the free and open-minded children of light. Perhaps *Emmett Burns,* in *The New Spoon River,* sums up most keenly his feeling about this blundering world:

> Passer-by, do you know who are the slickest schemers
> And the most excellent despots?
> They are those who say this is right and this is wrong,
> And who ascend the throne of what they call the right
> And then hedge the right with a law.
> Is there no way to beat these shallow souls?
> Follow me, passer-by:
> Be young, be wise,
> Be indifferent to good and evil

And the laws they make—
Seek only the truth,
And die!

And in *Anne Rutledge,* with its flashing side-light on
Lincoln, he presents life inexhaustible and triumphant:

Out of me unworthy and unknown
The vibrations of deathless music;
"With malice toward none, with charity for all."
Out of me the forgiveness of millions toward millions,
And the beneficent face of a nation
Shining with justice and truth.
I am Anne Rutledge who sleep beneath these weeds,
Beloved in life of Abraham Lincoln,
Wedded to him, not through union,
But through separation.
Bloom forever, O Republic,
From the dust of my bosom!

Mr. Masters has little patience with the "Europe-
blinded." Here at least is a poet who makes full use of
our rich "epic material." If he satirizes the republic
and its individual citizens, he also glorifies them. He
makes no apologies to the past or the far-away, he deals
with the stuff of his own time and place, and he is absolutely fearless and sincere. At the heart of his philosophy is love of the race and a fierce desire for its "pursuit of happiness" and reasonableness; but with humor
putting all this in perspective and tempering his bitter
wrath with a laugh.

If this poet is fundamentally epic in the sweep of his
vision, his prolific art indulges also other moods. Certain
fine poems of more or less cosmic motive are epic corol-
laries, no doubt—such things as *The World's Desire, The
Loom, The Star, Silence, Worlds.* And many poems

about real or typical characters—*Autochthon, William Marion Reedy, Cato Braden, Widow La Rue, Emily Brosseau, Sir Galahad* and others—as well as out-door poems like *Grand River Marshes, The Landscape,* and the supremely joyous *Lake Boats,* may be classed as details of that story of his place and people which is his chief legacy to art.

Sometimes his prolific genius is tempted by the past, and we have monologues from Shakespeare, Byron, Voltaire, and others. These are always interesting, whether one agrees or not with the poet's analysis of motives. But such excursions are tangents from the main curve of his orbit, and when they are pursued too deliberately, as in certain dialogues in *The Open Sea,* which elaborate the Brutus theme through the centuries, they become the most ineffective chapter of Mr. Masters' artistic history. Occasionally, however, one finds an intensely vivid study of remote and alien character, as in that rather early lyrical ballad *Saint Francis and Lady Clare,* which has all the emotion of a personal song.

Now and then he utters a real lyric cry. One would like to quote such poems as *I Shall Never See You Again, Song of Women, Poor Pierrot, Recessional, My Light With Yours, Sounds Out of Sorrow, The Sign*—poems which make a strong bid for remembrance because their intense rhapsodic passion burns away all imperfections and sweeps the reader along in its flame of beauty unstudied and sincere. Even the poet's technique, so often slipshod, has nobilities of its own at ecstatic moments. Perhaps the great thing about him is that he is *capable* of ecstasy, that he lives hard and deep, and knows the extremes, the agonies. Thus his art is sincere, convincing; one never doubts the emotion behind it. And to a poet who believes, who feels to the utmost, much may be forgiven.

THERE are delightful paradoxes in the career of Robert Frost. A Yankee to his finger-tips, he was born in San Francisco and "raised" mostly in the West. A poet intensely loyal, in subject and feeling, to New England, he was first published in London. Profoundly humorous in the richest sense of the word, presenting with just a hint of salty satire the anomalous incongruities of human character which develop in an isolated environment, he can yet achieve the exquisitely delicate pathos of *The Hill Wife*—pathos so illumined by the beauty of the human spirit as to transcend all sorrow and become joy.

In short, this poet, however loyally local, is bigger than his environment; and his art, plunging beneath surfaces and accidents, seizes upon the essential, the typical, in the relations of men and women with each other and with the earth, the sky, and all that lives and moves between them. Such art passes local boundaries as lightly as an airplane, and swings out into wider circles of time and space.

Mr. Frost has never been in a hurry. Born in 1875, he was almost forty when his first book was published in 1913. And the title of that book was *A Boy's Will,* as if, at thirty-eight, he had just got around to the business of growing up. Probably we shall never know what hard discipline his muse had been subjected to during the twenty or so previous years. No doubt she was of slow growth also; and if she inspired her embryo poet with crude uncouth verse-exercises, he punished her with reticence, and, moved by a certain inborn decorum, refrained from giving them to the world. I doubt if he ever moved before he was ready; but, unlike some slow-stepping philosophers, he has always known when he was ready and has not hesitated when the moment arrived.

He was ready in 1912, and therefore was not to be stopped when the publishers in his own country refused him a hearing—for he had a firm faith in his long-suffering muse, and a will as hard as his New Hampshire granite. The lady had waited patiently and been true to him—it was time for her reward. If she could not get it in America, he would try England.

In London he fell in with Ezra Pound and other poets. *A Boy's Will* was accepted for publication, and soon *The Code,* travelling back to America and appearing in *Poetry,* introduced the new poet to his countrymen. *North of Boston* followed in 1914, and the next year the poet returned with his family to his own country and to a leisurely pursuit of the business of farming. But Cincinnatus was not allowed to turn stony furrows uninterruptedly. Amherst called him to her counsels in 1916, and in 1921 the University of Michigan. To these academic halls he has brought a most unacademic mind; to the standardizing processes of American education he has offered the tacit and half-humorous opposition of an unconquerable individualism. One may be sure that any student strong enough to stand alone would get a smile and a wink and a hand-clasp from Robert Frost.

"These people seem to think I have never before had any time to myself," Mr. Frost remarked à propos of

Michigan's proffered post of resident poet with nothing professorial to do. "They think they are giving me my first chance at leisure, but they don't know how lazy I have always been!"

It is a pity the promise of leisure was so difficult of fulfilment, the chance of productive laziness so slight. These academic years since 1916 have given us only two small books, *A Mountain Interval* and *New Hampshire.* To be sure, these are both precious, and it may be that this poet, whatever the course of his life, would never have been prolific. As he matured slowly, so he takes his own way through the middle years, never hastening his steps, or speeding on his serene, high-stepping and proudly companionable muse.

If Mr. Frost was working at his art during that score of formative years, I think he was studying chiefly the rhythms of speech. He felt, no doubt, that if he could satisfy himself that his verse presented the musical essence of his neighbors' talk, all the rest—subject, emotional motive, dexterity of technique—would be added unto him. At any rate he did not publish until his poems had caught those slow and simple, but oh, elusive and difficult, rhythms. He transmutes them almost always into a freely moving iambic measure, usually blank verse in the longer poems, and in the shorter ones rhyming couplets or stanzas. His metrical patterns are according to precedent —he tries no free-verse experiments; but there is a subtle originality, a very personal style, in his weaving of cadences over the basic metre. The music has more variety than one would admit at first. The blank verse of *New Hampshire,* for example, goes swinging familiarly along in a loose stride, while that of *Snow* rises to sym-

phonic eloquence in suggesting the preacher's duel with
the blizzard. And the quatrains of *The Hill Wife* play
a very different tune from those of *Brown's Descent.*
Yet in each case there is no mere facile music-making—
the speech-rhythms are intensified, patterned if you will
into melody, but not artificialized.

> Yankees are what they always were,

sings Mr. Frost in the above-mentioned delightfully
Yankeeish poem. And Mr. Frost is a thorough Yankee
—he, no more than Brown, "ever gave up hope," or
failed to reach "that which he headed for," even if he
had to "bow with grace to natural law,"

> And then went round it on his feet
> After the manner of our stock,

when the "slippery slope" proved impossible. Perhaps no
poet in our history has put the best of the Yankee spirit
into a book so completely, so happily, as Robert Frost.
Emerson, greatest of the early New England group, was
a citizen of the world—or shall we say of the other
world. Whittier was a Quaker, with something of the
Yankee thrift of tongue. Longfellow was a Boston
scholar, untouched by Yankee humor. Lowell had some
of the humor, but he condescended to it, lived above it.
Edwin Arlington Robinson came from New England,
but his spirit did not stay there and his poetry escapes its
boundaries. Amy Lowell in certain of her poems makes
a vivid and picturesque use of New England life and
legendry. But none of these is so completely the real
Yankee, and so content to confess it in his poetry, as this
"plain New Hampshire farmer," "at present living in

Vermont"—no, Amherst or Ann Arbor—whom we are now considering.

There are three or four facets of this local tang in Mr. Frost's art. One is the rural background—landscape, farms, animals. We have this more or less in all the poems, and specifically in a number—*Birches, The Woodpile, The Mountain, The Cow in Apple-time, The Runaway* and others. And close to these are the poems of farm life, showing the human reaction to nature's processes—*Mowing, Mending Wall, The Axe-helve, After Apple-picking, Putting in the Seed* and others. Then there are the narratives or dialogues presenting aspects of human character: some of them dryly satirical, with a keen but always sympathetic humor, like *The Code;* others, *Snow* for example, broadly humane and philosophic; a few lit with tragic beauty—*The Death of the Hired Man*, the agonizing *Home Burial,* the exalted and half-mystical *Hill Wife*. And lastly we have the more personal poems, never brief confessional lyrics of emotion such as most poets give us—here Mr. Frost guards his reserves—but reflective bits like *Storm Fear, Bond and Free, Flower-gathering,* or meditative monologues quaintly, keenly, sympathetically humorous, the humor veiling a peering questing wisdom, as in *Brown's Descent* above mentioned, or the more recent *New Hampshire*.

The poems of nature and of farm life all express delight, and some are ecstatic. The poet knows what he is talking about, and loves the country and the life. He gets a thrill out of birches in the sun, a cow running cider-wild (such real animals in these poems!), out of mending stony walls, planting seed, etc. His touch upon these subjects is sure and individual, the loving touch

[ 60 ]

of a specialist—we know he knows. And in the character pieces we feel just as sure of him. That mean little
spidery skinflint in *The Code*—who can doubt his absolute existence? And the pitifully futile "hired man"
with the two who sheltered him; the parson idealist in
*Snow;* the winged and wind-blown figure of *The Hill
Wife;* the bereaved and disillusioned woman in *Home
Burial*—these and others are intensely alive, caught in
the act of passion or aspiration.

When it comes to personal confession—to autobiography, so to speak—Mr. Frost refuses to take himself
seriously. He has to laugh—or rather, he has to smile in
that whimsical observant side-long way of his. This mood
greets us most characteristically in *New Hampshire,* the
long poem which, in painting a portrait, so to speak, of
his state, establishes a sympathetic relation with himself,
and paints, more or less consciously, his own portrait.
That is, he presents a spare, self-niggardly, self-respecting,
determined, uncompromising member of the sisterhood of
states, one which has "a specimen of everything" but
"not enough of anything to sell," one which keeps a firm
hold on her fields and mountains, her equal state rights
with New York and Illinois, even while she grins in-
wardly at getting the better of her large neighbors in
spite of her own slight stature. Mr. Frost's personal
attitude, if we may believe his poetry, is much the same.
He would probably say to himself: "I am a specimen
farmer, teacher, traveller, citizen, poet; and I haven't
enough of anything to sell; but I've got a few mountains
and valleys inside of me, and a bit of sea to look across,
and I'm headed for something somewhere, and I'm bound
to keep going."

It's a reasonable human attitude. Anyone with an ounce of humor must accept his own infinite unimportance in the universal scheme; but also he has a right to set up his own importance as an element in that scheme. New Hampshire and her poet both have character, as well as a penetrating, humorous and sympathetic quality of genius. They face the half-glance of the world, and the huge laughter of destiny, with pride and grit, and without egotism.

If *New Hampshire* presents this attitude with delightful whimsicality, a shorter poem in this same latest book tells more seriously the story of a poet's doubt and intuition and aspiration. So it may be fitting to conclude this brief and inadequate study with *For Once Then Something,* a poem as confessional as Robert Frost is ever likely to write:

> Others taunt me with having knelt at well-curbs
> Always wrong to the light, so never seeing
> Deeper down in the well than where the water
> Gives me back in a shining surface picture
> Me myself in the summer heaven, god-like,
> Looking out of a wreath of fern and cloud-puffs.
> Once, when trying with chin against a well-curb,
> I discerned, as I thought, beyond the picture,
> Through the picture, a something white, uncertain,
> Something more of the depths—and then I lost it.
> Water came to rebuke the too clear water.
> One drop fell from a fern, and lo, a ripple
> Shook whatever it was lay there at bottom,
> Blurred it, blotted it out. What was that whiteness?
> Truth? A pebble of quartz? For once, then, something.

"For once, then, something!"—it's about as far as any of us can go in the quest of truth. But even that far is "something."

### EDNA ST. VINCENT MILLAY

LONG ago, when I was mooning and dreaming through the pig-tail period, I used to think how fine it would be to be the greatest woman poet since Sappho. The audacity of youth—of near-childhood—would have scorned any lower goal; and the young aspirant, gazing aloft and afar, seemed to detect a smile of encouragement on the inhumanly beautiful visage which glorified an imaginary shrine.

Well, failure is the lot of all—it were shame indeed for ardent youth to set up any attainable goal. The dream must outrun the fleetest foot, or else the trophy will wither in one's hand. "Success—there's no such thing!" I once made a "successful" man say in a play. It is more reasonable to take pride in the degree of one's failure than to measure with facile vanity one's achievement.

But I am reminded by that old dream to wonder whether we may not raise a point worthy of discussion in claiming that a certain living lady may perhaps be the greatest woman poet since Sappho. After all, the roll contains few names. Who are they, the woman-poets of the past twenty-five hundred years? Possessing few languages, I am incompetent in the search, but I can remember no names of importance in the Greek, Roman or mediaeval literature. Folk-lore may hide under its anonymity a few women—its motive and feeling are often feminine; but no one can search them out. A wide shelf of more-or-less-modern anthologies—French, German,

Italian, Russian, Jugo-Slavian, Armenian, Ukrainian, Swedish and others—all these contain few feminine names, and apparently none of importance. Two or three oriental ladies have been listed, but of their quality we cannot judge.

In short, the woman-poets seem to have written almost exclusively in the English language. Emily Bronte, Elizabeth Barrett Browning, Christina Rossetti, Emily Dickinson—these four names bring us to 1900. Differing profoundly each from the others, these women were alike in this—they were all recluses by instinct, leading shy lives more or less aloof from the world; three of them spinsters, and the fourth protected and enveloped by a singularly potent and sympathetic marriage.

Emily Bronte—austere, heroic, solitary—is of course the greatest woman in literature. Not even Sappho's *Hymn to Aphrodite* (ignorant of Greek, I speak timidly) can surpass *Wuthering Heights* for sheer depth and power of beauty, or match it for the compassing of human experience in a single masterpiece. But *Wuthering Heights,* though poetic in motive and essence, classes as a novel rather than a poem; and, if one omits that from the reckoning, Emily Bronte's rank as a poet, or more specifically as a lyrist, rests upon a single poem, the sublime *Last Lines* which made her faith in life immortal—for her other poems, some of them fine, are scarcely important. As a poet, though no less intense than Emily Dickinson, she is less prolific; and she has not the scope, the variety, of Edna St. Vincent Millay, whose claim to pre-eminence we are considering.

Mrs. Browning?—well, some of the *Sonnets from the Portuguese,* another fine sonnet *Grief,* and lyric bits of

[ 64 ]

longer (usually too long) poems, are beautiful and poignant, sincerely feminine in their emotional appeal. But
they do not quite ascend to those higher levels which
we are now trying to explore.

Nor Christina Rossetti. Religious poems like *Paradise*
and *Marvel of Marvels* are finely fluted little altar-
candles—burning rather pale, though, beside those of real
ecstatics like Saint Teresa or Gerard Hopkins; and a few
songs—*When I am dead, my dearest,* and others—are
lovely in their sweet sincerity of renunciation. But these
also breathe not that rarer air.

Emily Dickinson climbs much higher than either
Elizabeth or Christina; in fact, she presents a formidable
claim to Sapphic honors. Her brief poems—many of
them—have a swift and keen lyric intensity, a star-like
beauty. They are sudden flashes into the deep well of
a serene and impregnable human soul, sure of the truth
in solitude. They celebrate the eternal theme—search
of the mystery, the meaning of life, the relation of the
human soul to the beloved of this world and of the
world of vision beyond; and especially they illumine the
soul's quest of the infinite, of God.

Edna Millay is a very different person from any of
these four. By no means a recluse, she has courted life
and shunned none of its adventures. Her youth has been
crowded with companions, friends, lovers; she has gone
through college, earned her living at journalism, has
travelled, acted, given readings, known poverty and comparative ease—in short, she has taken the rough-and-
tumble of a modern American girl's life and has reached
its usual climax, marriage. Beginning, before she was
twenty and while still a little tomboy of the Maine coast,

with *Renascence,* a poem of desperate faith, lithe as a faun in its naked search of the soul, the danger has been that life might lure her away from art. The complications of a hunted human soul in these stirring days—the struggle for breath, for food and lodging, the pot-boilers, the flirtations, the teasing petty trials and interruptions—how could the poet in her survive all these, and put out fresh flowers of beauty?

But the poet has survived, and the flowers have sprung up richly along her path. If *Renascence* remains the poem of largest sweep which Miss Millay has achieved as yet—the most comprehensive expression of her philosophy, so to speak, her sense of miracle in life and death—yet she has been lavish with details of experience, of emotion, and her agile and penetrating mind has leapt through spaces of thought rarely traversed by women, or by men either for that matter.

For in the lightest of her briefest lyrics there is always more than appears. In the *Figs,* for example, in *Thursday, The Penitent, The Not Impossible Him* and other witty ironies, and in more serious poems like *The Betrothal,* how neatly she upsets the carefully built walls of convention which men have set up around their Ideal Woman, even while they fought, bled and died for all the Helens and Cleopatras they happened to encounter! Such poems emphasize with irony the essential aloofness of the soul, and in *Feast* we find this bitter truth in bleak and naked clarity:

> I drank at every vine.
>> The last was like the first.
> I came upon no wine
>> So wonderful as thirst.

> I gnawed at every root.
>     I ate of every plant.
> I came upon no fruit
>     So wonderful as want.
>
> Feed the grape and bean
>     To the vintner and monger;
> I will lie down lean
>     With my thirst and my hunger.

In *Aria da Capo,* a masterpiece of irony sharp as Toledo steel, she stabs the war-god to the heart with a stroke as clean, as deft, as ever the most skilfully murderous swordsman bestowed upon his enemy. Harangues have been made, volumes have been written, for the outlawry of war, but who else has put its preposterous unreasonableness into a nutshell like this girl who brings to bear upon the problem the luminous creative insight of genius?

Thus on the most serious subjects there is always the keen swift touch. Beauty blows upon them and is gone before one can catch one's breath; and lo and behold, we have a poem too lovely to perish, a song out of the blue which will ring in the ears of time. Such are the "little elegies" which will make the poet's Vassar friend, D. C. of the wonderful voice, a legend of imperishable beauty even though "her singing days are done." Here are two of them:

### EPITAPH

> Heap not on this mound
> Roses that she loved so well—
> Why bewilder her with roses,
> That she cannot see or smell?
> She is happy where she lies
> With the dust upon her eyes.

### CHORUS

Give away her gowns,
Give away her shoes—
She has no more use
For her fragrant gowns.
Take them all down—
Blue, green, blue,
Lilac, pink, blue—
From their padded hangers,
She will dance no more
In her narrow shoes;
Sweep her narrow shoes
From the closet floor.

Thousands of stay-at-home women speak wistfully in *Departure;* and *Lament*—where can one find deep grief and its futility expressed with such agonizing grace? Indeed, though love and death and the swift passing of beauty have haunted this poet as much as others, she is rarely specific and descriptive. Her thought is transformed into imagery, into symbol, and it flashes back at us as from the facets of a jewel.

And the thing is so simply done. One weeps, not over D. C.'s death, but over her narrow shoes and blue gowns empty in the closet. In *Renascence,* the sky, the earth, the infinite, no longer abstractions, come close, as tangible as a tree. *The Harp-weaver,* presenting the protective power of enveloping love—power which enwraps the beloved even after death has robbed him, is a kind of fairy-tale ballad, sweetly told as for a child. Even more in *The Curse* emotion becomes sheer magic of imagery and sound, as clear and keen as frost in sunlight. Always one feels the poet's complete and unabashed sincerity. She says neither the expected thing nor the "daring" thing, but she says the incisive true thing as she has discovered it and feels it.

Miss Millay's most confessional lyrics are in sonnet form, and among them are a number which can hardly be forgotten so long as English literature endures, and one or two which will rank among the best of a language extremely rich in beautiful sonnets. It is a pity that the poet ever broke up the series of *Twenty Sonnets* published in *Reedy's Mirror* during April and May 1920, and afterwards scattered, all but two of them, through the volumes entitled *Second April, Figs from Thistles,* and *The Harp-weaver*. About three-fourths of the twenty belong together in a sequence which should be restored, a sequence which might be entitled *Winged Love* since it portrays the ecstasy and bitter brevity of passion. Among these are *Into the golden vessel of great song, Not with libations, Oh think not I am faithful to a vow, And you as well must die, Cherish you then the hope I shall forget,* and others in which verbal music, the winged phrase, the richly colored image, carry poignant emotion in triumph. One of these expresses the divided allegiance of the poet-soul, torn between human passion and the diviner troth with inexorable art:

> Cherish you then the hope I shall forget
> At length, my lord, Pieria?—put away
> For your so passing sake, this mouth of clay,
> These mortal bones against my body set,
> For all the puny fever and frail sweat
> Of human love?—renounce for these, I say,
> The singing mountain's memory, and betray
> The silent lyre that hangs upon me yet?
> Ah, but indeed some day shall you awake,
> Rather, from dreams of me, that at your side
> So many nights, a lover and a bride,

But stern in my soul's chastity, have lain,
To walk the world forever for my sake,
And in each chamber find me gone again!

Beyond these, outside the love-sequence, the Euclid sonnet stands in a place apart, of a beauty rarely to be matched for sculpturesque austerity, for detachment from the body and the physical universe:

Euclid alone has looked on Beauty bare.
Let all that prate of Beauty hold their peace,
And lay them prone upon the earth, and cease
To ponder on themselves, the while they stare
At nothing, intricately drawn nowhere
In shapes of shifting lineage. Let geese
Gabble and hiss, but heroes seek release
From dusty bondage into luminous air.
Oh, blinding hour—oh, holy terrible day—
When first the shaft into his vision shone
Of light anatomized! Euclid alone
Has looked on Beauty bare; fortunate they
Who, though once only and then but far away,
Have heard her massive sandal set on stone.

Other minds, searching the higher mathematics, have divined the central structural beauty on which all other beauty is founded, but if any other poet has expressed it I have yet to see the proof. That a young woman should have put this fundamental law into a sonnet is one of the inexplicable divinations of genius. Those shallow critics who decry the modern scientific spirit as materialistic, who find no creative imagination in such minds as Willard Gibbs and Wilbur Wright, would do well to meditate upon this poem, one of the great sonnets of the language. If Miss Millay had done nothing else, she could hardly be forgotten.

But she has done much else. Wilful, moody, whimsical, loving and forgetting, a creature of quick and keen emotions, she has followed her own way and sung her own songs. Taken as a whole, her poems present an utterly feminine personality of singular charm and power; and the best of them, a group of lyrics ineffably lovely, may ultimately be cherished as the richest, most varied and most precious gift of song which any woman since the immortal Lesbian has offered to the world.

THE typical well-read American girl appears and develops in Sara Teasdale's books—and develops, as sometimes happens, into something rarer and finer than her early promise foretold. We have, quite frankly presented, in the *Sonnets to Duse,* of 1907, and in *Helen of Troy and Other Poems,* of 1912, this girl's dream "crushes," her imaginary love-affairs, her tremors and bewilderments, her woes and delights. Even in *Rivers to the Sea,* of 1915, this girlish softness sometimes persists; but in certain of its poems one notes the beginning of a hardening process which is shaping the girl into a woman and her enthusiastic outpourings into poems—poems of a finished and delicate, if narrow technique. And in some of the new poems in *Love Songs,* of 1917, and in the more austere and mature *Flame and Shadow,* of 1920, a fully developed fine spirit expresses its sensitive reactions to life with an economy of phrase and a simple lyric intensity that show also matured art.

But let us follow her development more in detail. Girlishness has a right to state its case, no doubt; and we feel the authentic statement of it, sometimes prettily set forth, in those two early books of this rather frail and closely protected St. Louis girl who dreamed and rhymed over Duse's photographs, over those highly standardized and much poetized heroines, Sappho and Helen;

and now and then, quite shyly and wistfully, over some
passing and indifferent living boy.

> Your beauty lives in mystic melodies
> And all the light about you breathes a song,

she cries to Duse, whom she had never seen; and again:

> Yea, like a flower within a desert place,
> Whose petals fold and fade for lack of rain,
> Are these your eyes.

—lines that escape gush because of something perfumed
and fragile about them—a bud of talent just beginning
to open.  The Greek heroines and Guinevere and others
celebrated in the second book, are less fortunate—these
ladies indulge in long monologues; and if poets mature
and distinguished have failed to put effective words into
the mouth of Sappho, one could hardly expect the miracle
from a mere girl inexperienced in both life and art, and
of most undramatic talent.

In one section of this second book the poet begins to
seek her own element, but her wings flap with the rather
exaggerated action of inexperience.  This one is a girl's
theory of what unrequited love should be:

> Less than the cloud to the wind,
> Less than the foam to the sea,
> Less than the rose to the storm
> Am I to thee.
>
> More than the star to the night,
> More than the rain to the sea,
> More than heaven to earth
> Art thou to me.

But the illusion collapses at the first touch of reality:

> For though I know he loves me,
> Tonight my heart is sad—
> His kiss was not so wonderful
> As all the dreams I had.

[ 73 ]

In *Rivers to the Sea,* published three years later, the bud of girlish talent has opened into a flower. This book contains some of the poet's finest lyrics—*Morning, The Flight, The Answer, Longing, After Death,* and this much quoted one, *Debt:*

> What do I owe to you
>  Who loved me deep and long?
> You never gave my spirit wings,
>  Or gave my heart a song.
>
> But oh, to him I loved,
>  Who loved me not at all,
> I owe the open gate
>  That led through heaven's wall.

In this volume and the two later ones we have the material for a rounded estimate of a poet whose songs give the woman's version of the human love-story, or at least as much of it as one of the finer, more sensitive and protected women of our veiled and walled-in civilization may contribute to the whole vast epic of the race.

Sara Teasdale's study has been to express emotion in the simplest form of English lyric verse. Two or three quatrains of three- or four-footed iambic lines, each quatrain emphasized by a single rhyme, form usually the metrical structure of her songs. But the process is not so easy as it seems, as many would-be lyric poets have discovered at heavy cost. Miss Teasdale builds upon this simple structure subtle variants of rhythm and melody that weave to a climax expressing fitly some keen emotion. Her instrument is not rich and powerful, capable of chords; and it has more the aching quality of a violin than the plangent triumphant tone of a harp—a violin played with soft tenseness by feminine hands at twilight.

One comes upon her music unexpectedly, so to speak, and when she is in her best mood the reward is singularly pure and fine.

Let us try two or three more. Here is a *Wood Song:*

> I heard a wood thrush in the dusk
>     Twirl three notes and make a star.
> My heart that walked with bitterness
>     Came back from very far.
>
> Three shining notes were all he had,
>     And yet they made a starry call—
> I caught life back against my breast
>     And kissed it, scars and all.

This is called *On the Dunes:*

> If there is any life when death is over
>     These tawny beaches will know much of me—
> I shall come back, as constant and as changeful
>     As the unchanging many-colored sea.
>
> If life was small, if it has made me scornful,
>     Forgive me—I shall straighten like a flame
> In the great calm of death, and if you want me
>     Stand on the seaward dunes and call my name.

And this, also from *Flame and Shadow,* is one of the loveliest of all:

> Let it be forgotten, as a flower is forgotten,
>     Forgotten as a fire that once was singing gold.
> Let it be forgotten for ever and ever—
>     Time is a kind friend, he will make us old.
>
> If anyone asks, say it was forgotten
>     Long and long ago—
> As a flower, as a fire, as a hushed footfall
>     In a long forgotten snow.

These songs give Sara Teasdale's rhythmic range—narrow, but within its limits delicately varied. The fall of slow syllables in the last is especially adroit, lengthening out the *for ever* into quiet deeps of remoteness. And if her rhythmic range is narrow, her subjects also follow pretty closely the single track of personal emotion. One feels behind the poems a straight clear-thinking mind, but the poetic motive comes from feeling rather than thought; and the feeling springs from common human experiences, not from intellectual passion of acceptance or revolt. Her mind is conscious of standing idly by, conscious that her poems do not tell the whole story:

> What do I care, in the dreams and the languor of spring,
>   That my songs do not show me at all?
> For they are a fragrance, and I am a flint and a fire;
>   I am an answer, they are only a call.
>
> But what do I care, for love will be over so soon—
>   Let my heart have its say, and my mind stand idly by.
> For my mind is proud, and strong enough to be silent—
>   It is my heart that makes my songs, not I.

It follows that her poems do not present the unexpected intuition, do not flash their light into depths of subconsciousness and make us thrill with a sense of discovery. Their weakness is a temptation toward the easy and obvious. Their strength is the emotional intensity and the clear swift artistry with which they often succeed in expressing the reaction of a finely feminine spirit to the beauty of nature and life, the ecstasy of love, the threat of pain and death, and the transitoriness of all these things.

Her reactions are always serious. Now that women are becoming more articulate, and we detect soprano and contralto voices among the tenors and baritones who have hitherto monopolized the lyric field, one may hear a few high notes of ironic laughter to match the gayety, or even ribaldry, of masculine songs which have played up the moods and aspects of love. But mostly the feminine voices are serious to the point of poignancy—love especially, to most women, is a serious, if not indeed a tragic adventure. Sara Teasdale's love-songs may be high-hearted almost to the point of gayety, but they are always serious. And always there is in them, as in all her singing, something fugitive—the emotion, so keen at the moment, will soon be gone. If Sara Teasdale has a message for us, perhaps it is summed up in these two lines from *The Voice:*

> Seek for Beauty—she only
> Fights with man against Death.

One element of strength in her poems is that within their outspoken emotion one feels the hidden and secret fire of a spirit essentially shy and reserved. The poet may seem to be frank, but she does not say quite all. This power of personality in her may prove the strongest factor in the persistence of her fame—indeed, fame, in the ultimate analysis, is always based on personality. For a few of her lyrics will certainly flare above the others as time goes on, and be cherished for their beauty and clarity, like finely cut jewels of warm pure color offered by a woman's hand to the rich treasury of English song.

## AMY LOWELL

*[It is difficult to recognize the grim decree of fate by considering Amy Lowell's work as finished. Indeed, the materials for rounding the circle are not yet before us, for two posthumous books will complete the record. The study of her poetry which follows was written a few months before her too early death, and it may be best not to change its tenses or spirit. If it suggests a great woman in full career of unexhausted power it will give a truer impression of the poet than could any study written under the immediate influence of the loss of her.]*

ONE may as well begin by granting Miss Lowell everything but genius. There is a rumor, probably too plausible to be true, that she once said, "I made myself a poet, but the Lord made me a business man." Did I say everything but genius?—but she has genius, only not of the kind we usually imply when we talk of the few fortunate poets who possess it. Her genius is that of the commander, the organizer; and she has chosen to organize herself as well as the world, and bring to bear all the resources of her imagination, temperament and scholarship in the service of a varied and practicable literary talent.

Even genius can't burn very long or strong without that sober persistent feeding of its flame which character alone may accomplish. History is full of "brilliant magnificent failures," the little heaps of ashes where its ineffectual fires, which had flared up with noise and blaze, fell to embers and went out. There are so many chances against genius that the rare cases of its self-fulfilment seem almost miracles. But character, when aided by intelligence, may go a long way without genius, as countless famous names, highly honored in their day and still lingering on history's pages, may be invoked to prove.

It has interested Miss Lowell to explore many fields and study all forms. Beginning—in the *Atlantic* about fifteen years ago—with sonnets and other exactitudes, and writing her 1912 book entirely in rhyme or blank verse, she was attracted by the imagists from their first appearance toward the end of that year, studied their ideas and technique, and joined the group to the entent of appearing in the three *Some Imagists* anthologies of 1915-16-17. In her six books of verse are lyrics, grotesques, narratives; in rhyme, blank verse, free verse and the "polyphonic prose" which, with scholarly intuition of values, she adapted and modified from the French. And two other books, *Six French Poets* and *Fir-flower Tablets,* prove her skill in adapting to English the elusive meanings of modern French poets, and even, with the aid of her friend Mrs. Ayscough, of old Chinese. Also, in *A Fable for Critics,* she has tried her hand, like Byron, at a lightly running satirical handling of her contemporaries.

In all this astonishing variety one feels power. Behind it all is the drive and urge of a rich and strong personality. The force which Miss Lowell's New England ancestors put into founding and running cotton-mills, or belike into saving souls, she puts into conquering an art and making it express and serve her. And with what success! Most poets and prosers are remembered because of what they wrote, details of biography and character being of little consequence. Others—Pope and Byron are examples, and our own Eugene Field—have instinctively dramatized themselves before the world, so that their books become but one element in a memorable career, a career which sets its mark upon a period and proves typical and permanently interesting.

Amy Lowell is such a figure. Certain of her poems might survive even if someone else stood behind them: *Patterns,* for example, says a true thing, a thing close to people's lives and hearts, with beauty and concentrated force; and a few lyrics are delicately wrought on a motive of poignant wistfulness. But backed as they are by her magnificent authority, not only these will be cherished, but also enough others to round out and complete the portrait for the next age. People will feel the sweep and luxury of her brilliant passage through a sober world, and will keep in touch with it through the gaudy colors of *Can Grande's Castle,* which, whether or not it proves her case for polyphonic prose, presents to the limit its author's commanding audacity and love of color and drama. And they will admire the cosmopolitan intelligence which breaks through New England boundaries of mood and method, and searches the earth from Peru to China for gorgeous exotic flowers, in *Legends* and other sumptuous "pictures of a floating world."

I shall be accused of saying that Miss Lowell will be remembered more as a person than as a poet, and to a certain extent this is true. But if her commands to the goddess have been a little too dictatorial, still she has put that elusive personage through some lively experimental paces, and taught her a thing or two worth knowing. The New England muse has been shaken out of her cosy provincialism by this daughter of the Caesars, and set upon the doorstep of a larger world; and Boston, aghast but inspired, acclaims while it doubts this Lowell of the new day and the wider horizon.

One detects a certain scientific rapture in many of Miss Lowell's interesting experiments in technique. She delights in the rush and clatter of sounds, in the kaleidoscopic glitter of colors, even though the emotional or intellectual motive goes somewhat astray among them. In a few poems in the imagist anthologies—*Spring Day,* for example—one's ears and eyes feel fairly battered; still more in the *Can Grande* essays in polyphonic prose. She is most definitely true to the imagist technique in brief poems like some of the *Lacquer Prints*—the *Fuji* one, or *Paper Fishes.* *Patterns,* while not slavishly in that method, benefits by its exacting discipline; and such lyrics as *Venus Transiens, A Gift, Solitaire* owe to it their fine precision and fragile beauty. Also the two which follow:

### OMBRE CHINOISE

Red foxgloves against a yellow wall streaked with plum-colored
    shadows;
A lady with a blue and red sunshade;
The slow dash of waves upon a parapet.
That is all.
Non-existent—immortal—
As solid as the centre of a ring of fine gold.

### NIGHT CLOUDS

The white mares of the moon rush along the sky
Beating their golden hoofs upon the glass heavens;
The white mares of the moon are all standing on their hind legs
Pawing at the green porcelain doors of the remote heavens.
Fly, mares!
Strain your utmost,

Scatter the milky dust of stars,
Or the tiger sun will leap upon you and destroy you
With one lick of his vermilion tongue.

But imagism could not hold her in, nor any other system of technique. She has used for her own purposes the training it gave her, just as she has used her study of prosody, and her wide reading of poetry in English and French, and, through translation, in other languages. No doubt it has sharpened her style, made it more direct and firm, even in the long narratives in *Legends,* and the picture-stories, if one may so call them, in *Can Grande.* Of these two books, I get more fun personally out of *Legends. Can Grande* seems too explanatory, too much a literary exercise, an effort to see what may be done with polyphonics in presenting characters, scenes, impressions, stories. Its colors and sounds hurtle against the mind with kaleidoscopic intensity from beginning to end of each narrative, so that one gets tired and loses all sense of climax. Also the form itself becomes monotonous with its teasing internal rhymes and assonances; it is ingeniously effective in the direction of virtuosity rather than beauty.

But in *Legends* she is less absorbed with technique, and so more free in the handling of her various methods. Her presentation of the stories selected from folk-lore and legendry here, there and everywhere may not be so mediaeval as the old ballads, so oriental as Lafcadio Hearn, so aboriginal as Lew Sarett or Natalie Curtis or Frank Cushing's Zuni medicine-man, but it is a clever and effective interpretation by a modern poet-scholar accomplished in the study of literature and rhythms. And the book is immensely entertaining. The stories are told with gusto by an up-to-date enthusiast, an artist who does not dawdle or grow weary or lose control of her method. And they are full of astonishingly good figures and picturesquely vivid descriptive passages; one is carried along with a sense of swift and expert movement.

The best of these "tales of peoples," in my opinion, are *Many Swans,* derived from our own aboriginal folk-lore, the knightly ballad *The Ring and the Castle,* the pretty Chinese *Legend of Porcelain,* and the New England murder-story *Four Sides to a House.*

A number of Miss Lowell's New England narratives are in the form of monologues in dialect—mostly character-sketches of lonely souls, pushed by a bitter fate to extremes of agony. The people in these poems seem to me authentically alive, and certain ones—*Reaping, Off the Turnpike,* the clock poem, *Number 3 on the Docket*—suggest strongly the weirdness of isolation on some of those decaying farms—human beings with nerves drawn tense to the verge of insanity. The free-verse rhythms may be rather ragged, but it is a harsh unmusical habit of speech which the poet is trying to suggest, and more flowing measures would destroy, rather than express, whatever poetry is inherent in the situation. If some of them touch on the grotesque, they are all the more expressive of their author, for her sense of humor takes that direction.

In fact, Miss Lowell, as well as certain other modern poets—W. C. Williams, Alfred Kreymborg, Marianne Moore *et al*—have reminded us that the grotesque, even in poetry, is an authentic artistic motive. If a Japanese ivory-carver may put his sense of absurd incongruities into a netsuke, or a Gothic stone-cutter into a gargoyle, there is no reason why a poet should not take and give similar delight in such a grotesque as *Red Slippers,* which I quote as one of Miss Lowell's most brilliant successes, and also as a characteristic example of her polyphonic prose:

### RED SLIPPERS

Red slippers in a shop-window; and outside in the street, flaws of gray, windy sleet!

Behind the polished glass the slippers hang in long threads of red, festooning from the ceiling like stalactites of blood, flooding the eyes of passers-by with dripping color, jamming their crimson reflections against the windows of cabs and tram-cars, screaming their claret and salmon into the teeth of the sleet, plopping their little round maroon lights upon the tops of umbrellas.

The row of white, sparkling shop-fronts is gashed and bleeding, it bleeds red slippers. They spout under the electric light, fluid and fluctuating, a hot rain—and freeze again to red slippers, myriadly multiplied in the mirror side of the window.

They balance upon arched insteps like springing bridges of crimson lacquer; they swing up over curved heels like whirling tanagers sucked in a wind-pocket; they flatten out, heelless, like July ponds, flared and burnished by red rockets.

Snap, snap, they are cracker sparks of scarlet in the white, monotonous block of shops.

They plunge the clangor of billions of vermilion trumpets into the crowd outside, and echo in faint rose over the pavement.

People hurry by, for these are only shoes, and in a window farther down is a big lotus bud of cardboard, whose petals open every few minutes and reveal a wax doll, with staring bead eyes and flaxen hair, lolling awkwardly in its flower chair.

One has often seen shoes, but whoever saw a cardboard lotus bud before?

The flaws of gray, windy sleet beat on the shop-window where there are only red slippers.

One finds a similar quality in *Balls, Fireworks,* the *Stravinsky Trilogy* and other poems. In fact it colors

her work generally, for it is one of her vital and control-
ing characteristics.

In summing up, one might inquire whether Miss
Lowell has gone further as a lyric or a narrative poet,
using *narrative* to cover all her various presentations of
episodes of historic, legendary or more individual human
adventure. Probably the latter direction has given more
scope to her fecundity and energy, her love of color and
sound and drama. The richness and luxury of her product in this kind contrasts strangely with the delicacy of
her personal lyrics, which are mostly in a minor key of
wistful sadness. On the whole she has been generously
expressive. Her six volumes of verse and three of prose
present, with singular completeness, a commanding—nay,
enthralling—personality. Such energy, fecundity, persistence, intelligence, appearing in this world of com-
promises and half-successes, rebukes people less forceful,
less unified, by achieving to the very limit of its power.
And, as we suggested above, her books are only one
element of the drama which she has impressed upon the
literary history of our time.

### JOHN GOULD FLETCHER

A PAINTER-poet, a landscape-poet, a colorist—one searches in vain for the descriptive word. For Mr. Fletcher's keen eye for surface beauty is but one outlet of a subtle metaphysical mind, a mind which has gone questing far and wide for intimate responses—through travel, through reading, through strange tongues, through the arts and philosophies, as well as through life's closer contacts. His Pegasus has had a weight to carry, and sometimes its wings have trailed in earthly dust; one has felt thought dragging too hard upon inspiration, sheer flight impeded by a prodding intellect.

It is a question how far deliberation is creative. One rarely feels in Mr. Fletcher's art the true lyric rapture, the emotion that seizes the singer and carries him away. But one does feel something only a little less impassioned —the absorption of the contemplative spirit in its object, the self uplifted and transcended into ecstasy. This latter mood or method, while more conscious than the other, while invoked rather than inspired, is but a little less authoritative in all the arts. It implies an imagination sensitive and worshipful, keen to accept and reflect all of this world's varied manifestations of beauty.

> Brown bed of earth, still fresh and warm with love,
> Now hold me tight;
> Broad field of sky, where the clouds laughing move,
> Fill up my pores with light!—

This is Mr. Fletcher's cry in *Irradiations*. And through-out this group of nearly forty poems—indeed, in all the *Preludes and Symphonies*—the poet celebrates his love of earth and sea and sky in all their magic transformations. Also he sometimes presents those infinities of nature as modified and framed in by man's building of houses, cities, ships; it was a city-flight of clouds which excited his most famous, and perhaps most colorful lines:

Over the roof-tops race the shadows of clouds;
Like horses the shadows of clouds charge down the street.

Whirlpools of purple and gold,
Winds from the mountains of cinnabar,
Lacquered mandarin moments, palanquins swaying and balanc-
    ing
Amid the vermilion pavilions, against the jade balustrades.

Glint of the glittering winds of dragon-flies in the light;
Silver filaments, golden flakes settling downwards;
Rippling quivering flutters; repulse and surrender,
The sun broidered upon the rain,
The rain rustling with the sun.

Over the roof-tops race the shadows of clouds:
Like horses the shadows of clouds charge down the street.

Here is Mr. Fletcher's real love affair. The more personal love poems in *The Tree of Life* are comparative-ly unconvincing. Through the *Symphonies—Blue, Black and Gold, Green, Golden, White, Orange, Red, Violet, Grey, Scarlet*—he records the meditative imaginings ex-cited by his adoration of beauty. London, Arkansas, Arizona, French battle-fields; streets, flowery meadows, the forest, the desert—all these move him to worship as he passes from scene to scene of the earth's enormous pageantry:

[ 87 ]

I am the wanderer of the world—
No one can hold me:
Not the cannon assembled for battle,
Nor the gloomy grain of the hollow,
Nor the house where I long time slumbered,
Nor the hilltop where roads are straggling.
My feet must march to the wind.

Indeed, he finds motive enough, emotion enough, in the earth-drama, and instinctively shuns the clash and fever of human contacts:

Now that all the world is filled
With armies clamoring,
Now that men no longer live and die one by one,
But in vague indeterminate multitudes;

Now that the trees are coppery towers,
Now that the clouds loom southward,
Now that the glossy creeper
Spatters the walls like spilt wine:

I will go out alone
To catch strong joy of solitude
Where the tree-lines, in gold and scarlet,
Swing strong grape-cables up the smoldering face of the hill.

Rarely does his art make room for fellow-creatures. The two or three primitives in his Arizona group are an integral part of the desert, like its cactus. The lady in *The Tree of Life* remains, in spite of all her poet-lover's eloquence, an abstraction. Mr. Fletcher is most convincing when most alone.

A close study of this poet's technique would show him a somewhat rebellious imagist, experimenting in and out of their tense method but profiting by its discipline. The "vermilion pavilions" passage shows how swiftly his lines may follow the bright-colored racing clouds. In *Down*

*the Mississippi*, by way of contrast, we have a succession
of slow movements, beginning:

Dull masses of dense green,
The forests range their sombre platforms.
Between them silently, like a spirit,
The river finds its own mysterious path.

Loosely the river sways out, backward, forward,
Always fretting the outer side;
Shunning the invisible focus of each crescent,
Seeking to spread into shining loops over fields:

Like an enormous serpent, dilating, uncoiling,
Displaying a broad scaly back of earth-smeared gold;
Swaying out sinuously between the dull motionless forests,
As molten metal might glide down the lip of a vase of dark
    bronze.

Everywhere a sensitive ear for word-harmonies and time-
values; everywhere persistence in seeking, through the
intricacies of language, his own personal rhythm.

Sometimes, as with most other poets, his technique lags,
seems labored. His polyphonic prose, with its endless
tinkle of internal rhymes and assonances, is, like Miss
Lowell's, an interesting experiment in a highly artificialized, and therefore unresponsive, form; at best a perfervid
eloquence, too monotonous in its cadences. But mostly
he prefers free verse, and uses it, according to the mood
of the poem, with a delicate and subtle variety of sound
and tune.

Mr. Fletcher's excursive mind has led him to a study
of oriental technique in various arts, and the brief poems
in his *Japanese Prints* are an effort, not to imitate or
translate, but to interpret in our own terms the spirit of
the Japanese hokku, tanka, etc. The result seems slight
and frail, on the whole the book does not lead us very far

toward either East or West; but three or four of its tiny poems are very delicate—for instance, *Fugitive Beauty:*

As the fish that leaps from the river,
As the dropping of a November leaf at twilight,
As the faint flicker of lightning down the southern sky,
So I saw beauty, far away.

Or this one:

A piece of paper ready to toss in the fire,
Blackened, scrawled with fragments of an incomplete song:
My soul.

In spite of his cosmopolite wanderings and foreign residence, there is something indestructibly of his own country about John Gould Fletcher. No one but a southerner brought up during the decay of the old regime could have written *The Ghosts of an Old House,* a poem perfumed with fading elegance and melancholy with vanished grandeur. And even apart from the implications in many of his subjects—*New York, Chicago, Skyscrapers, The Grand Canyon, etc.*—a certain type of much travelled, much educated, serious-minded American is manifest in all he writes. If he lacks humor, he makes up for it by a deep strain of imaginative mysticism which he has not yet fully expressed, and which may be his next note. Of late his work in verse has lacked something of the earlier fire. But one feels this slowing down as an interlude— his thoughtful philosophic mind is leading his imagination into new fields. One would not be surprised if his art should flower again in a stimulating new birth of power.

In *The Tree of Life* the finest of the love poems express foreboding—for example, *The Offering,* very lovely with its haunting refrain,

Dead leaves, dry leaves;

and we find it also in this briefer lyric, *The Silence:*

> The silence that I hear is more than words;
> The silence that I breathe is more than thought;
> The silence that I know is more than life;
> It is a silence of all silences.
> For ever and ever, to eternity
> It goes, and I go with it, well content.

But no poet goes to eternity content with silence. If Mr. Fletcher can hear the song in that silence that is "more than life" we may have from him poems more profoundly beautiful than he has yet achieved.

THE astonishing thing about H. D.'s poetry is the wildness of it—that trait strikes me as I read her whole record in the *Collected Poems* recently published by Boni & Liveright. She is as wild as deer on the mountain, as hepaticas under the wet mulsh of spring, as a dryad racing nude through the wood. She is never indoors, never even in a tent. Her feet know the harsh rocks, but never the ordered hardness of pavements. Her breath is drawn from bright breezes and bold winds, but never from the walled-in atmosphere of rooms. She is, in a sense, one of the most civilized, most ultra-refined, of poets; and yet never was a poet more unaware of civilization, more independent of its thralls. She doesn't talk about nature, doesn't praise or patronize or condescend to it; but she is, quite unconsciously, a lithe, hard, bright-winged spirit of nature to whom humanity is but an incident.

Thus she carries English poetry back to the Greeks more instinctively than any other poet who has ever written in our language. Studying Greek poetry, she finds herself at home there, and quite simply expresses the kinship in her art. For the Greeks, like all singers of primitive races, were never indoors, and their gods were effluences of nature, personifications of her forces. Compared with the Greeks, the inhabitants of little England have been shut-ins ever since the language formed itself out of the ruins of Latin and Gothic tongues. And their

poets have written in houses; they have sung gloriously
of nature, but they have looked at her through windows—
they have not been one with her.

It would be an interesting speculation to consider how
much H. D. owes to the pioneers whom all Americans
descend from more or less. The pioneers took a shut-in
race out of doors, exposed it to nature's harsh activities,
and thus restored a certain lost fibre to its very blood
and bones. H. D., eastern born and bred as she was,
has inherited from them rather than from the barons and
carls of England's past. And her poetry is more akin
to that of our aborigines than it is to the Elizabethans or
Victorians, or any of the classicists or romanticists between them. The English poet Winifred Bryher said,
in reviewing *Hymen:*

> To people born in England H. D.'s work is peculiarly Ameri-
> can—American with a southern flavor and a singularly native
> strength.

Her technique, like her spiritual motive, is lithe and
nude. The free-verse forms she chooses are not even
clothing, so innocent are they of any trace of artificiality;
they are as much a part of her spirit, they complete it as
essentially, as harmoniously, as the skin which encloses
and outlines the flesh of a human body.

One may follow her flight from worldliness in all her
poems, but perhaps it is most explicit in two of them.
*Sheltered Garden* is a protest—observe that even her
protests are uttered out-of-doors:

> I have had enough—
> I gasp for breath!

she cries; and after a few lines continues:

[ 93 ]

> I have had enough—
> border-pinks, clove-pinks, wax lilies,
> herbs, sweet-cress.
>
> Oh for some sharp swish of a branch—
> there is no scent of resin
> in this place,
> no taste of bark, of coarse weeds,
> aromatic, astringent;
> only border on border of scented pinks.
> . . . . . . . . . .
> For this beauty,
> beauty without strength,
> chokes out life.
> I want wind to break—
> scatter these pink-stalks,
> snap off their spiced heads,
> fling them about with dead leaves;
> spread the paths with twigs,
> limbs broken off;
> trail great pine branches,
> hurled from some far wood
> right across the melon-patch;
> break pear and quince,
> leave half-trees, torn, twisted,
> but showing the fight was valiant.
>
> Oh to blot out this garden,
> to forget, to find a new beauty
> in some terrible
> wind-tortured place.

And here, in *Huntress*, we find her dryad spirit free
again, in its own element:

> Come, blunt your spear with us—
> our pace is hot,
> and our bare heels
> in the heel-prints—
> we stand tense—do you see?
> are you already beaten
> by the chase?

We lead the pace
for the wind on the hills.
The low hill is spattered
with loose earth—
our feet cut into the crust
as with spears.

We climbed the ploughed land,
dragged the seed from the clefts,
broke the clods with our heels,
whirled with a parched cry
into the woods:

*Can you come,*
*can you come,*
*can you follow the hound trail,*
*can you trample the hot froth?*

Spring up—sway forward—
follow the quickest one—
aye, though you leave the trail
and drop exhausted at our feet.

There is a bold and trained athleticism in such poetry as this. H. D.'s art has not the unstudied spontaneity of folk-lore, often so beautiful in its naiveté; it is shaped by an artist, carefully wrought to an effect of seeming improvisation. Its lines are simple in their strict firmness, but their simplicity is the result, not of instinct alone, but of right instinct sternly educated and disciplined. The keen rhythms of her poems respond with lyric magic to a spirit ever accepting nature's rhythms, a spirit growing with the grass, circling with the sun, racing with the wind, resting with the rocks on the slow beating-out of seasons.

In a certain sense she is inhuman, or perhaps superhuman. Her art is above and beyond little individual loves and hates; these, if they appear at all, merely serve to emphasize passions more ascetic in their indestructible hardihood. One feels that she has lived through and left behind the fierce surge of emotion which drowns so many souls; addressing a god, she says in *Adonis:*

> Each of us, like you,
> has died once.
> Each of us has crossed an old wood-path
> and found the winter leaves
> so golden in the sun-fire
> that even the live wood-flowers
> were dark.

Perhaps, in the last analysis, the much abused word mystic should be invoked to describe the super-sensuous significance of her poetry. Her real subject is the experience and aspiration of the human soul—the flowers and trees she writes about, the rocks and winds and mountains, are symbols of the soul's adventures, of a soul which discards and transcends and sublimates the daily events and emotions of ordinary life. In *Pygmalion* we hear her asking agonized questions of the infinite, when the sculptor's marble gods "have melted into the light" and departed "each from his plinth":

> Now am I the power
> that has made this fire,
> as of old I made the gods
> start from the rocks?
> Am I the god?—
> or does this fire carve me
> for its use?

In one of the most ecstatic of her poems, *The Shrine,* she seems to present inviolable Beauty—"great, fierce, evil"—

> You have tempted men,
> but they perished on your cliffs.

Beauty imperious and relentless, whom men seek forever through storms and agonies of the soul, but whose ultimate consolation they never quite attain:

> You are useless,
> O grave, O beautiful;
> the landsmen tell it—I have heard—
> you are useless.
>
> And the wind sounds with this,
> and the sea,
> where rollers shot with blue
> cut under deeper blue.
>
> Oh but stay tender, enchanted,
> where wave-lengths cut you
> apart from all the rest—
> for we have found you,
> we watch the splendor of you,
> we thread throat on throat of freesia
> for your shelf.
>
> You are not forgot,
> O plunder of lilies.
> Honey is not more sweet
> than the salt stretch of your beach.

The agony of beauty is often her theme—for, as Amy Lowell said of her, "To this poet, beauty is a thing so sharp as to be painful, delight so poignant it can scarcely be borne." In *The Gift* we find her longing for rest from this agony:

> I reason:
> another life holds what this lacks,
> a sea, unmoving, quiet—
> not forcing our strength
> to rise to it, beat on beat;
> a stretch of sand,
> no garden beyond, strangling
> with its myrrh-lilies;
> a hill, not set with black violets,

> but stones, stones, bare rocks,
> dwarf-trees, twisted—no beauty
> to distract, to crowd
> madness upon madness.

There is in this poet's work a cool hardness—indeed, the parallel is with sculpture in bronze or marble. *Hymen* carves a marble frieze, stained with clear colors in the old Greek or Chinese fashion—a frieze along which the nuptial procession marches with appropriate recitative and choral song. The mood, and the April-of-life freshness of it, are sustained by an art singularly serene and sure.

The later poems, *Heliodora* and the rest, are further testimonies to this poet's quality, enriching her fame though scarcely advancing it. She has rarely done a lovelier thing than *Fragment Thirty-six,* her variations on a Sapphic theme. And we may reasonably hope that her work is not yet half done, for her firm and practiced art is no mere passing impulse of youthful talent.

H. D. has been called "the most imagistic of the Imagists." When some of her poems first appeared in the fourth number of *Poetry* (January, 1913), following Richard Aldington's beautiful *Choricos* in the second, it was evident that a new spirit was in the air, a spirit demanding for the art precision, economy of word and phrase, rhythm personal and not metronomic or derived, and direct presentation of the image, stripped of superfluous ornament. Her own stern instinct had been verified and strengthened by Ezra Pound's harsh discipline, and reticence had saved her from exposing immature work to the world. Thus there are no juvenilia in her record —she was a finished product when she began.

She began, rather shyly, with a few of those translations, or "reflections," from the Greek anthology which
are probably as close to a revelation of the original as any
translator may achieve. And the *Heliodora* section of
her *Collected Poems* includes more recent fragments from
Greek lyrists, whose singing suffers only a sea-change to
another magic in passing through the mind of a modern
artist akin to them.

IT is a platitude, no doubt, to assert that the poet is not a man of action. Shelley goes so far as to deny poets any share of the common urge toward action when he calls them "the trumpets which sing to battle and feel not what they inspire"; and his grandiloquent phrase, "Poets are the hierophants of an *unapprehended* inspiration," seems to mean that they don't know what they are talking about with their trumpets, songs, prophecies, and other evidences of lyric rage. Shakespeare's temperament was so averse from action that most of his heroes are weak men lifted impotently to places of power, and his only negligible characterizations are of strong men, like Cæsar and Henry V, who act by plan and force of character and not by impulse. And so on—one might multiply examples; the poet usually retires to a corner to look on, and when, as rarely happens, he rises and marches forth to lead the world, his course is not likely to be the path of wisdom.

So T. S. Eliot, seeking refuge in his library and in ancient ritual from the bewildering chaos of the modern world, is no exception to the species. One might allege that he is not even one of the unfeeling "trumpets which sing to battle," but probably it would be too much to expect any modern sophisticate to be the hierophant of any inspiration he did not thoroughly apprehend. Mr. Eliot stays in his world, the world of the library and the established church, and through its criss-cross of shaded window-panes he looks out on the tempest and turmoil, and presents at least the confusion of the battle which even our most active fighters hardly pretend to understand.

If any plausible complaint is to be registered against this poet, perhaps one may question whether he has not been too much the slave of his temperament. Always he seems to have retreated instinctively from adventurous experience, and apparently no cruel decree of fate has forced experience upon him. A Puritan-descended Saint Louis boy, he early joined the group of sophisticated cosmopolites in London, working at his exacting art through tumultuous years on the basis of a bank-clerk routine. A close analysis of his small books—reticent, yet confessional, all of them—would show with what a shudder of sensibility to the grotesque he cringes before the outrageous attacks of life. It would be unfair, perhaps, to call Mr. J. Alfred Prufrock a self-portrait, yet the bitter humor of its delicate caricature offers a figure as recognizable as Wyncie King's masterly drawing of Joseph Pennell—as recognizable and as pitiful in its tragi-comic questioning of the meaning of life. Absurd, thinks the battered hero, that such as he, thin and bald and puny-hearted with the wearing years, should be calling on his soul for a momentous decision!

> Do I dare
> Disturb the universe?

And again:

> I have measured out my life with coffee-spoons. . . .
> Then how should I begin
> To spit out all the butt-ends of my days and ways?
> And how should I presume?

And in a few later lines of Mr. Prufrock's love-song

we have the whole story of the super-sophisticated twentieth-century worldling whose searching mind has been imprisoned by walls and roofs and indoor philosophies:

Should I, after tea and cakes and ices,
Have the strength to force the moment to its crisis?
But though I have wept and fasted, wept and prayed,
Though I have seen my head (grown slightly bald) brought in
    upon a platter,
I am no prophet—and here's no great matter.
I have seen the moment of my greatness flicker,
And I have seen the eternal Footman hold my coat, and
    snicker—
And in short, I was afraid.

The tragedy of inadequacy, so common in every clime and time, is emphasized to poignancy, not only by the poet's sharp and wounding edge of humor, but also by the blinding flame of beauty perceived or imagined.

I have heard the mermaids singing, each to each.
I do not think they will sing to me.
I have seen them riding seaward on the waves,
Combing the white hair of the waves blown back
When the wind blows the water white and black.

Beauty is almost unbearable with this poet; we get it from him in keen flashes—a vivid image, a few lines of wilful tenderness, a vagrant unexpected rhyme, a rush of colored words. Rarely does he indulge it to the length of even so brief a poem as *La Figlia che Piange*. But his sense of humor—humor satiric and yet piteous—is always present. It stands at the gate of his mind, not to keep emotions out, but to whip them as they come in. "Cousin Harriet" and "Aunt Helen" are not merely laughed at, they are forlornly loved in their pretentious absurdity. And the Sweeney grotesques have just that quality of delighted wonder at life's oddities which one may find in a Hokusai drawing.

It is this mixture of perceptions and emotions which makes *The Waste Land* so alive. The poem, kaleidoscopic, profuse, a rattle and rain of colors that fall somehow into place—gives us the malaise of our time, its agony, its conviction of futility, its wild dance on an ashheap before a clouded and distorted mirror.

I will show you fear in a handful of dust,

the poet cries, and he shows us confusion and dismay and disintegration, the world crumbling to pieces before our eyes and patching itself with desperate gayety into new and strangely irregular forms. He gives us, with consummate distinction, what many an indoor thinker thinks about life today, what whole groups of impassioned intellectuals are saying to each other as the great ball spins.

Yet all the time there are large areas of mankind to whom this thinking does not apply; large groups of another kind of intellectuals whose faith is as vital and constructive as ever was the faith of their crusading forefathers. To the men of science, the inventors, the engineers, who are performing today's miracles, the miasma which afflicts Mr. Eliot is as remote a speculative conceit, as futile a fritter of mental confectionery, as Lyly's euphemism must have been to Elizabethan sailors. And these men are thinkers too, dreamers of larger dreams than any group of city-closeted artists may evoke out of the circling pipesmoke of their scented talk. These men are creating that modern world which the half-aware and over-informed poets of London and Montmartre so darkly doom.

So one cannot trust utterly people of idle hands and muscles and supersensitive brains. The story they tell may not be the complete "tale of the tribe"—myopic vision and narrow experience may shut off the far horizons where devoted pioneers are discovering new domains of thought. But the hero, and the epic bard chanting his victories, were a fashion of more primitive times than ours, and *The Waste Land* has become a point of departure for prophets less intuitive and poets less inspired than Mr. Eliot to play their symphony of discords. Their revelations, however incomplete, may give us a near view of the confusion that besets us and the destruction that threatens our civilization unless the chaos is resolved.

Thus Mr. Eliot's glistening, swiftly flowing poem of human and personal agony has acquired almost the distinction of prophecy, of a Jeremiad implying social upheaval and readjustment. No doubt the poet himself would be the first to disclaim such an intention—he would probably say that *The Waste Land* is the reaction of a suffering valetudinarian to the persistent after-the-war chaos in Europe, with its tumbling-down of old customs and sanctities. It is a condition, not a theory, which confronts him; and he meets the condition with an artist's invocation of beauty. One would expect a certain deliberateness in Mr. Eliot's art, but this poem surprises with an effect of unstudied spontaneity. While stating nothing, it suggests everything that is in his rapidly moving mind, in a series of shifting scenes which fade in and out of each other like the cinema. The form, with its play of many-colored lights on words that flash from everywhere in the poet's dream, is a perfect expression of the changing tortures in his soul. If one calls *The Waste Land* a masterpiece of decadent art, the word must be taken as praise; for decadent art, while always incomplete, only half-interpretive, is pitifully beautiful and tragically sincere. The agony and bitter splendor of modern life are in this poem, of that part of it which dies of despair while the world is building its next age.

If Mr. Eliot's subject, in *The Waste Land,* is essentially a phantasmagoric fade-out of God, his later poems—*Ash Wednesday,* and the brief *Song for Simeon, Journey of the Magi, Animula*—are the record of his despairing desperate conversion—his half-hearted clutch on the God of his Puritan fathers, but disguised in Anglican vestments and ritual; the systematized God whom, in his irreverent American days, he had denied, indicted, even parodied. His "reversion to moral absolutism," together with his acceptance of the quaint conventions of the English social system, have had an unfortunate influence, however, upon his art, which loses the blithe or pathetic humor of *Prufrock* and the early satirical poems, and the incisive tragic realism of *The Waste Land,* and assumes a distinguished mournfulness, set out in slow rhythms by a master-poet seemingly self-convicted of sins artistic as well as moral. As yet his conversion gives the poet no joy, and the religious motive brings nothing of the rich and generous inspiration of his early irreverence. Let us hope that British citizenship, implying a formidable caste system and the Anglican ritual, have not dampened his poetic ardor, and that we shall yet have from him the great modern religious poem which will restore the splendor of the faith.

THOUGH Elinor Wylie died at forty-two, in a sense her work was complete, was finished. She had perfected her style and delivered her message. Death merely rounded the circle, gave her career a wholeness, a symmetry, as when a thorough-bred racer wins a trophy at the goal which was his starting-point a few minutes before.

Her first poems, like the racer's first paces, were of an instinctive yet trained precision; there was no fumbling or halting, never a stumble or a false step. To be sure, she began later than most poets, never discovering her literary gift until she was well past thirty and disciplined by a tragic experience of life. Still, waiting beyond youth for one's debut in any art does not imply adequate practice in technique—a late beginning tends to make the first steps slow and painful. Not so, however, in Elinor Wylie's case; the four poems printed in 1921 in *Poetry,* which she called her "first acceptor," showed her a master of her tools, capable of artistry which admitted no compromise. She never surpassed the muted music of *Velvet Shoes,* and in *Fire and Sleet and Candle-light* she traced what became a favorite rhythmic pattern:

> For this you've striven
> Daring, to fail;
> Your sky is riven
> Like a tearing veil.

> For this you've wasted
>     Wings of your youth;
> Divined, and tasted
>     Bitter springs of truth.

.   .   .   .   .   .   .

> Your race is ended—
>     See, it is run:
> Nothing is mended
>     Under the sun.

> Straight as an arrow
>     You fall to a sleep
> Not too narrow
>     And not too deep.

Here we have at once that exactness of method—the true word, the balanced line, the close rhyme-scheme, in short, the skill and polish—which characterize all her work. We have also the personal significance—her own friendships, loves, joys, agonies implied but never stated, suggested but never sentimentalized. *Atavism,* in this earliest group, may be a literal confession of her own feelings; yet, reading it, one gets no facts, but merely a kind of aura surrounding a distinguished human spirit, an aura defending her against mysteries beyond.

The contents of her first three small books of verse are just one hundred poems, most of them very brief, two or three of about fifty lines, and one of nearly two hundred. What she seems to say in the sharp intensity of these poems is the fragility of life in its well-nigh intolerable beauty, and she says it with a sparkle of rich many-colored glazes, like eighteenth-century French porcelains. Her art, indeed, allies itself with the eighteenth century, not so much with the poetry of that period as with those other arts, at once hard as jewels and supremely delicate, which must pass through fire to earn perfection. Like them, she protected emotion with an armor of artificiality, she glazed it with shining colors. And like those rigid old porcelains, so enduring in their fragility, her poems would seem to be protected by their quality, as faultless exhibits from our multi-varied century set up for future generations to wonder at.

It would be interesting to trace the emotional motive in such art. In a picture like Millet's *Angelus,* in lyrics like Sara Teasdale's, the emotional motive is stated in the simplest terms of beauty. But one may be deeply stirred also by a Watteau picnic, or by such a poem as *A Strange Story,* even though the emotion here is corseted and veiled and embroidered in all the artificialities of a super-subtle civilization. Not that Elinor Wylie is a Watteau—she is too much a creature of her own time to use his particular kind of elaborately costumed images; but she sees life, as he did, encumbered with all the paraphernalia of civilization, and she goes further than he did in finding it almost overwhelmed under the load.

Condemned prisoners, we are told, take refuge from the sense of doom in little things. Elinor Wylie's sense of the tragedy of life led her to such beflowered and beribboned refuges as *Jennifer Lorn, The Venetian Glass Nephew,* and *Mr. Hodge and Mr. Hazard.* The first of these novels—the earliest—has always seemed to me a masterpiece of its kind. There is never a false note, never a trace of reality in the whole elaborate concoction; its puppets move with precise grace through a delicately patterned satire of the human comedy as their manager pulls the intricate strings. In *The Venetian Glass Nephew,* on the contrary, the threads are too finely spun—they break, and the brittle figures shatter until nothing is left but dust. *Mr. Hodge and Mr. Hazard,* which I have not read, would seem to be of similarly tenuous structure; and I shall never dare attempt *The Orphan Angel,* which resuscitates Shelley and brings him to America, even though Mrs. Wylie made a sincere effort to express in this book her life-long hero-worship of the English poet.

To return to the poems, which, as her most important work, should alone engage us. I have quoted half of a poem from her first book, with its short lines and staccato rhythm. This pattern delighted her to the end for purposes more or less satiric; we find her using it in *Peregrine,* the longest poem in her second book, *Black Armor,* and doubling it into the tetrameter lines of *Miranda's Supper* in *Trivial Breath.* The swift steps of the measure accept happily that intricate play of highly original rhymes in which she delighted; she tosses them like a juggler his balls, and catches them dangerously at the end of a line as they seem about to escape her handling. They are clever, witty, miraculously effective; but more than that, they are robust, muscular—they carry the light texture of these poems with authority and power.

But these quick-stepping staccato rhythms were merely the lighter resource of her skilful art. From the first she used the sonnet form now and then, *Atavism* being her earliest sonnet, winning from it slow sweeping rhythms. And one of the most beautiful poems in *Trivial Breath, Desolation is a Delicate Thing,* trails still slower cadences in lines of variable length. Each new volume shows increased technical expertness, a new delight in fitting her ideas and emotions to the exact forms that reveal them most effectively, and the rhythms that accept most musically her highly figurative language.

*Angels and Earthly Creatures,* the posthumous book of forty poems which she had arranged just before her sudden death, gives evidence that her art fed and grew to the end upon an ever-enriching spiritual experience. The nineteen sonnets which open the volume form one of the memorable love-sequences of a language supreme in such confessional records of human passion. But even here Elinor Wylie preserves her reticence, speaks proudly from behind a luminous veil of figurative denial:

> Although these words are false, none shall prevail
> To prove them in translation less than true,
> Or overthrow their dignity, or undo
> The faith implicit in a fabulous tale.

Through the richly colored texture of these sonnets one discerns that they are dedicated to a lover of mythical range in tragic power:

> The shadow of its light is only this:
> That all your beauty is the work of wars
> Between the upper and the nether stars;
> Its symmetry is perfect and severe
> Because the barbarous force of agonies
> Broke it, and mended it, and made it clear.

And the sequence as a whole expresses the age-old womanly tribute to masculine strength, the feminine feeling of deprecation in giving to the partnership merely its more fragile and decorative elements. One might quote almost any sonnet to prove this worshipful posture—here is *V:*

[ 110 ]

The little beauty that I was allowed—
The lips new-cut and colored by my sire,
The polished hair, the eyes' perceptive fire—
Has never been enough to make me proud;
For I have moved companied by a cloud,
And lived indifferent to the blood's desire
Of temporal loveliness in vain attire:
My flesh was but a fresh-embroidered shroud.
Now do I grow indignant at the fate
Which made me so imperfect to compare
With your degree of noble and of fair;
Our elements are the farthest skies apart;
And I enjoin you, ere it is too late,
To stamp your superscription on my heart.

Besides this sequence, other poems in this book are done on a large scale—they give one a sense of size and mastery in the contemplation and artistic expression of love and death, the two universal elements of the human problem which enthralled her heart and imagination as if with a premonitory warning. Toward the end of her life she seemed to breathe

> the honey breath
> Issuing from the jaws of death.

The splendid *Hymn to Earth* and *This Corruptible* celebrate the triumph of death. Almost she begins to accept the ultimate dissolution in a high spirit of reconciliation.

Life for Elinor Wylie was not a simple affair of obvious choices; it was a conflict between, not spirit and flesh, but spirit and intellect. In the *Song* in *Black Armor*, she says wistfully:

> When I am dead, or sleeping
> Without any pain,
> My soul will stop creeping
> Through my jewelled brain.

[ 111 ]

Her jewelled brain defied the claims of the flesh and challenged the claims of the spirit; it dramatized and adorned the hazards of life:

> In coldest crucibles of pain
> Her shrinking flesh was fired,
> And smoothed into a finer grain
> To make it more desired.

She could not accept the obvious happiness or the common woe; thought crept in to torture her emotions and temper her art. It gave to her nature a spiral twist and spring, and to her poetry the hard keenness of knowledge. For her there was no peace, except perhaps in another world. But she loved this world of search and strife; in *Last Supper* we find her ecstatic over the beauty of it, even while she tastes the pomegranate of Proserpine, and feels in her mouth the seven seeds of death:

> Now that the shutter of the dusk
>   Begins to tremble in its groove,
> I am constrained to strip the husk
>   From everything I truly love.
>
> So short a time remains to taste
>   The ivory pulp, the seven pips,
> My heart is happy without haste
>   With revelation at its lips.
>
> So calm a beauty shapes the core,
>   So grave a blossom frames the stem,
> In this last minute and no more
>   My eyes alone shall eat of them.

It may be proper to close this brief study with a sentence or two from the last letter I received from this poet of high desires and deep despairs. This letter, which was sent from England six weeks before her death in grateful acknowledgment of the Levinson Prize, ends with a reference to her convalescence after the accident of the previous summer:

Being unable to write novels, I wrote some forty poems of a certain merit. So do you really think it was an "unfortunate accident," or are you not convinced for the thousandth time of an astonishing beauty and strangeness of life?

The beauty and strangeness of life—these she felt intensely and expressed to the limit of her power, like all poets who, in the brief years accorded to them, struggle to give utterance to the inexpressible.

## ARCHIBALD MAC LEISH

ONE morning in late April of 1931 a modest, melancholy, implacably sincere young man faced an audience of two or three hundred persons in the Arts Club of his native city of Chicago. The modernistic setting of the room—suave, never violent, a faultlessly tempered simplicity—was in harmony with the poet's mood; against it the beauty of his cadences was like the sound of a fountain in a garden, and through the windows the incessant motors slipping along Michigan Avenue struck the bass notes of a perfect chord.

It was manifest that a thinker confronted us, and that he was using his slow quantitative elegiac rhythms to express the break-up and remolding of the world. It was as if he saw some mighty hand crumbling the dried clay of worn-out systems to moisten and reshape it into a form unforeseen and strange. He stood beside the adventurous molder sensitively aware of risk, trembling lest the huge and massive figure of human society, still in the rough, should prove less symmetrical than the one now dissolved to powder, should prove indeed incapable of symmetry, casting upon the new age a gigantic shadow of ugliness.

As the poet read the prologue of his Mexican epic, *Conquistador,* one felt that he was using the fury and splendor, the clash of ideals and civilizations in that old sixteenth-century war, as a symbol of the modern worldwide clash of systems and ideas; that Cortez and Montezuma seemed to him not more different, not more violently opposed in every thought and custom, than the separatist feudal world from which we are emerging and the steel-linked radio-bound international world which already holds us in its enormous grip. One felt that this poet realized the threat of tragedy in the situation of the human atom caught in immensities, realized the grotesque heroism of the atom's conquest of gigantic tools, of his puny leap into infinities of knowledge. His imagination seemed to be aware of the modern clash of forces, and one queried his future, wondering how profoundly and prophetically he would be able to symbolize this conflict in *Conquistador* and later poems.

My mind wandered back over this fellow-citizen's history. Born in a Chicago suburb to a typical well-to-do family, childhood and school life; Yale, graduating in 1915; the Harvard law school for two years; marriage; the War, and as he volunteered and left his wife and infant son for service in France, his first book of creditable youthful poems was edited and brought out by a young Yale professor, his friend; service at the Front in the Field Artillery; after a year of it ordered home in August, 1918, to train soldiers to handle big guns; the Armistice, just as he and his troops were about to embark for France; demobilization, followed by three years' practice of law with a firm of repute in Boston; all very like other American boys from well regulated suburban homes; typical, except for the soldiering, of the youth of our fathers and brothers, perhaps of our sons and grandsons. And then a breaking away from tradition at the thrill of a new discovery, a new purpose—that not law but literature was his vocation, not legal oratory but poetry. Then came a burning of bridges, and flight across the sea with his family, this time to a France at peace. And after a few years' sojourn back again to his own country, and the purchase of an old farm in Massachusetts.

Perhaps it was necessary and inevitable that the embryo poet should go abroad to enforce the change—his only way of making a complete break with his conventional and professional past, of escaping the doubts and queries of puzzled and well-meaning friends. Also he needed Paris esthetically at that time more, probably, than he realized; he needed the ferment, the intellectual hostilities and loyalties, the provocative rages against everything conventional or old-fashioned. He needed a thorough stirring-up that his art might be enriched beyond the mild flavor of his first book; and if his enthusiasm for the new contacts carried him too far, tempted him toward derivation and imitation, that was a phase to be easily outgrown, in all probability, as his work developed.

*The Happy Marriage* (1924) and *The Pot of Earth* (1925) were the first fruits of the new passion. In reviewing them in *Poetry* I said in part:

These two books are "tone-poems" played with muted strings; played in the half-light or the half-dark when rapture and anguish, however real, become suspect of dreams. What we all fear, the poet sees come to pass—life blurs and dissolves before his eyes; lovely concords are hushed; beauty that is too beautiful perishes of its own fragility, like a soap-bubble vanishing with its flicker of iridescence.

All this is not expressly said, any more than in music. In the earlier book we have indeed the delicate raptures of a happy marriage—love as fleet as a fawn to tempt and elude, as warm as a bird in the nest to cherish and guard; but the poet, singing the changes of joy, feels always how perishable is joy in this vibrating, swinging, dissolving world. And he knows that the soul can not be bound, but must beat away from the closest contacts. . . .

In *The Pot of Earth* we find the poet's instinct for rhythms and tone-values developed almost to virtuosity. A certain relation to *The Waste Land* is obvious. Mr. MacLeish, either consciously or unconsciously, has set himself to study Mr. Eliot's wavering variable rhythms, his way of neither beginning nor ending, of leaping backward and forward, and somehow reaching his goal by wayward paths no other poet could travel. But if the younger poet has taken a few hints from the elder one, he has shown extraordinary intelligence in recognizing their adaptability to his theme, and in heeding them just so far as they suited his purpose. In other words, *The Pot of Earth* is beautifully done.

From this book to *Streets in the Moon* was a long leap. In a year the poet had gained firmer ground to stand on, and though we still hear echoes of Eliot, and both hear and see reminders of the *transition* experimenters with rhythm and typography, the poet is developing his own style and using it to express his own personality. The book contains such modernistic meditations as *Einstein,* such self-questionings as *L'an trentiesme de mon aege* and the beautiful *Signature for Tempo,* such grotesques as *March* and *Man!;* and everywhere the expert touch, the delicate manipulation of rhythms, the fine, sometimes almost-too-studied phrasing. In the latest book, *New Found Land,* we find a further development of these qualities: poems of rare and usually melancholy beauty, like *Immortal Autumn* and *Epistle to be Left in the Earth* —a beauty marred only by eccentric typography and troublesome lack of punctuation.

Through all these books the poet's philosophy of life— or perhaps one should say the instinctive feeling about life which becomes the underlying motive of his art—is less

[ 117 ]

hard in texture and brazen in tone than most of the
Parisian-American group could sympathize with; there
is room for human pity in it, and even for human love—
that love of the race which, implying the merging of the
individual in the mass, may be the democratic, or at least
the communistic, ideal—an ideal difficult, perhaps well-
nigh inaccessible to the poet, who is always by inborn impulse an individualist.

We find this instinct of human pity underlying the self-
analysis presented as the artistic motive of *The Hamlet of
A. MacLeish*.  Here the Elizabethan doubter shrinks into
the modern agonist, and "the King his father's ghost,"
revisiting the glimpses of the moon, becomes the symbol of
the world's irrevocable past, of dead generations and their
dreams:

> Where is thy tongue, great spectre?  Hast thou not
> Answered to others that with hearts like ours
> Followed thee, poets, speakers in the earth?
> Didst thou not show them?  For they were as sure,
> Returning, as those men whom the great sea
> Chooses for danger. . . .

In *Conquistador* the poet strikes out into a more
spacious primitive world.  To simplify his story of the
Conquest of Mexico, to make it an epic of races rather
than heroes, he bases it on the "true history of those wars,"
a book written in old age by Bernal Diaz del Castillo,
who, as a young soldier, had fought with Cortez from
Cuba to Montezuma's capital.  This soldier is the narrator throughout, and through the poet's imaginative in-
tensification of his tale we get the fierce courage of the
lawless adventure: the dash into unknown seas and lands;
the battles with formidable tribes—horde after horde

pouring upon the invaders, and their killings avenged by
massacres; the ruin of cities and confiscation of treasure;
the obliteration of a whole civilization and its literature
and arts——

And the town gone—no stone to a stone of it——
And the whole thing was a very beautiful victory——

and finally the building of Spanish cities and the settle-
ment of that "good land" by its conquerors.   The poet
unrolls before us the violence and terror and blood-lust
of the onslaught, the rich propitiatory gifts sent by "the
king of that country," followed by desperate and san-
guinary resistance; the mysterious religion with its holo-
causts; the retreats and ambushes and despairs—all set
against a background of incredible beauty, of unparalleled
scenic magnificence.   It is a great story, and the poet
meets it expertly with a pounding and pouring of broken
rhythms as regular—and irregular—as waves under
changing winds.

As yet this is Mr. MacLeish's most powerful work—
the biggest scheme, handled most adequately, of anything
he has as yet attempted.   It increases one's hope of this
poet's ability to express his time, one of the most creative
periods in the world's history; to answer back in song
the god-like or demoniac power of its men of science—
the engineers, builders, inventors, explorers, who have
piled Ossa on Pelion of miraculous discoveries, and made
over the world for the next age.

ONE winter evening in 1918, after a lecture on modern poetry at the University of Illinois, a number of faculty members and their guest from Chicago gathered around blazing logs for a talk. The late Stuart P. Sherman, always courteous in manner and distinguished in bearing, was there to lead the discussion—it was two or three years before he gave up teaching and became literary editor of the New York *Herald-Tribune*. Regional and racial influences on our literature soon became our topic, whereupon a quiet shy dark young man at the edge of the group found something intelligent to say about the poetic inheritance of our aboriginal tribes. Gradually, as we prodded him, we discovered a rich store of experience and knowledge, and at last he responded to our urging by giving us some Chippewa songs in the original, to a wild piano or dance accompaniment.

The beauty of this modest little performance, its testimony of enthusiastic loyalty to aboriginal friends, delighted the dark young man's audience, and I urged him to translate or interpret some of the songs in free verse. The result was *The Blue Duck* and *Chippewa Flute Song,* which first appeared in *Poetry* for November 1918.

Later I learned how Lew Sarett, the son of immigrants descended from half the crowded races of Central Europe, had acquired his intimacy with one of our aboriginal tribes. As a boy in northern Wisconsin he loved the primitive forest and its wild beasts and birds. As a youth, escaping from the city slums whither his parents had brought him, he pushed out into our northwestern wilderness and accepted with joy its harsh discipline—indeed, many a tale of stout adventure might be told to prove his prowess. To pay for a college course, he guided hunters and fishermen for nine seasons through the Chippewa country, thereby gaining a knowledge of aboriginal feeling and customs which has been a fertile inspiration of his poetry. And not only is he the most sympathetic imaginative interpreter of aboriginal feeling and rhythms, but he brings to us, in many poems, a stronger suggestion of the true spirit of the pioneers than those poets who have more directly undertaken to tell the epic story of their conquest of the West; for he reveals with finer art the love of adventurous men for the wilderness, their delight in animals and birds, in forests, plains, mountains and all free spaces.

*The Blue Duck* was Mr. Sarett's first important adventure in the interpretation of aboriginal life and art. It is a plunge into the wilds to watch him beat out with voice and feet and arms the breakneck rhythms of this poem; and even those who, less fortunately, read it merely with the eye, can hardly fail to feel in it the rush of feet and the lilt of chanting voices. It begins:

> Hi′! Hi! Hi′! Hi!
> Hi′! Hi! Hi′! Hi!
> Hee′ya! Hói-ya!
> Hee′ya! Hói-ya!
> Keetch′-ie Má-ni-dó, Má-ni-dó!
> The hunter-moon is chipping at his flints,
> At his dripping bloody flints;

> He is rising for the hunt,
> And his face is red with blood
> From the spears of many spruces,
> And his blood is on the leaves that flutter down.
> The Winter-maker, Beé-bo-an',
> Is walking in the sky,
> And his windy blanket rustles in the trees.

Other poems in Mr. Sarett's first book—*Rain Song, The Squaw Dance, Chippewa Flute Song,* etc.—are scarcely less successful interpretations of the Indian's highly figurative lyric moods and the rhythms of his song. Such poetry comes close to the beat of the red man's music, and makes a spontaneous use of his symbolism. And the *Council Talks*—Chippewa monologues of protest against the specious white man's encroachments —give us the authentic flavor of his irony.

This poet's faith in life is attested also by narratives and lyrics of men and animals—people as simple-hearted as beasts, animals who suffer like children. Who can forget the *Four Little Foxes* in his third book, *Slow Smoke?*

> Speak gently, Spring, and make no sudden sound;
> For in my windy valley yesterday I found
> New-born foxes squirming on the ground—
>     Speak gently.
>
> Walk softly, March, forbear the bitter blow.
> Her feet within a trap, her blood upon the snow,
> The four little foxes saw their mother go—
>     Walk softly.
>
> Go lightly, Spring—oh, give them no alarm!
> When I covered them with boughs to shelter them from harm
> The thin blue foxes suckled at my arm—
>     Go lightly.
>
> Step softly, March, with your rampant hurricane.
> Nuzzling one another, and whimpering with pain,
> The new little foxes are shivering in the rain—
>     Step softly.

*The Box of God* is a more ambitious development of the
same theme, a summing up of his spiritual experience in
these contacts with wild life.   This poem is an outdoor
man's profession of faith—the creed of the pioneer, of the
explorer, the discoverer, the inventor in whatever field;
of the man who sees something beckoning ahead, and who
must follow it, wherever it leads; of the hero with the
future in his keeping, who, though called by different
names in different ages, is always the same type.   Mr.
Sarett makes an Indian guide his spokesman—an Indian
guide who rebels against confinement in that ritualistic
"box of God," the little Catholic church in the mountains in which his "conversion" had been registered:

> Somebody's dere. . . . He's walk-um in dose cloud. . . .
> You see-um?  Look!  He's mak'-um for hees woman
> De w'ile she sleep, dose t'ing she want-um most—
> Blue dress for dancing.  You see, my frien'? . . . ain't?
> He's t'rowing on de blanket of dose sky
> Dose plenty-plenty handfuls of white stars;
> He's sewing on dose plenty teet' of elk,
> Dose shiny looking-glass and plenty beads.
> Somebody's dere . . . somet'ing he's in dere . . .

We have in this poem a modern reversion to the hero
type as a subject of poetry; and essentially its central
motive, as of all heroic song, is the search for God, for a
larger God than men have ever entrapped in the churchly
boxes they have made for him.   The forthright faith of
the man of action is in it, something of the force of the
world-builder, wherever he is found.   We live in a
period of swift and tremendous change: if many of our
poets feel it as chaos and disintegration, Mr. Sarett feels
it as a new and larger summons to faith in life and art.

[ 123 ]

*The Box of God* is so inspired, and in it his art is of a rich and nobly beautiful pattern and texture.

The poems in Mr. Sarett's two later books, *Slow Smoke* and *Wings Against the Moon,* are more episodic, less epic in motive; but the best of them follow out-of-door trails. There are Amerindian narratives of absolute authenticity, some of them showing the exact aboriginal inflection of shrewd humor. And there are animal poems which show Mr. Sarett as the most intimate friend of wolves, mountain goats, the lynx, the deer, the coyote, and other beasts of our western wilds, of all the poets, living or dead, who have written about them. He knows the feelings of wild beasts from close and sometimes dangerous contact.

Lew Sarett's poetry suggests the wealth of our aboriginal inheritance—an authentic primitive tradition which has enthusiastic interpreters and students in our western states and the nations to the south, and is destined to influence profoundly American art. As our wilderness narrows and our aborigines assume the customs of their conquerors, it becomes increasingly important that the record should be set down in enduring art; and in these days, when most of our poetry is conceived and written indoors, when much of it smells of the lamp and delves into dark places of the human mind, it is refreshing to read a poet whose every gesture, every idea and figure of speech, is drawn from a life of action in wild places. There is no cheapness, no facile sentimentality in his poems of "tooth and claw," "tinder and flint," and the dark people who know nature in her harshest moods, but there is the stern sympathy of a man who has shared their sorrows, and also the grim humor of one who understands their laughter.

## MAXWELL BODENHEIM

IN nineteen-thirteen and fourteen, when *Poetry* was in
its first and second years, a blond youth used to appear
at the office now and then, bearing innocent young rhymes
written out in an incredibly large round babyish hand.
Of all the young poets who have called on us—so numerous, and of so many aspects, origins, and degrees of fortune—this usually silent figure was perhaps the most
unpromising and forlorn. He always looked hunted and
haunted, as if half-starved and half-ill. Nor had his
manner acquired its later audacity.

At that time Helen Hoyt was the "subscription department" of *Poetry,* and Alice Corbin Henderson the associate editor, and we all used to feel sorry for this pale
young prentice-poet, to the point of inviting him to stay
and read the books and magazines which were already
bringing us new voices from all over the world. We
wished we might accept his rhymes—alas that we did not
preserve a few to confirm or deny the justice of those
early rejections! Now probably they are lost forever,
for the author himself has rejected them.

So it was a pleasure to "the staff" when this frail pale
visitor surprised us one day with some free-verse experiments which we were able to print. At last Maxwell
Bodenheim had caught on to "the new movement"—it
was new indeed at that time—and these *Sketches,* in
*Poetry* for August, 1914, were a not inadequate introduc-

tion of his inquisitive ironic mind and his slantingly searching art. One finds in them some of his characteristic phrases—"the surliness of the ditch," the miner "bending under thick knowledge," the steel rail's "stiff smile at Time—a smile which men call rust." And his irony is there, though serious and inherent, not uttered with a smile.

Well, after that Mr. Bodenheim's rise was rapid and his hitherto subdued manner became adventurous—nay, insistent and emphatic. His bitter childhood and youth urged him to a dark literary revenge—letters full of malign, carefully sculptured phrases of denunciation, began to descend upon his recent friends—a harmless pirouetting which kept his mind agile for the more serious exercise of his art. Life was a theatre for Mr. Bodenheim, in which, as a proud poet, he felt bound to play his heroic role jauntily, let the sword-play fall where it might. And of course the stage was none too stable—financial props and pillars were very shaky if not utterly lacking, and the social background of his little scene—the great rough-and-tumble world whose commands he ignored—was unsympathetically discordant. Thus the drama came to many a point of strain, with Comedy and Tragedy offering their masks in the wings.

He fell in with Ben Hecht, and they were friends at intervals between pranks and rages. He was one of the early contributors to that high-stepping and gaily careering periodical, *The Little Review*. He discoursed and read poems at the Dill Pickle and other gathering-places of storm-tossed souls. In short, he sharpened his keen wits against whatever he could find of adroit and sophisticated in Chicago before he shook its dust from his feet and its smoke from his eyes, and made off to New York to become a contributor to *The Century* and a prickly pillar of the Poetry Society of America.

Meantime, while he was lifting himself by such contacts out of the slums and stupidities which fate had tried to assign him to, what was he achieving in his art? From the first the critics began to notice his phrase-making, his adroit manipulation of words. It is true that he has a caressing way with words, that he turns them to strange uses, making the familiar old coins seem newly minted and patterned. He is a lover of words; he studies their color and savors their "bouquet" like a winebibber. But this is not his whole story, though perhaps it is more of it than truly great art would confess. If words have been an intense preoccupation with him, that is a consistent detail of a spirit keen, narrow and ironic rather than rich, big and generous.

Though his sensitive feeling for words betrays him sometimes into preciosity, mostly he makes it serve his purpose. For his is an art of veiled and egoistic emotions, in which the immediate subject, be it a lady or a buttercup or the rear porch of an apartment building, reflects, like an actor's practice-mirror, the poet's swiftly changing expressions and attitudes. This is not said in dispraise— there is a sense in which it is true of every artist; indeed, one's self is so important that the most outward-gazing soul can not escape it. But with Mr. Bodenheim it is the one all-engrossing phenomenon of the universe. Standing before the mirror, he is kindled to frozen fires of passion over the ever-changing aspects of his thought in its mortal sheath; he is intrigued—nay, moved to the white heat of ice by the subtle workings of his mind,

[ 127 ]

trailing off from the central unreal reality there visible out to nebulous remote circumferences of an ego-starred philosophy. The eyes he looks into are his own; the bluebird flies with his own wings; the planets whirl through space to "drop little gestures upon my forehead."

The inevitable answer of egoism to the world's enormous disregard is irony—Mr. Bodenheim's artistic motive is ironic always. Sometimes the irony is veiled and delicate, almost invisible, like that of a man blowing bubbles against the pitiless destructive sunlight:

> Your cheeks are spent diminuendos
> Sheering into the rose-veiled silence of your lips,

he cries, and with sarcastic satisfaction he watches the gossamer words dissolve unheeded. His "Minna whose smile is my throne" is as theoretic an abstraction as the Elizabethan lady whose gallant sang,

> Her eyes are sapphires set in snow,
> Refining heaven with every wink.

But he celebrates his literary loves with a dark modern seriousness and intensity unknown to Lodge and Lyly.

One watches the development of his art with much the same feeling which a gaping crowd lavishes on a tight-rope athlete dancing over perilous abysses. Graceful and marvellously expert are the steps he wastes in merely asserting his expertness. A paradox is to him an irresistible temptation—he must set out to prove it though truth freezes on her mountain-top. At first, when beauty was his paradox, some of the proofs he offered had an exquisite grace. The poems in free verse in *Minna and Myself* on death and *To Our Dead,* the lovely *Make of Your Voice*

*a Dawn,* and a few others, make one forget the attitude.
Here is one called *Love:*

> You seemed a caryatid melting
> Into the wind-blown, dark blue temple of the sky.
> But you bent down as I came closer, breaking the image.
> When I passed, you raised your head
> And blew the little feather of a smile upon me.
> I caught it on open lips and blew it back.
> And in that moment we loved,
> Although you stood still waiting for your lover,
> And I walked on to my love.

The rhythms of these poems are his own, dangerous but
perfectly achieved, like the disembodied figures of speech
which he plucks from somewhere out of the soaring air.
Here, as rarely elsewhere, he achieves ease.

But ease cannot be maintained on a tight-rope, and
proving the paradox does not produce great art. The
super-athletic attitude becomes a strain. Already in Mr.
Bodenheim's second book, *Advice,* one feels weariness; the
rhythms are not so sure, and the motives are much more
perfunctory. The best poem in it, *Advice to a Bluebird,*
is deliberate rather than spontaneous, and bears no comparison with the earlier lyrics above mentioned. In later
publications he quite silences the lyric note; and when,
in certain rather expository poems, he experiments with
rhyme and metrics, even to the point of writing sonnets,
one is forced to wonder how a rhythmic instinct once
sensitive and original could become so tame.

The later books are mostly confessedly satiric—the
irony hitherto implied is now stated. In *Introducing
Irony* and *The Sardonic Arm* the super-athletic attitude
is frankly maintained, but with an engaging and insolent
humor. The unexpected is ushered in with a flourish, the

fantastic is gaudily paraded. Wit is so agile that one misses half its leaps and bounds. Life circles around us like a three-ringed circus whose countless stunts have agility but neither motive nor meaning. Mr. Bodenheim, as ringmaster, greets his whirling world with a wide malicious grin, and whips it cruelly along on its path of pain. Always, here also, the behold-me attitude; always the super-athlete putting words, characters, conceptions through incredible paces.

Sometimes one responds with a grin to the delightfully demoniac topsiturviness of it all. The heroin-peddler,

> Immersed in that brisk midnight known as crime.

The lively dead in a morgue, whose talk

> Accepts the jest of a universe.

The acrobat, violinist and chambermaid celebrating the "geometry of souls." Even

> Death,
> Grandiosely hackneyed subject,

does not escape this sardonic jester. In his cemetery, where Shaw and Maeterlinck are put lightly underground with Shakespeare, the poet reflects:

> Being finalities, the grass and trees
> Find no need for rules of etiquette.

He salutes "the old gravediggers"—

> From their faces adjectives have fled,
> Leaving the essential noun.

And he bids us

> Imagine the perturbation
> Of a stone removed
> From the comprehension of a mountain,
> And branded with the name of A. Rozinsky!

But witty lines, brief extracts, slander this poet by seeming more humane than his intention. To get the sardonic flavor of his satirical accusation of life one must read entire poems, entire books. Of late he has written two novels: the first one, *Blackguard,* has not reached me; the second, *Crazy Man,* I have just read. Following its keen and sympathetic portrait of the dance-hall girl, with its clever use of her swift-winged slang, I wondered whether at last Mr. Bodenheim had forgotten his pose, abandoned his quest of the paradox. But no— enter the noble thief, who, being handled with a singularly voluble prosiness, turns the tale to sentimental bunk and holds it there to the end.

What drop of poison in this poet's blood, embittering his thought, threatens to nullify the higher reaches of his art? One thinks of the great satirists, of Cervantes, Aristophanes, Rabelais, of Swift and Gay—men bigger, more generous than their private grudges at untoward fate; men whose laughter is rich and round as it still rolls heartily over the world. What Freudian tragedy of suppression and deprivation through this poet's childhood may have turned his blood to gall, and the wine of his satire to vinegar? Will he never work himself free of the inferiority complex which twists his art?

MRS. SEIFFERT'S earlier art was music. At Smith College, under a progressive instructor, she robbed other courses to devote herself with feverish energy to musical composition. "And I know my songs were good," she says today. "But they lie packed away, not quite completely finished; and I feel toward them as I should toward a dead child."

After college, after marriage, after maternity, "it was impossible ever to get four uninterrupted hours—and musical composition requires at least that." So another art, one apparently less exacting, allured her. She felt a musical invitation in words.

This is not to say that she twisted her talent in order to cultivate an art alien to her temperament. Some minds are resourceful, adaptable. Her instructor had discovered in his brilliant pupil power of self-expression in music, and had guided her toward that technique. When that art failed her, she discovered in herself power of self-expression in poetry, and found that her musical technique, while different, was suggestive and helpful in this art, by no means impossibly antagonistic.

It was a singularly well endowed mind which proceeded to practice the new technique to a point of rare sensitiveness and expertness; and it was a keenly emotional spirit which used it, but one saved from solemnity and egoism by an unfailing and altogether delightful whimsicality.

[ 132 ]

One of Mrs. Seiffert's earliest printed poems, *The Portrait of a Lady in Bed*—appearing, I think, in *Reedy's Mirror* early in 1916—showed that here was that rare phenomenon, a poet capable of wit, not wit superficial, concerned only with turns of phrase and tricks of humorous observation, but wit profoundly inherent in the subject and in the philosophical attitude of the poet's mind. This kind of wit is rare in English poetry; it is much more Gallic than Anglo-Saxon. In Mrs. Seiffert's later rhymed dialogue, her modern "morality play," *The Old Woman,* we find what may rank as a masterpiece in that particular genre. This poem says so much about life and death, about custom and adventure, about the imperishable and immortal human soul and body, about the desperate and unsolvable mystery of it all, that it leaves us gasping. I, who have read it countless times in the course of putting it through the press, voting to award it a prize, and often renewing my pleasure in it, still wonder whether I have caught the full circle of deep and serious meaning which the poet draws so lightly, so easily, with such gay audacity, that one's first, and possibly last, reaction must be merely a smile.

This dialogue opens Mrs. Seiffert's book, *A Woman of Thirty,* published in 1919 by Alfred A. Knopf. No doubt it is the most important poem in it, but there are others almost as good, whether in a similar vein or one more obviously serious. Before passing on to the latter, I cannot forbear quoting the delicious *Ode in the New Mode,* in which the dexterous wit is simple and light, concealing no deep surprises. This skit in free verse was written under the masculine pseudonym of Elijah Hay, as one of Mrs. Seiffert's contributions to the *Spectra* hoax

[ 133 ]

through which her friends Arthur Ficke and Witter
Bynner set out, with her aid, to satirize the much-talked-
of imagists. Here is the poem:

> Your face
> Was a temple
> From which your soul
> Came to me beneath arched brows;
> And my soul knelt at your feet.
>
> Then
> Inadvertently
> I saw your leg
> Curved and turned like a bird-song,
> Dying into ecstatic silence at the garter. . . .
>
> Wretched
> Woman!
> When you are wholly lovely
> Man cannot forget either of his two afflictions—
> Soul, or body!

The third section of the book, called *Studies and De-
signs,* opens with a poem as crisp and metallic as a hum-
ming wire. It is merely a description of *A Japanese
Vase,* whereon

> Five harsh black birds in shining bronze come crying
> Into a silver sky—
> Piercing and jubilant is the shape of their flying. . . .

Yet it contrives to suggest the "unswerving flight" of
the human spirit toward some dream of "a shore of gold."

This poem and others testify to the richness and variety
of the poet's culture. She has traveled far and wide, not
only physically but mentally, and she feels, sympathetically and instinctively, the art of other races. There is,
however, no parade of knowledge or exceptional experience—her culture has entered into her being, and her art

inevitably expresses it. The following poem on *The Moonlight Sonata* shows, especially in its beautiful third line, her emotional indebtedness to music:

> My soul, storm-beaten as an ancient pier,
> Stands forth into the sea: wave on slow wave
> Of shining music, luminous and grave,
> Lifting against me, pouring through me, here
> Find wafts of unforgotten chords which rise
> And droop like clinging sea-weed. You, so white,
> So still. so helpless, on this fathomless night
> Float like a corpse with living tortured eyes.
> Deep waves wash you against me: you impart
> No comfort to my spirit, give no sign
> Your inarticulate lips can taste the brine
> Drowning the secret timbers of my heart.

There are, however, many lyrics of simple human experience—love, motherhood, friendship, emotional illusions and disillusions. *Maura* is a fine sequence of half-fulfilled, half-frustrated love, a sequence which tells not quite the whole story. The *Singalese Love Songs* question the illusion:

> You think you seek my love,
> But you seek
> My denial.

And *The Pathway of Black Leaves* cryptically asserts the captivity of those who "walk free at last."

Then we have certain penetrating observations, cast often in imagistic form. Here is one called *Sorrow.*

> Sorrow stands in a wide place—
> Blind—blind.
> Beauty and joy are petals blown
> Across her granite face;
> They cannot find
> Sight or sentience in stone.

[ 135 ]

> Yesterday's beauty and joy lie deep
> In Sorrow's heart, asleep.

In two later books, *Ballads of the Singing Bowl* and *The King with Three Faces,* Mrs. Seiffert veils her modern thinking in rhymed measures of short lines. The ballads, especially, compress into allegorical brevity secret chambers of feminine emotion which few poets of either sex have explored. Not so succesfully *The King,* which leads into a maze of somewhat fumbled figurative personalities, as in such bitterly cryptic narratives as *Ballad of the Dolphin's Daughter, Rad and Beeling,* or *Two that Feasted.* And often one finds extremely vivid lines, figures swift and beautiful, which prove the poet's mastery of her difficult technique.

Sometimes, as in that legend of old Egypt, *Ballad of a Queen,* the story is more direct and realistic, less weighted with allegory. And in *Noah's Ark: A Play for Toys,* which closes her latest volume, the allegory is reduced to terms so simple as to be accessible to childhood, HE, the gigantic owner of the toy-figures, serving as Deity to the tiny inhabitants of the Ark, so confused and impotent in the drama of their emotions. The poet's stern authority, which forces her toy-actors to present the whole human story in baby rhymes wrought with words of one syllable, makes this brief dialogue a miniature of skilfully significant design, presenting a tragedy in little whose puppets say much more than they know.

In noting the advance in courageous thinking and original artistry shown in her later work, one may look forward confidently to further discoveries of Mrs. Seiffert's questing mind.

A N insinuating, quizzical, inquiring spirit; sometimes
a clown, oftener a wit, now and then a lyric or dramatic poet—such is Alfred Kreymborg. He trips about
cheerfully, among life's little incongruities; laughs at you
and me and progress and prejudice and dreams; says "I
told you so!" with an air, as if after a double somersault
in the circus ring; grows wistful, even tender, with
emotions always genuine even though not too deep for
momentary tears. And always, whatever his mood,
whatever his subject or purpose, he is, as becomes the
harlequin-philosopher, entertaining.

Mr. Kreymborg's "free forms" suit his temperament,
and they present his thought fitly, with the delicate
aplomb of the mandalute which he so often uses to ac-
company them. As a rule they are extremely *staccato,*
a movement that tires if one reads too many, though
usually any incipient yawn turns into a smile. Who
could resist the deftness of this bit of wit—an epigram
called *Life?*

> I met four guinea-hens today,
> Creaking like pulleys.
>
> "A crrk," said one;
> "A crrk," said two;
> "A crrk," said three;
> "A crrk," said four.
>
> I agree with you cheerfully, ladies.

And here is another from the same laughing philosopher:

> Tiny boy,
> staring at me
> with eyes like toy balloons;
> That broom is much bigger than you—
> put it down.
> You won't?
> Then don't put it down.

And I should like to quote also the divertingly true *I am four monkeys;* but that is already famous.

Are these poetry? Why not? Did not Horace write satires long ago, and successfully "put them over" with the Romans—yes, and with sober-minded professors of Latin even to our own day? Are these not as much poetry as Pope's diffuse and ingeniously rhymed satirical skits, which were gulped down, though with wry faces, by the "wits and beaux" of that "Augustan age"? Is there no room for satire in modern poetic art? "Because thou art virtuous, shall there be no more cakes and ale?"

I own it doth amaze me to hear some critics solemnly reading the law against Messrs. Kreymborg, Eliot, Williams, Cummings, and others whenever they indulge in contemporary satire. As if the muse must always march grandly to heroic tunes, or dance to approved classic measures, and never while away a more intimate hour, to steps of her own devising, among our own hidden and cherished frailties! These poets are witty in a modern fashion. They give us satirical verse of a kind more fit for our telegraphic age than Horace's sententious periods or Pope's ingenious couplets; but verse as well entitled to be called poetry as theirs in this kind.

I do not mean that **Mr. Kreymborg** is always a satirist.

Even in his most serious moods, however, he keeps his light touch-and-go manner and his telegraphic, almost telescopic, style. His "free forms" are not always so good a fit for the serious as for the whimsical mood; their rhythms become as obvious in their way as certain familiar hymns are in theirs. But sometimes he does a thing worthy of that over-used adjective, exquisite, like this wistful *Dance:*

> Moon dance,
> You were not to blame.
> Nor you,
> lovely white moth.
> But I saw you together.

Again, as in one or two of the group *To My Mother,* a feeling delicately tender is set to soft music. *Entity* perhaps came by wireless, yet I find it not quite unworthy of the muse:

> I am.
> And you.
> And atoms.
> Censure?
> Forgiveness?
> Why?

*America* suggests rather bravely the big swinging march of a young nation. And here is a portrait admirable in precision, *Cézanne:*

> Our door was shut to the noon-day heat.
> We could not see him.
> We might not have heard him either—
> resting, dozing, dreaming pleasantly.
> But his step was tremendous—
> are mountains on the march?
>
> He was no man who passed,
> but a great faithful horse
> dragging a load
> up the hill.

In his *Plays for Poem Mimes* Mr. Kreymborg's free forms accept expertly the theatric test. These brief dramas act well, they play better than they read, which is the final test of a playwright's instinct. Moreover, he is in the advance guard—the trend of the new poetic drama toward pantomime and ballet is nowhere more delicately illustrated than in the dramatic monologue *When the Willow Nods,* wherein the single speaker accompanies with rhythmic talk the symbolic action of the character. Certain farces—*Lima Beans,* for example— also pattern the action with just enough conventionalization of dialogue and posture, though in others of these *Plays for Merry Andrews* the effect of repetition in re-echoing dialogue seems overdone, becomes a clatter.

Alfred Kreymborg has adventurous and forward-looking ideas in any art he practices. If only he were a man profoundly impassioned and possessed, he might be one of the poets of power in the making of the new age. But he lives more lightly, more pleasantly, than the great; his feeling moves in ripples, not in strong waves. And so his delicate insight and sure touch are expended upon the lesser triumphs of the art, upon feathered shafts of satire, rainbow glints of beauty, tenderness, pathos. And there is much charm in his glance beyond, in his way of suggesting more than he tells.

THE voices of women have been heard in full antiphonal strength through the lyric chorus of the past fifteen years. Soprano voices, mezzo, contralto—voices of different power and quality, of all varieties of timbre and tone—have sung out the sensations, emotions, ideas of women with a frankness rarely before attained. There has been little imitation of men, almost none of that envious reaching-out for virility which feminine artists have often been guilty of in periods less hospitable than ours to their efforts at self-expression. And consequently their poetic utterance becomes remarkable not only for its clarity and beauty, but also for the frank sincerity of its revelation of the feminine point of view. The women poets of our time, in short, have been content to be women; and in thus accepting their destiny they have invaded a field comparatively open to their advance.

I have studied a number of these poets in this series of articles, but it would take many more such screeds to present in due detail the special values of even the more prominent women whom one finds in any modern list. And perhaps their variety of mood and manner, their dramatic contrasts of temperament, may be more sharply suggested by considering them together.

One feels impelled to group them roughly in two classes—the subjective and the objective; the first group preferring, as a rule, to express their own emotions, and the second the emotions of others. If I mention Helen Hoyt as typical of the first group, and Agnes Lee of the second, we are reminded at once of the two extremes of feminine temperament. With Helen Hoyt as in the main subjective, each in her very individual way, we might group Louise Bogan, Aline Kilmer, Muna Lee, Léonie Adams and Leonora Speyer. And with Agnes Lee as instinctively observant of others, are Eunice Tietjens, Alice Corbin, Lola Ridge, Marion Strobel, and a group of women still more reflective, like Hazel Hall and Genevieve Taggard, who look in and out with philosophic minds. But in the very act of grouping one feels how fluid are all human currents, for no individual can be precisely defined, and each of these poets gets out of bounds to range the other fields.

I have described Helen Hoyt as typically subjective because it is always her own feeling which interests her, her own reaction to the beauty of nature or the thrill of experience. This is as evident in her park poems—the oft-quoted *Ellis Park,* for example—as in the love poems to which her first book, *Apples Here in My Basket,* is devoted. But it is in her love-lyrics, whether the verse be metrical or free, that she speaks most spontaneously, most poignantly, with a voice that is her own and by no possibility another's. And because of this intense emotional sincerity, which is matched by rhythms as direct and simple, she speaks for thousands of other women. .

She has an extraordinary way of putting into a few lines some detail of feminine emotion which seems never to have been quite said before. And she always speaks with singular precision, satisfied with one motive, and

never continuing after the thing has been said.  **Here is**
one of these shining facets of feeling, *Difference:*

> I say so many things,
> I cannot understand your silence.
> I give so much,
> I cannot understand your always taking.
> I change myself so willingly to please you,
> I cannot understand
> That you have never thought of changing.

And *Refuge* has the same kind of spontaneity and beauty:

> I took my sorrow into the forest—
> Oh, do not hurt the forest with your sorrow!
>
> I took my bitterness to the sea;
> But the sea answered,
> *The brine of my own bitterness is bitter enough.*
>
> I could not reach into the sky's height and calm;
> I was ashamed to lay my weeping on the bosom of the earth.

There is always a touch of distinction in Helen Hoyt's
handling of themes which, with many women poets,
would become mawkish.  Her passion is never cheap, even
when it is joyous; and when, through the joy, she discerns inevitable sorrow beyond, we have such a lovely
wistful poem as *Words Out of Waking* or *Rain at Night.*

Love is "woman's whole existence" far less today than
it was when Byron wrote the line, but it is still her
favorite theme in lyric poetry, as indeed it is, to a less
degree, with men.  Muna Lee's method is nearer to
Sara Teasdale than to Helen Hoyt.  Such a poem as
*The Thought of You,* in two quatrains, belongs to the
pure lyric school and attains that effect of song in flight
which only a few lyrics give:

> The thought of you is taller than the sunset
> Flaming up above the world's crumbling edges.

> The thought of you is shyer than the lizard
> In a cleft of the limestone ledges.
>
> The thought of you is wilder than the wild birds
> Whose only joy is in their own wild flying.
> The thought of you is lovelier than starlight,
> And sadder than a young child's dying.

And the sonnet sequence in *Sea-change* is a beautiful celebration of a woman's passion, baffled yet in a sense triumphant.   Here is the final sextet of the series:

> I am not I who come back to old ways—
> Not I, but what a dream has made of me,
> Beyond earth's power to alter or undo.
> And if I must walk quietly all my days,
> As once I walked, content that this should be,
> God must remake the world, or me, or you!

With Aline Kilmer the problem of a woman's emotional life is more subtle.

> Many die when they see
> That the terrible thing is true.
> But it has been easy for me—
> I always knew.

And out of bitter knowledge she reminds us that passion is unreasonable, inconsequent, ephemeral, and that perhaps only a woman's children find something in her that is steadfast.   Such a poem as *The Heart Knoweth its own Bitterness* digs under the dead leaves of convention; and *If I had Loved You More* is another agonized word of self-suspicion, the soul's confession of inadequacy when bereavement has made all previous daily living seem trivial.   In many poems this note is struck—the last stanza of *Things* gives it sharply:

> For life seems only a shuddering breath,
>   A smothered desperate cry,
> And things have a terrible permanence
>   When people die.

Indeed, the tenor of Mrs. Kilmer's poetry is an accusation—of herself primarily, and thence of all these pitiable human souls who long so ineffectually for light and power and joy. And the least of her songs records, in its delicate ever-moving gleam and rhythm, the beauty of a spirit which demands too much of itself—of life.

Louise Bogan's book, *Body of This Death,* is a still harsher challenge:

> Love me because I am lost;
> Love me that I am undone.
> That is brave—no man has wished it,
> Not one.
>
> Be strong to look on my heart
> As others look on my face.
> Love me—I tell you that it is a ravaged
> Terrible place.

She feels a bitter scorn of herself, of all women:

> Women have no wilderness in them,
> They are provident instead,
> Content in the tight hot cell of their hearts
> To eat dusty bread.

The dark mood runs through the book—its rhythms sound the tragic self-communings of youth unanswered and unsatisfied.

The poems of Léonie Adams are less agonizing in motive than Miss Bogan's—theirs is a somewhat gentler "strangled passion of desolation". Their quiet mournful rhythms seem set to a subtle half-interval scale, and she tunes them adroitly to respond with beauty as she utters her wayward and elusive criticism of life. Brief quotations hardly suffice, but this *legato* sonnet, *Thought's End,* may give a hint of her temper and method:

[ 145 ]

I'd watched the hills drink the last color of light,
All shapes grow bright and wane on the pale air,
Till down the traitorous east there came the night,
And swept the circle of my seeing bare.
Its intimate beauty like a wanton's veil
Tore from the void as from an empty face.
I felt at being's rim all being fail,
And my one body pitted against space.
O heart more frightened than a wild bird's wings
Beating at green, now is no fiery mark,
But heaven empty of accustomed things.
Be self no more against the flooding dark:
There thousandwise sown in that cloudy blot,
Stars that are worlds look out and see you not.

Leonora Speyer's earlier instrument was the violin—
it is not often that one may change in mid-career from
one art to another, and develop proficiency in a new
technique. Her second book, *Fiddler's Farewell,* is much
better than her first, even though the title-poem and
certain others are too deliberate. The *Ballad of a Lost
House* is the most sustained of the longer poems; the
emotion is carried to its climax without strain in a form
of extreme simplicity. And the eloquence in *Of Mountains* rises in a few passages to a more potent lyricism.

Certain poems show keen insight into human nature's
problems; among them *Onlooker, Little Lover, Affinity,
Kleptomaniac.* And two—the sonnet *Protest in Passing,*
and the book's brief epilogue—offer a high-hearted,
almost gay, salute to death. Here is the second of these:

Let not my death be long,
But light
As a bird's swinging;
Happy decision in the height
Of song—
Then flight
From off the ultimate bough!

> And let my wing be strong,
> And my last note the first
> Of another's singing.
> See to it, Thou!

I have spoken of Agnes Lee as a typical figure in the other group—those women poets who are instinctively observant and dramatic. Agnes Lee's is the questing mind that delves into strange places for blooms no other would suspect. "Faces and open doors" lead her within them; some little thing startles her to emotion which tugs at her heart and brain, and we have a poem piteous, wistful, whimsical according to the kind of sympathy which inspired it, but recording imaginative rather than personal experience. An account of an accident reaches her, and we get the reaction of that accident on the victim's parents in the tragic sketch, *Evening*. The joy and pathos of motherhood is suggested to her not so much by the infant Christ as by the infant Iscariot in his mother's arms. A tale of leprosy from Honolulu is transmuted into that agonizing dialogue, *The Asphodel*. And a name in a newspaper police report gives us *Mrs. Malooly* done to the life:

> Mrs. Malooly has gone to her rest,
> Who scrubbed Manhattan's marble aisles.
> She has forgotten, forgotten, forgotten
> The mop and broom
> And the patterned tiles.
>
> Mrs. Malooly has gone to her rest
> In the smooth-dug loam—to a rest so deep
> She has forgotten, forgotten, forgotten
> The unmade bed
> And the whiskey sleep.

Indeed, Agnes Lee's poems are dramatic lyrics or lyric dialogues. She is absorbed, to the point of intense emotion, in the emotions of other people; and the only personal utterances one finds in her books are quiet reflections like *Numbers* or *At Dawn*. She has always had a musician's instinct for sound, but her earlier poems were often too loosely constructed on themes too expansively indulged. Gradually, however, she has sharpened her technique to a finer edge.

Of course these women poets have their confessional moments, even though I class them here as mainly observant or dramatic. But though they may have written love lyrics in the most approved moods and forms, their more distinctive work records, more or less reflectively, impressions of other people.

Eunice Tietjens, for example, is more convincingly herself in her *Profiles from China* and *Profiles from Home* than in the most personal lyrics of *Body and Raiment;* and her art is more effective in the free-verse forms which she theoretically questions than in the rhyme and metrics which she prefers. In the *Profiles* a wise-woman seems to take us by the hand and point out odd corners of human destiny along travelled highways far and near. If she presents with slanting irony our petty inadequacies, yet her touch is sympathetic, or even tender; and her art can rise to keener heights of joyous or tragic beauty in such poems as *The Wall* and *The Most Sacred Mountain*. In these there is exaltation: at the summit of "Tai Shan the beautiful, the most holy," she is blown by "the twelve clean winds of heaven"; and on the wall, in the presence of China's agony, she can cry,

> Who am I, that I should die for these?

With Alice Corbin the aboriginal and Mexican life

around her, set against a background of desert and mountains, has absorbed of late her artistic energies. The old Mexican woman, the goat-herd Juan Quintana, the tribal dance-festivals—the various details of life left over from long ago in the midst of our modern world—these have been the theme of her too infrequent art. But her earlier lyrics were more personal in their joyous reaction to the mystery and immensity of the universe. She is always aware of larger spaces behind our little lives; the five quatrains of *Nodes* express this consciousness with singular intensity:

> The sun and all the planets in the sky,
>   Beside the sacred wonder of dim space,
> Are notes upon a broken tarnished lute
>   Which God will some day mend and put in place.

And such poems in free verse as *Music, In the Desert,* the lovely *One City Only,* beat slow rhythms like muffled drums.

Grace Fallow Norton seems also aware of other worlds. One feels in her work a certain shyness of withdrawal, a reluctance to confess herself fully. She makes lyrics about other people—the sick in a hospital, the mythical miller's daughter—as a veil to hide behind with her doubts and questions. And her singing voice, slight and delicate, is musical and full of feeling.

With Lola Ridge this world is enough. Its beauty of nature and of human struggle stir her lyric passion, and its injustices fire her proud spirit to rebellion. In many poems she beats the drum and cymbals of anger to arouse the defeated, the disheartened. She cries in *Débris:*

> I love those spirits
> That men stand off and point at,
> Or shudder and hood up their souls—
> Those ruined ones
> Where Liberty has lodged an hour,
> And passed like flame,
> Bursting asunder the too small house.

The fire in her, that kindles for beauty in such poems as *The Song* and *The Edge,* flames out with destructive fury in *The Song of Iron.* But if much of *The Ghetto* is almost propaganda, its fierce rhythms and impassioned imaginings lift it into poetry:

> I would be a torch unto your hand,
> A lamp upon your forehead, Labor,
> In the wild darkness before the dawn
> That I shall never see.

Marion Strobel, in her first book, *Once in a Blue Moon,* gives us the modern girl, the modern young woman —the various rainbow colors of her prismatic emotional experience, registered in a technique audaciously personal and felicitous. Her flirtations are here, in all their ephemeral intensity; her friendships, even her atheltics; also her observations of characters and situations, presented with irony, compassion, or reverence, but always with a keen sense of drama. We have her whole vivid and varied experience of life, an experience unusually fortunate, ending with ·the charming *Songs to Sally,* a fresh and fair revelation of young motherhood. There is exquisite tenderness in such poems about her friends as *A Bride, Pitiful in Your Bravery*—indeed, all the *Seven Brave Women;* as also in this brevity, *Little Things:*

Little things I'll give to you—
Till your fingers learn to press
Gently
On a loveliness.

Little things and new—
Till your fingers learn to hold
Love that's fragile,
Love that's old.

The other poets on our list are moved more by ideas
than by the emotions of their own hearts or their observations of other people. With Genevieve Taggard emotion
waits on thought, and both are imaginatively enticed.
Her spirit impersonates the sun-child, or runs with the
panther in *Epithalamium,* or shivers in predicting the
*Ice Age:*

Noiselessly the planets will blow by,
Like smoke, like breath, like driven snow;
Frost-bitten suns on on, on on will blow;
Over earth's curve, the moons, like birds, will fly,
Making no noise and only vague shadow.

And spider snow will spin and spin
A tangle of frost to snare earth in.

And even in her love-poems one feels a certain remoteness and austerity. Her mind looks on from afar.

Hazel Hall and Gladys Cromwell both died in the
youth of their achievement, and yet the work of each is
singularly well rounded and complete. Both were held
aloof from life, the one by her wheeled chair, the other
by a spiritual isolation—for Gladys Cromwell lived with
her twin-sister in a companionship so close as to re-enforce
her shyness, making life's ordinary contacts impossible,
and its extraordinary ones—which the sisters rashly invoked in their war work—in the end destructive.

*The Crowning Gift, Folded Power, The Mold*—these and other poems are austere in their shapely beauty, like a bas-relief carved in gray stone. Among her briefer utterances, perhaps *The Christian* will suggest Miss Cromwell's temperament and the tenor of her thinking:

> I was free. But now in a net I am caught;
> In a delicate net of love I am taken.
> I, the lonely whom nobody sought,
> Can feel the poor and the sorrow-shaken
> Draw the line of their yearning taut;
> I am held by experience. When I die
> Their net will draw me through fathoms of sky;
> I cannot evade immortality.

Hazel Hall was less instinctively shy, and she lived more emotionally in the lives of people she worked for or whose passing she watched from her window. Her needlecraft became a symbol; of the millions of women who have stitched the raiment of the world, she alone, so far as I remember, has recognized its universal significance. Here, from a number of needle-poems, is *One by One:*

> One by one, one by one,
> Stitches of the hours run
> Through the fine seams of the day;
> Till like a garment it is done
>     And laid away.
>
> One by one the days go by,
> And suns climb up and down the sky;
> One by one their seams are run—
> As Time's untiring fingers ply,
>     And life is done.

And in *Walkers* we have the sound of many feet passing by—a sensitiveness to footfalls on the part of this listening paralytic girl which reminds one of Helen Keller's uncanny sensitiveness to the feel of hands. In *Hunger* she gives almost the whole story of her life:

> I have known life's hunger,
> Though by other name;
> It has been dream and singing,
> Faith and the whip of shame.
>
> Not until I listened
> To sounds of a world swept by,
> Did I learn to hear my own heart,
> And hear all life in its cry.
>
> Not until the hunger
> Of all the world was blown
> Like a wind against my window,
> Could I name my own.
>
> And I have learned that only
> This is not proved vain:
> Hunger by which a world is fed
> As I am fed by pain.

A poet earlier dead than either of these, one singularly modern in feeling and method yet already a classic, may fitly close this brief sketch of song-impassioned women of this century. Adelaide Crapsey, dying at thirty-five in 1914, used her art like a sword to defend herself bitterly against the threatening enemy. Frail and aloof, she wrote of the fulness and glory of life, of *Birth-moment* and *The Mother Exultant*. From her death-bed she uttered, to "the dead in the graveyard" under her window, a fierce protest against their thwarted lives. In her heart is never "resignation, sister to defeat." She cannot veil the cold agony of death with theories or dreams, but gives us in a number of poems its naked

[ 153 ]

horror.   *John Keats,* for example, has lines like these:

> Yea, now, caught in
> The aghast and voiceless pain
> Of death, thyself doth watch
> Thyself becoming naught.

In her *Cinquains* Miss Crapsey invented a highly distinguished form which no imitator has used so well. No doubt she had in mind the severity of certain Japanese lyric forms, for these delicate exaltations of her mind rise and pass like perfume in mysterious concentrated beauty, somewhat in the wistful manner of a *hokku*. In none of her longer poems, beautiful and nobly impassioned as they are, has she quite equalled the curved and polished perfection of these.   Here are two of them:

### TRIAD

> These be
> Three silent things:
> The falling snow . . . the hour
> Before the dawn . . . the mouth of one
> Just dead.

### FATE DEFIED

> As it
> Were tissue of silver
> I'll wear, O fate, thy grey,
> And go, mistily radiant, clad
> Like the moon.

And so, "mistily radiant," she was led off by the conqueror—but not to utter silence and darkness, for the shadowed fire of her spirit burns on with singular intensity in her small book of tragic but exultant song.

## CERTAIN POETS OF YESTERDAY

*Chaucer and Langland*
*Shakespeare*
*Shelley*
*Keats*
*Byron*
*Matthew Arnold*
*Walt Whitman*

WHEN the English language was in the making—
the English language, which the Germans call
"the bastard tongue," "the insignificant pirate dialect,"
in comparison with their own throaty and mouth-filling
speech; when English was taking unto itself Saxon
strength, Norman splendor, and a touch of the more
southern Latin grace, to become that powerful, flexible,
and richly tuned organ which was to be heard around the
world: even in those half-articulate and illiterate centuries the shaping influences were yet more or less conscious, and more or less incarnate in human beings of
different minds. The singers who wandered from castle
to castle, or from hamlet to hamlet—ambassadors and
newsmongers to the lords and the folk—chanted their
sagas and romances in forms derived from Norse, Teu-
tonic or French tradition, and fought on English soil
the war of *kultur* even then.

It was fitting, and singularly dramatic, that the final
battle of this war should have been delivered over to two
such sturdy champions as Chaucer and Langland. The
time was the militant and imaginative fourteenth century
of Edward the Third, of his knightly son the Black
Prince, and his work-hating, beauty-loving grandson
Richard the Second; the fourteenth century of amazing
contrasts—extravagance and starvation, beauty and loath-
someness, jewelled embroideries and vermivorous rags.

And the scene was mostly London—London of the Norman court and the Saxon people, of lords and starvelings, castles and hovels, pageants and pests; little London, already rising into glory out of the slime of the river Thames.

Not that the two champions consciously faced each other in their intellectual lists. Neither may have known of the other's existence; or, if they ever met in those narrow mudways, no doubt the courtly Chaucer smiled when surly "Long Will" refused to make way for him, or take off his ragged cap to this retainer of kings. Neither suspected, probably, that the future of England, or at least of English, lay between them, that one or the other of them was molding a world-encircling language and cutting the patterns of an immortal art.

Of course all the odds were with Chaucer; then, as now, he was irresistible. Well born, well reared, learned in three or four languages, a cosmopolite who had carried his king's messages to Italy—Italy, then mothering the Renaissance—and withal, one of the most engaging and sympathetic beings who ever took human shape, it was no wonder that Chaucer had it all his own way, and that English poets have done his will for centuries. Reared in the Norman court, chanting French romances from childhood, he naturally preferred rhyme and the three-time iambic measure to the alliterations and assonances, and the harsh irregularities, of the pounding four-time measure derived from that Saxon tradition which was still dear to the hearts and sweet to the ears of the common people. Indeed, it was a proof of Chaucer's broad sympathy, of his strong mind and big heart, that he did not abandon English altogether, that he, like Dante, insisted on writing his poems in his mother tongue instead of in courtly French or learned Latin. It was a fortunate day for us all when Chaucer said:

> Let clerks enditen in Latin, for they have the property of science and the knowinge in that faculty; and let Frenchmen in their French also endite their quaint terms, for it is kindly to their mouths; and let us show our fantasies in such words as we learneden of our dames tongue.

So, though Chaucer did not introduce the French forms into the new combination language, it is not too much to say that he domesticated them. He made rhyme, and the iambic measure, as much at home in English as they ever have been in the romance tongues, and he opened the way for some of the greatest rhythmists who ever lived—Shakespeare, Spenser, Milton, Coleridge, Shelley, Swinburne and others—whose verse-structure, however varied, is almost entirely based upon the three-time iambic foot or bar, their four-time experiments being comparatively slight and incidental.

Thus Langland was left far behind, *Piers Plowman* was forgotten except by scholars. From his time until Shelley's, four-time measures were almost abandoned, being found only in a few Elizabethan songs, in parts of Dryden's two music-praising odes, and in a few other experiments. The iambus "reigned supreme," usually in the five-footed line which Chaucer's fine instinct had preferred to the French hexameter as better suited to the genius of the new language. And even when Coleridge—in the *Ancient Mariner* and a few other poems, Shelley—in *The Cloud, The Skylark,* and others, and Byron—in *There be none of beauty's daughters* and one or two other songs, began to vary the music of English verse with four-time measures, their experiments bore little relation to Langland, or to the earlier Saxon bards. And while Swinburne's varied rhythms wove with infinite delicacy new renaissance patterns, they never went back to the stern old Gothic motive.

The first great modern poet, no doubt, to put aside altogether the renaissance patterns was Whitman. In doing so, he did not consciously return to the music of the sagas—the Gothic motive, as it may be called—yet his free verse is more allied to Langland than to Chaucer; it has more in common with the old Anglo-Saxon bards than with Shakespeare or Milton or Swinburne. It does, in short, remind us once more of the older tradition— older, that is, in English poetry—though the reminder is far-away and indefinite, a matter of feeling and flavor and general rhythmic pace, rather than of form or tune.

But in the impetus toward free verse which Whitman led, and which is evident in so much modern poetry— French and Italian as well as English—it is possible that Langland and his Old-English predecessors will have increasing influence. Indeed, we have evidences of this— in such modern presentations of mediaeval music as Mr. Ezra Pound's truly wonderful paraphrase, *The Sea-farer,* for example. Those old poets will be studied, not from the point of view of academic scholarship, but from that of immediate beauty and fecundity. We shall have a new realization of their power of imagination and of the splendor and variety of their rhythms.

And thus Langland, after more than five centuries, may come into his own at last. The world may rediscover that modern socialist, anarchist, anti-militarist, who in the king-ruled, monk-ridden, war-lorded fourteenth century, lifted up his prophet's voice for the brotherhood of man, and was called crazy for his pains. Chaucer took his world as it was, and left us a Holbein portrait-gallery of the people he saw around him; loving the processional pageantry of the life of lords and commons, and ignoring the invisible and inarticulate miseries of the forgotten remnant—the poor who froze and starved in hovels, and died in battles and periodic plagues. Langland, on the contrary, felt these miseries of the poor as the only fit subject for tragic passion: a great democrat, he made the crowd the subject of his epic; a great seer, he looked forward to the end of their miseries, not through mythical compensations in heaven, but through increase of justice on earth.

The urbane Chaucer for five centuries has led the poets his successors: in motive as well as technique they have been mostly of his mind, accepting his aristocratic point of view, his delight in the upper-class pageant, and almost entirely ignoring the burden-bearing poor. But perhaps Langland is like to bridge the centuries and clasp hands with the poets of the future, the prophets of the new era, toward which the world is marching through blood and fire, through faith and dreams.

WHAT manner of man was this who peopled a provincial stage, made music of a barbarous tongue, played a few parts, dreamed many dreams, set up an estate in his native village, and died in his prime over three hundred years ago? What manner of man was it whose name, during these three centuries, has been rung on all the bells of fame, whose people are the friends of all the world, whose thinking washes under all our cargoes, and whose rhythms are the waves on which our visions ride? Everywhere he is present—we cannot escape him; he passes current like the coin of the realm. He is part of our language, of the phrasing and movement and beat of it; and when we are silent the very winds and stars march to his music. What manner of man was this who has become so much more important to the world than he ever was to himself?

Of course there is only one word that a man can write with whatever expenditure of ink—the word *myself*. Shakespeare has been called impersonal, but he could no more escape this word than the clamorous egotist who shouts "I! I! I!" on every page. If he hides behind his characters, he is nevertheless there, and the search for his evasive personality is the central and secret fascination of his work. Some writers are easy to find in the books they leave us, and when found they may be no great matter; others reveal themselves only to their friends, and reward them with special intimacy; others pause for a beautiful gesture, a smile, almost a touch, and are off again, always alluring and eluding. But this poet, who, giving himself away in thirty-seven plays and an hundred and fifty-four sonnets, was yet the most reserved of men, this poet is the most magnetic of all. The things we discover of him—that sympathy and insight, that humor and shrewdness, that love of all life and passion for all beauty, that poignant tenderness at the edge of a grave, that strange worldliness and baffling indifference to his art—these are but the beginning of his self. His secret is always deeper within, further beyond. The more we get—those of us who get beneath the surface at all—the more awaits us.

Because this poet does not wear his heart on his sleeve or explain himself to the passer-by, and because a certain type of mind delights in puzzles and cryptograms and facile interpretations, we have had a thousand misreadings of his character; and even huge and elaborate Baconian theories to rob us of our Shakespeare, and substitute for that large figure something small and definite and precise. The "myriad-minded," we are told, must have been a soldier to reveal war, a lawyer to understand law, a courtier to present princes, and the domineering Frank Harris has soberly asserted that he must have been a madman to compass the madness of Lear. What are these foolish commentators doing but exposing their own folly? The colossus stands there unshaken, smiling his enigmatic solemn smile, with that same look of pity and tenderness in his eyes.

It takes a poet to interpret a poet. Holbein might have painted Shakespeare if he had lived long enough, or Dürer might have made a copperplate of him as mysterious as the *Melancolia*. But no meaner imagination can quite compass that soul adrift between hell and heaven, devoured by earthly desires and divine despairs, writing immortal plays as a kind of lucrative by-play, a sop and solace to his tyrannous imagination, which clamored for freedom in worlds greater than his own. Now and then, during these three centuries, someone has cast a flash-light on this figure, but no one has yet revealed all the pride and power of it, all the sorrow and weakness. Even Mr. Edwin Arlington Robinson, in his illuminating monologue, *Ben Jonson Entertains a Man from Stratford,* though he gets nearer to the heart of his subject than any of the thousand-and-one critics and panegyrists before him—even he does not strip that spirit bare.

The littleness of man, his inadequacy, his inefficiency—this seems to have haunted Shakespeare's imagination. Man's impotence to will, to do, to achieve, in spite of intellect, beauty, charm, goodness, in spite of all qualities which should make him powerful—the poet is haunted by this theme; he rings the changes on it in all the great tragedies, and pursues it in many of the comedies. Apparently he searched history and human life in vain, as Nietzsche did, for the throned and sceptred figure of the man of power. Not finding him in either Plutarch or Holinshed, or among Queen Elizabeth's courtiers and freebooters, he presented again and again, as the supreme tragedy of life, the pathetic figure of the weak man in a great place. Power unused, or inadequately or criminally used, was the universal spectacle on a chance-blown planet, the one central cause of all our woe, for Shakespeare as for Nietzsche. But the German poet-prophet, living after Darwin, would not despair of his hero. Non-existent today, the man of power might yet be evolved. So he set up, before the mind's eye of the struggling race, that ideal of the super-man which thrilled his people like some ichor from the table of dead war-gods, and sent them forth to conquer the world.

Apparently Shakespeare did not believe that the race could ever produce the efficient man—for him it was not in the stars. Again and again he balks at the hero: he turns his back on Edward III and his warrior son, and makes of Henry V a picturesque stage monarch, a royal bravo with a Prince-Hal past, created as an attempt to satisfy the red-blood British patriotism of his day; and his Caesar is a pitiful weakling who gives the lie to history, and proves the poet's lack of faith in man's power to play a god-like role.

With what infinite variety, what deep tenderness of love and pity, Shakespeare studied human inadequacy, revealed human littleness, almost any of the plays may bear witness. But his favorite version of the theme, as pre-eminently in *Hamlet,* is the man on a throne, or near it, who cannot answer the summons of ironic destiny to be a leader, a ruler; the man who can see all around a deed, divining motives and consequences, yet is powerless to prepare it and do it, powerless to act except on impulse. Again and again he found this inadequate king in Holinshed and the other chroniclers: in John, Richard III, Henry IV, Henry VIII, he read him as the half-great, foiled by his own lusts or ambitions, his muddled thought or misty vision; in Henry VI he was the well-meaning self-baffled theorist, motionless on a tumbling throne; and in Richard II he was the artist, the poet, absorbed in creating a refuge of beauty away from the mud-stained, blood-splashed world.

His own inadequacy for action—this was the tragedy Shakespeare knew best, the tragedy which humiliated him to the dust and poisoned his pride of intellect. And he was merciless with himself; for, having probed to the secret source of his own inefficiency, he set it on a throne for all to see. He placed it where immediate and decisive action was continually required as the final fruit of noble and developed character, and showed how, without that, all subtlety of thought, fire of passion, desire of beauty, intuition of truth, became the source of chaos and confusion, and ended in blood and ashes.

Usually the poet drives his lesson home, at the end of the play, by leaving lesser men, second-rate in everything but will, to obliterate the hideous waste of life and restore the order of the world—as when Fortinbras takes the dead Hamlet's throne. Apparently he set a higher value on this power of action, which he had not, than on all the dreams and visions of his poet-heroes—their audacity of intellect, their unfailing beauty of speech, their tenderness and loving kindness, their heroic desires and ideals.

Shakespeare confessed his tragedy, of course, in the sonnets, besides his less deliberate confession in the plays. The sonnets present his supreme experiences—exquisite emotion, love exalting or degrading, conviction of sin, conviction of fame, the sense of unendurable beauty, the magnanimity of unalterable love, the blight of decay and death, the glory of spiritual life. But through the poem runs his ever-present theme, his sense of personal futility, of inadequacy for life: self-torture over doing always the wrong thing while seeing the right, self-disgust that his lady's other lovers can outplay him, that any fool can seize the moment for action better than he.

Perhaps nowhere else, in English personal poetry, does one feel so sure of the poet's absolute uncompromising sincerity. In Shakespeare's sonnets a wide range of human experience is transmuted into the subtlest music ever wrought out of English words; and so, for one who knows and loves them, they reach the heart of any mood, like a dear friend's voice. Seek them as a relief from petty cares and they soothe like running waters; go to them in grief and they are elegies, in joy and they chime like bells, in triumph and they sing paeans. Remorse, despair, pity, love, worship—the most diverse emotions— all find their answer here. It is as though the poem had been sung for the special mood we bring to it, so intimately, so healingly, does it touch each wound and fill the chambers of the soul with beauty.

The sonnets record a period of passionate experience in a life whose serenity is elsewhere its strongest note. They are the forty days of struggle in the wilderness, and they bring, not bitterness or violence, but surer vision and deeper sympathy. They lead from the comedies to the tragedies, from *Much Ado About Nothing* to *Macbeth* and *Antony and Cleopatra* and *King Lear*.

It is my feeling that from the time of the sonnets to his death—about fifteen years—the poet steeled himself against devastating emotional excitement and took refuge in his imagination. One thing seemed about as important as another in the actual world; he felt something of that illumined apathy which Browning ascribes to the resurrected Lazarus. The people around him became part of the dream, gaining color and significance but losing substantiality. Gradually his serenity regained its poise: we have the proof of this in *The Tempest,* and we might have had more in that unwritten greatest play of all had he lived to grow old in Stratford.

One of Shakespeare's love lyrics—perhaps the most magical—has long seemed to me expressive of a larger meaning:

> Take—oh, take those lips away
>   That so sweetly were forsworn;
> And those eyes, the break of day—
>   Lights that do mislead the morn;
> But my kisses bring again,
>   Bring again—
> Seals of love, but sealed in vain,
>   Sealed in vain!

I do not know what lady first heard that madrigal. To inspire it was worth a life of care, and we may well hope that this high service to the world may have short‑ ened the purgatorial pains she had to suffer for her per‑ fidy. But perhaps we should think of her as a symbol of something less tangible, a symbol of life itself. Surely it was thus that Shakespeare knew and loved his world. Tantalizing mistress, what vow could bind her to his soul forever? Elusive and unconquerable, her trustful eyes could turn from him, her smile could pass to another before it had time to fade, her oaths were broken even in the uttering. Royal and bountiful she is, beautiful and strong; but unremembering and insecure. For a time her treasures crown him, and all her raptures fall about his soul. But even in the moment of ecstasy he knows the vanity of these sensuous joys. Then, above all, he feels the infinite summons. The world and its accepted values fade off into nothingness, time loses its brief space in the eternal years, knowledge is drawn up like a curtain before the unfathomable mystery, and all our human pride becomes the shadow of a dream. Before that inescapable vision what are life and song and fame? Bubbles to be blown for a toy, to rise and gleam and vanish and be thought of no more. And so, deeper than his love of life was his indifference to it, wider than his knowledge of the world was his recklessness of its applause. Flowers or ashes—he cared not; kisses or broken vows—he could live and love for either.

Thus in his personality there is something selfless and inscrutable which from age to age has fascinated the world. We feel him vast, impartial, beneficent, like light and air. We return to the old simile and liken him to the ocean for universality and strength and poise. And we feel in his presence, as before these natural forces, that he tells not all, he gives not all. We take from him *Hamlet, Lear, The Tempest* unsatisfied, wondering what he could have done if he had ever put forth his utmost power. We diagram his greatness, we explain it in terms of earth and in terms of heaven. We theorize and define and dream, but the heart of his mystery still eludes us. We are baffled by his impenetrability, and we cast him from our hearts into the outer darkness of intellectual admiration, and clasp once more the familiar idols— those lesser heroes whose limitations make them kin to us. And he knows that we are faithless, that we take him for what he is not, that our hearts are cold to him. He had foreseen it all—that fame is but a breath, that immortality is but light across a grave. He was not deceived, and his love can never change with the altering

of ours. Still out of the deeps of time his voice seems
calling to the approaching years:

> Take—oh, take those lips away
>   That so sweetly were forsworn;
> And those eyes, the break of day—
>   Lights that do mislead the morn;
> But my kisses bring again,
>     Bring again—
> Seals of love, but sealed in vain,
>     Sealed in vain!

IN these days of revolutionary changes it was appropriate to be reminded of Shelley by the centenary of his death; and the reminder may well lead us to a deeper study of the man and his work than a casual reading of *The Cloud* and *The Skylark*. For of all the ranking English poets, Shelley was preëminently the poet with a message—a type somewhat decried by modern esthetic theorists, who would not permit the muse to stiffen her lips with didactic emphasis. Even Milton, the Puritan partisan of Cromwell, pleader for free speech, free thought, free divorce and other heresies, was a conservative conformist beside Shelley, whose stark idealism accepted no compromise, whose ardor for a complete revolution in human society would have been, like Lenin's, "the same in act as in desire" if he also could have faced the tragic ironies of fate by achieving political power.

Of course we have only the beginning of Shelley's thinking, for he was under thirty, and young for his age, when he died. Yet there is a kind of finality about it, for he seems youth incarnate, youth immortal; and perhaps, as with the great mystics among whom Mr. Yeats classes him, old age with him would have been but a diviner childhood. Aflame with reformatory zeal, he theorized with complete conviction; and his theoretic picture of a perfect world was as untroubled by common sense as a cubistic painting, and as unaffected by the humane perspectives of humor. He had youth's single-mindedness, single-sightedness; perceiving a vivid truth, he struck out toward it through all obstacles, no matter how many conventions, laws, or even human hearts were broken on the way; only to be deflected from the immediate goal by the more flaming ardor of a newer revelation.

His creed was essentially Godwin touched by emotion, eighteenth-century radicalism transfigured by a poet's dreams. Freedom, sacrosanct and glorified, was its cardinal principle: evil is an accident; could man always have been free he would never have wandered from virtue—"government is but the badge of his degradation." Lift from man's past history the incubus of the law, with its consequences of obedience, "fear, faith and slavery"; grant him through all his course freedom of thought, of action and of love, and the human race would have enjoyed one long millennium of universal justice. And now this long-delayed peace on earth must be invoked on the instant by chosen souls. Live out your life, fulfil all natural impulses so long as your heart is pure, restrain neither thought nor deed, and "neither change nor falter nor repent"—such was the counsel of perfection which his impulsive "practicalness" urged upon his puny neighbors and flaunted brightly in the face of the canting world. He had no time to wait or think. If his intellect built too slowly, his imagination lightly overleapt logic and perched upon cloudy ramparts for a sunrise song.

The lyrics by which he is chiefly remembered were mere tangents from the rounding circle of his message—he would rather have destroyed them, probably, than let his fame rest upon such slight sparks of personal emotion, such flashes of joy or love or despair as were thrown off casually while, from *Queen Mab* to *The Triumph of Life,* he was summoning to action the hosts of the hapless world. The language of his summons was clear. In *The Masque of Anarchy* and certain more directly political poems of anathema, his faith in the power of the human soul utters a command to the proletariat of his time:

> Rise, like lions after slumber,
> In unvanquishable number!
> Shake your chains to earth like dew
> Which in sleep had fallen on you.
> Ye are many—they are few.

In *Prometheus Unbound* this faith becomes an assertion of man's ultimate supremacy, when "the painted veil . . . called life . . . is torn aside":

> The man remains—
> Sceptreless, free, uncircumscribed, but man;
> Equal, unclassed, tribeless and nationless;
> Exempt from awe, worship, degree; the king
> Over himself; just, gentle, wise—but man.
> Passionless?—no; yet free from guilt or pain,
> Which were, for his will made or suffered them;
> Nor yet exempt, though ruling them like slaves,
> From chance and death and mutability—
> The clogs of that which yet might oversoar
> The loftiest star of unascended heaven,
> Pinnacled dim in the intense inane.

With a zealot's precision Shelley demanded the absolute. His was a religious spirit, always fascinated by the supernatural, seeking communion with an impalpable divine essence. Therefore, in spite of the buffetings of fate, he stands for the revelation to men of ineffable spiritual realities beyond the reach of sensuous experience.

His soul flamed upward like Blake's, though with less detachment. He explored the empyrean, he touched the intangible; his poetry brought down to earth the vision of supernal beauty which had eluded even the blind eyes of Milton. Through him the vitality of mystical abstractions, the power and sweep of subtle unseen forces, the loveliness of secret beauty, the glory of naked truth, and the upward reach of the human mind toward the infinite splendor, are given the fiery proof of song. On earth he was ill at ease; in the highest heaven of imagination his poise was perfect. He never wavered in his flight, never stooped to catch the popular ear, never degraded for the sake of transient rewards a mission which seemed to him the holiest of all confided to mortal man. For poetry he held to be the noblest and most universal of the arts by which truth is made manifest to men, language being "as a mirror which reflects," and the materials of other arts "as a cloud which enfeebles, the light of which both are mediums."

One is tempted to quote whole pages of his magnificent *Defence of Poetry* in this connection, an essay which makes a royal progress through the universe, and shows that the spirit of poetry is the manifestation of the eternal order and harmony, the vitalizing and regenerating principle, the exemplar of wisdom and the revealer of love, the soul of aspiration, "the echo of the eternal music"; the destroyer, too, of wrong—a "sword of lightning, ever unsheathed, which consumes the scabbard that would contain it." As an art, "poetry redeems from decay the visitations of the divinity in man," being "the record of the best and happiest moments of the happiest and best minds." He defends these happiest and best minds, who "make immortal all that is best and most beautiful in the world," from the charges the world has brought against their lives; insisting that their frailties are merely the rebound of what is animal and passionate in their nature from a spiritual exaltation they experience and express but do not understand.

Poets are the hierophants of an unapprehended inspiration; the mirrors of the gigantic shadows which futurity casts upon the present; . . . the trumpets which sing to battle and feel not what they inspire; the influence which is moved not, but moves. Poets are the unacknowledged legislators of the world.

He at least would be true to his high office. He would illumine a path for men's hopes to travel even though they mocked him. The glorious vision of an exalted destiny for his race was before him, and in the fit disclosure of that vision he felt secure of immortal influence, even though the world rejected him in life. And the world did reject him. He threw down the gauntlet and his country took it up. His name was the synonym for unspeakable crimes, his poems were a target for the wrath and ridicule of reviewers, their small editions lay unsold with his publisher, and his sympathetic readers could be counted on the fingers of one hand. It was long after his death that the song of "the nightingale who sat in darkness" began to penetrate to men's ears.

For in form, as well as in feeling, Shelley was a revolutionist, and therefore unwelcome. English poetry was but newly awake from its eighteenth-century trance. Coleridge, Burns and the quiet Wordsworth had brushed away forever those reams of rhymed eloquence with which Pope and his kind had smothered the goddess; but the world was as yet scarcely aware of it, preferring the old heroics. Though Byron was forcing down its throat his modern message, Shelley and Keats were still exotics— outlandish birds singing a wild strain. Perhaps Shelley himself scarcely realized how different his style was from all that had been so long in vogue. Like every true poet, he had an instinct for form; and it was probably by instinct, rather than deliberate intention, that he followed Coleridge in breaking the long reign of the iambic measure, that he played with anapaests and spondees, and surpassed in delicate complexity of rhythm even the gay Elizabethans. For the expression of modern subtleties he added more strings to their instrument, and passed it on to us enriched with new notes and capable of a broader range.

Beauty, love and freedom are the triune chord at the basis of Shelley's song. We hear it again and again, like the Holy Grail motive in *Parsifal*. *Prometheus Unbound* is the spirit of freedom, braving omnipotent tyranny for love of the human race, who still declares, after aeons of agony:

> I would fain
> Be what it is my destiny to be,
> The savior and the strength of suffering man,
> Or sink into the original gulf of things—

and at whose release and reunion with Nature, when Eternity has conquered the evil principle of Power, all earth and her children rejoice in the ecstasy of inextinguishable love and holiness and peace. The choruses reach a celestial height of lyric exaltation; whether spirits or echoes or furies speak, they speak with eternity behind and before them, reveal to us birthless and deathless minds.

*Prometheus* and *Adonais* and the lyrics are the best of

Shelley; for in most of the longer poems, as even occasionally in these, he does not escape grandiloquence. With Coleridge and Burns and Keats he restored the lost Elizabethan tradition, resumed the grand manner, even though his one deliberately Elizabethan experiment was a failure. It is curious that this radical could not carry his radicalism into the theatre. *The Cenci* is, in my opinion, an imitative dramatic essay rather than a drama, an experiment in the Elizabethan manner modified by classic austerities. It out-Websters Webster in horrors, but misses Webster's vitality; its characters are premeditated types rather than suffering men and women.

Shelley met the world of men and women with the solemn, unquestioning belief of some flower or child, and when things proved not what they seemed he thought they must be the exact reverse. The strength of the recoil was the natural result of the violent eagerness of the attack, and it was all a part of his passionate youthfulness. For not only the glories of youth but its weaknesses were his—its irreverence, its fiery impatience, its haughty intolerance of the work-a-day world, its inability to laugh at itself or take an all-round rational view, its reckless daring in the first onset flagging under prolonged effort. Thus it is by his upward reach more than his capacity for sustained flight that Shelley wins his place among the masters. For this reason his lyrics are the most typical expression of his genius. These are the record of his ardent emotionalism; each one comes fresh from a burning mood. There is no time for inconstancy, for the dulling of the fine edge of inspiration, such as makes even the *Prometheus* strongest in its first act, a thing which can not be said of a faultless work of art.

If he had lived to be old the record might be different. But as yet his thinking had not passed through youth's sense of dissonance and unreality. When he died he was still aloof from life: "As to real flesh and blood," he said, "you know I do not deal in these articles;" and he called himself "the knight of the shield of shadow and the lance of gossamere." Humanity disappointed him, and even the momentary joy of dreams brought despair in its wake. It was because of the very ardor of his ecstasies that life was for Shelley a series of disillusions. One after another the raptures of his youth went out, and his path grew darker and more lonely to the end. He died at a crucial point in his development, when everything seemed to be falling away from him, when the struggle with despondency was tempting him to suicide, "that golden key to the chamber of perpetual rest." If he had lived longer he must either have withdrawn more and more from actualities or have emerged into a more mature and humane wisdom.

But we need not quarrel with his fate, or lament that his eager, restless, baffled spirit found swift repose in death. Life could scarcely have satisfied him—in the very exaltation of his purpose lay its doom. As it is, we may recognize in him the spirit of immortal youth, who had scarcely time to cry, "Then what is life?" before fate sealed his lips. In *Adonais* he prophetically praises death as if for his own burial, but in that last moment of the storm on the Gulf of Spezia he might have sung a still finer song. For he was glad to die. He was one of

> . . . the sacred few who could not tame
> Their spirits to the conqueror, but as soon
> As they had touched the world with living flame
> Fled back like eagles to their native noon.

THE year 1921, the one-hundredth since the death of Keats, was sacred also to Dante, who died at Ravenna September fourteenth, 1321, leaving his work achieved and complete after a rounded life of fifty-six rich years. Of all English poets since Shakespeare there may be two, Keats and Synge, who gave promise of genius as powerful and shapely as Dante's, and of mind and will as capable of fulfilling its high serene commands; and these two, by the same tragic hazard, were fatally interrupted by illness and early death.

The *Quarterly's* reception of Keats' first book has become a byword—it is so easy for the casual inheritor of opinions to be wise after the fact. But, after all, the youthful bard was trying out a new instrument; and even Shelley himself was not at once impressed, for he said of *Endymion,* "The author's intention seems to be that no person should possibly get to the end of it;" not to speak of Byron, whose remarks are almost unprintable. So far as this luscious and exuberant exercise of youthful genius is concerned, I sympathize with Shelley, for I never could read it through without liberal skipping. Ditto *Hyperion*—but then, my appetite for modernized Greek myth is distinctly limited; I cannot "appreciate the intensity and complexity of symbolic and spiritual meaning" which Keats and many other poets have read into, and wrung out of, a folk-lore beautiful in its original primitive simplicity.

[ 179 ]

*Isabella, or the Pot of Basil* was a more Chaucerian stunt of verse-narrative—a tale drawn from Boccaccio's rich mediaeval storehouse: a pretty thing, but slight—even the poet soon tired of it, called it "mawkish." *Lamia* also did not quite "come off." And the beauty of *The Eve of Saint Agnes,* exquisite as it is, is of the fragile, the dreamily artificial kind, like a Venetian goblet blown in many-colored glass.

These all were preparatory. What have we to assert triumphantly the immortality of Keats the master? We have a half-dozen lyrics of beauty incredible and supreme, beauty which admits this youth to the innermost magic circle of all the rich domain of English lyric poetry, the circle haunted by Shakespeare's voice, by a few strains from Marlowe and Spenser, from Coleridge and Shelley and Blake; while beyond, near but not quite within, one may hear the chanting of Milton and of old John Donne, and perfect chords from Burns, Byron and Poe, leading on many others, a number of moderns among them—poets ever to be remembered, who have sung a few songs, or maybe only one, too beautiful to perish.

The *Ode to a Nightingale,* and the ballad *La Belle Dame sans Merci*—any long life were richly charged with these two poems alone. And when we add to these the other great odes—the *Grecian Urn, Autumn, Melancholy, Bards of Passion and of Mirth;* and certain sonnets *On Chapman's Homer, When I Have Fears, Bright Star* —one must say "Wonderful—wonderful!" and feel that what Death robbed us of might have added to the mass, but hardly to the splendor, of this poet's gift. For in his best work, he had the ineffable magic; he had that dizzy sweep of imagination which takes one's breath away, which finds the secret of utterance as surely as the lark or the wind.

This is the final miracle in poetry, and Keats achieved it. It is this miracle which proclaims the pre-eminent masterpiece, whether that be a song like Marlowe's *Come Live With Me,* a tragedy like *Antony and Cleopatra* or *King Lear,* an ode like the *Nightingale,* or a ballad like *La Belle Dame sans Merci.* Keats achieved it in two or three poems of longer, higher and more sustained flight than the brief and beautiful songs which flash like so many bright-winged birds in English poetry; his bird soars off into the blue and wheels toward the sun in magnificent disdain of earth.

But what a man gives, be he poet, beggar or king, is always himself; and the fascinating thing about Keats' imperishable gift is the torch-like beauty of that glorious spirit which went flaming through the cluttered world for a few brief years, leaving a cleared path for men's souls to walk in. He saw through the perplexities and distractions of his age:

> Beauty is truth, truth beauty—that is all
> Ye know on earth, and all ye need to know.

To him Byron's rebellions, Shelley's reforms, were negligible details in the rounded spiritual experience of man. To him, as to Blake, "nothing is pleasing to God except the glad invention of beautiful and exalted things." He knew that beauty includes all perfections sublunary and subliminal; that it is the magic circle which encloses them all, giving form and symmetry to the created universe— and to that infinitesimal detail of it, the life and dreams of man.

[ 181 ]

And then the tragic poignancy of his suffering—for unfulfilled love and early death caught his spirit unready and unreconciled; and the great things he had done seemed slight to his despair in contrast with those "high-piled books" unwritten in his "teeming brain." Of course we know now that his disease was a direct infection from the young brother whom he had nursed tenderly to the end; and that the medical malpractice of his time speeded him off as fast as possible by prescribing bleeding and a starvation diet. It is small consolation to feel that today a science more enlightened might have saved him to round out Dante's fifty-six years and rival the majestic mass of the great Italian's completed labors. Fortunately there is a higher consolation: a few perfect poems, which, being perfect, are therefore in themselves complete, sufficient.

O N the nineteenth of April, 1824, died George Noel Gordon, Lord Byron—poet, peer, personality of international importance. One of the most dramatic figures of a dramatic epoch rounded out fitly his spot-light career by dying in full armor, so to speak, as general in command of troops fighting for freedom on soil sacred to beauty. Even the fates assisted him to expire at the romantic moment, by making his physicians rob his fevered body of twenty ounces of blood four times in two days, so that there was nothing for an empty heart to do but stop its ineffectual beating.

And the heart of Europe, in sympathy, almost stood still at the news. No Englishman who had ever lived— not Shakespeare, Marlborough or Newton, not Elizabeth or any lesser king—could so have silenced for a moment the nations of the earth, or wrung such sorrowful tears from millions of eyes.

> And one is born
> To make the sun forgotten,

said Emerson. In Byron's day he was that one—whatever he did struck a bell that was heard around the world, a bell whose echoes we still detect after a clamorous century of loud voices and great events.

It was not merely that he was a poet—Shelley, Keats, Coleridge, his contemporaries, were never heard of outside of England, and very little inside. It was not that he was a peer—British lords kept to their caste at home and made little stir abroad. It was not that he was romantically beautiful to behold, with a beauty intensified and darkly stained by that bitter scar of the twisted foot. It was not that he was a gay Lothario, with a string of feminine hearts to his credit, mysteriously knotted with purple deeds. No, it was none of these, nor all of them combined. For besides all these there was that indefinable magic which still sets all of us on the quest. It was "personality plus"—and then plus once again.

Of course Byron knew what was going on in the world —in whatever world, social, intellectual, political, he moved in. For under all his poses and passions a shrewd sense of humor and a fundamental common-sense prompted one of the keenest, most observant minds in Europe. His letters show him probing the cant of his time, penetrating individual and national hypocrisies with swift precision. And they show him also a sincere and practical enthusiast for human liberty, hating and working against oppression wherever he found it. But he was no fanatical doctrinaire, like Shelley, who would make over rock-bound institutions in a day. He took his world as he found it and played his part in the drama according to its rules, but played it for all he was worth with the true, if somewhat theatrical, sincerity of a great actor vaunting a proud role.

He never missed a point, and, as with all keen players for whatever stakes, instinct served him better than reason. Was the world weary of the placid pentameters of Cowper and Thomson, and eager for pure romance?— even while he enthused theoretically in praise of the old fashion, and strung out *Hints from Horace* to prove it, he

had *Childe Harold* up his sleeve. Was his age tired of
the Georges and the Bourbons, and hopeful of "liberty,
equality and fraternity"?—Byron, while accepting jeal-
ously every privilege of rank and wealth, while using his
peerage as a vantage-ground, railed at all the feudal
tyrannies in poems and letters, and fought for the freedom of Italy and Greece, as he would have fought for that
of England, with his money, his pen and finally his sword.

But did ever a major poet begin so mildly! Reading
*Hours of Idleness,* I reflect upon the swift dismissal which
such freshman verses would be punished with by any
modern editor. And even the first two cantos of *Childe
Harold,* which made him famous and gave him the London smart set to play with—even these are juvenilia,
rhymed eloquence draping a melodramatic attitude struck
to satisfy his instinct for giving the people what they
secretly wanted. And he went on responding to their
romantic desire, perfecting the orotund-eloquent style in
the second half of *Childe Harold*, piling Ossa on Pelion
of romantic adventure in *Lara, The Corsair, The Giaour,*
and other poems and plays "written for women" which
betrayed the poet's genius by their rush and color and
occasional flashing lines.

All this while he was falling into and out of love with
debonnair insouciance, writing innumerable letters to his
mentor, Lady Melbourne, and various younger ladies,
getting married and unmarried and exiled for his virtues
as well as his sins, taking refuge in the beauty of nature
and of old Italian towns, and renewing his inspiration in
fresh love affairs under the blue skies of Venice and
Ravenna.

Well, as a poet where does he stand after these hundred

years?—for it should be our business to strip his work of all those so potent glamours of personality, rank, beauty, amatory indiscretions, political enthusiasms; to disregard as well the over-severe reactions of contempt which these glamours have evoked during the past century; and to judge his poems as works of art.

If the romantic poems are mostly in the orotund-eloquent style, still few English poets have used it so effectively as Byron in, for example, the Waterloo passage and the "deep and dark blue ocean" passage in the latter half of *Childe Harold*—stanzas which, as every school-boy knows, roll magnificently off the tongue. If not the purest type of poetry absolute, orotund-eloquent verse of this quality is yet of proud and authentic lineage, the Elizabethan drama and *Paradise Lost* having admitted it freely to their sacred pages except when the muse demanded higher service. Byron could swing it almost to grandeur when moved by his genuine love of wild nature, or by proud and tragic episodes of human history; and moreover he used it to dignify contemporary events, and to describe out-door magnificence which he was often the first to praise. So the best of the plays, *Manfred* and *Cain,* have similarly a true, if somewhat pompous, sincerity of motive, and an organ-richness of sound and movement; if not man communing, naked and in secret, with his maker, they are at least man richly robed among all the scenic splendors and thunders of a great stage, proclaiming to a rapt audience the bitter rebellion of his heart against the tragic sorrows of his fate. At least Byron's plays are not, like *The Cenci,* imitations of the Elizabethan model, which indeed he was far from admiring. Their inspiration, if hardly either Elizabethan or classic, was perceptibly Gallic.

Somewhat demoded now, perhaps, are these proud poems which marched so triumphantly around the world, though most of the moderns may well envy their passion and power. At least he was no "wax lily" but very much alive; he had guts as well as five active senses; and moreover, he loved Swiss mountains better than English gardens, and democratic simplicities better than caste conventions. Today, however, it may be in order to inquire in which poems he made most effective use of his volcanic temperament and his swift and often too facile style. What poems are the finest and frankest expressions of his genius, the most beautiful and the most profoundly sincere?

Well, *Don Juan*—the earlier cantos—is Byron's masterpiece, no doubt; *The Prisoner of Chillon,* as a dramatic monologue, rises to a fierce beauty beyond the rhymed-eloquence class, while the *Sonnet to Chillon* and two or three lyrics (*She Walks in Beauty, Oh Snatched Away in Beauty's Bloom,* and especially *There Be None of Beauty's Daughters*) are among the treasures of the language. Let us pause long enough to quote the last of these, which changes, in the middle of each stanza, from four-time to three-time with a truly Shakespearian loveliness:

> There be none of Beauty's daughters
>   With a magic like thee,
> And like music on the waters
>   Is thy sweet voice to me:
> When, as if its sound were causing
> The charmed ocean's pausing,
> The waves lie still and gleaming
> And the lulled winds seem dreaming.

> And the midnight moon is weaving
>     Her bright chain o'er the deep,
> Whose breast is quietly heaving,
>     As an infant's asleep.
> So the spirit bows before thee
> To listen and adore thee,
> With a full but soft emotion
> Like the swell of summer's ocean.

In *Don Juan* Byron essayed a mode new in English, which suited his temperament admirably, both as poet and man of the world—a mode of conversationally familiar narrative verse, mainly satirical but rising at the call of the theme to higher levels of seriousness and beauty. Chaucer, in his *Prologue,* had used a familiar style; the eighteenth century, from Pope to Goldsmith and Cowper, had been busy with familiar satires and everyday descriptive narratives; but no one had effected quite this combination of lightly touched humorous satire, sharp description, and narrative covering episodes amusing, pathetic, tragic, absurd—indeed, sometimes all four together, with the careless inconsistency of life itself. It was an unshrinking realism then new to poetic art, and not yet improved upon by any of the moderns who have worked in this genre.

The stanza Byron chose would have been difficult for any poet less facile to handle; but he plays delightedly with its triple many-syllabled rhymes, and evidently enjoys its adaptability to every mood, from trivial to tragic. No touch could be lighter than his in the passage about his hero's mother, for example. Here is one stanza:

> Now Donna Inez had, with all her merit,
>     A great opinion of her own good qualities.
> Neglect indeed requires a saint to bear it,
>     And such indeed was she in her moralities.

> But then, she had a devil of a spirit,
>   And sometimes mixed up fancies with realities,
> And let few opportunities escape
> Of getting her liege lord into a scrape.

Contrast such trifling with this famous stanza from the farewell letter of Don Juan's first love:

> Man's love is of man's life a thing apart—
>   'Tis woman's whole existence.  Man may range
> The court, camp, church, the vessel and the mart;
>   Sword, gown, gain, glory; offer in exchange
> Pride, fame, ambition to fill up his heart—
>   And few there are whom these can not estrange.
> Men have all these resources, we but on
>   To love again, and be again undone.

The ghastly shipwreck episode or the Haidee love-story might be quoted to show the poet handling pathetic or tragic incidents without forsaking the conversational tone, lit even here by grim humor.  Of course he carries the thing too far—in the later cantos of the unfinished "epic" one gets very tired of the Empress Catherine, and the fresh humor hardens into a dry cynicism.  But the poem throughout is the straight, sincere, satirical utterance of a clear-sighted, keen-witted, not wholly cynical man of the world, whom life had favored with more than her usual allowance of roses and rotten eggs.

Byron, being a lord, was cursed with snobbish friends, and the worst snob of them all was his biographer Tom Moore, whom he had so gallantly saluted in one of his most quoted poems:

> My boat is on the shore,
>   And my bark is on the sea;
> But before I go, Tom Moore,
>   Here's a double health to thee!

> Here's a sigh to those who love me,
>   And a smile to those who hate;
> And, whatever sky's above me,
>   Here's a heart for every fate.

When Moore and Murray burned Byron's memoir, which he had entrusted to Moore as his most mature and sincere work, they committed a crime against him and us for which contempt is too slight a punishment. "Most of my poems have been written for women," said Byron; "this memoir is written for men." The two sycophants trembled, no doubt, before its frank discussion of contemporary people, ideas and events—the truth must be hidden forever! And so these illuminating pages were destroyed. We can hardly over-estimate the loss; for though critics may differ about Byron's poetry, there can be no two opinions about his prose. His letters are almost incomparable as the searching, flashing, wholly sincere confidences of a man profoundly and humorously aware of himself and the world. The memoir could have been no less; it may have been even more.

In these hundred years and more since his death Byron's fame has been blown back and forth by many winds. But today he would seem to be secure of his rank among the great poets of his time. And if not the greatest soul among them, at least we may grant him the clearest head and the most compelling personality.

MATTHEW ARNOLD is still remembered in this country by those who thronged to hear his lectures back in the eighties, five years before his sudden death. Shy and unaccustomed to audiences, he made a typically British figure as he stood stiffly erect, reciting without a single gesture the essay on Emerson which he had written and learned by heart. The squareness of his face was emphasized by straight lines of hair and side-burns, and of his body by an arm horizontally immovable except that its fingers fumbled a handkerchief.

The essay—now one may read it, of course—was a just and appreciative estimate of Emerson, but not quite of soul-satisfying enthusiasm to an American audience of that period. On the whole, neither lecturer nor audience warmed up or got together. A little humor, a smile somewhere, would have saved the situation; but although Arnold's friends used to insist that he had plenty of this benign quality, he must have kept it for home consumption—he did not bring it across the sea. On the whole, it was personally unfortunate, however financially profitable, that a man so modest and retiring should have been received and escorted across the continent by all the sensation-machinery of *réclame* which our newspapers, even then, knew so well how to prepare.

It was as an apostle of "sweetness and light," rather than a poet, that Arnold was welcomed; but today his poems already overshadow his prose—the poet obscures the prophet. In anticipation of his recent centenary I took down from a high shelf the two morocco-bound volumes of his poems which had been gathering dust during the decade of my deep plunge into the troubled waters of modern verse. How would this austere Victorian, dead now for thirty-five years, strike me after these years in another world?

Well, I confess he has changed, like an aging friend after a long absence. The eye is less keen, the skin less firm, the step less proud, than they seemed at our last meeting; and the raven locks are sprinkled with ashes. Little details of old-fashioned manner or attire stand out with a new conspicuousness—I see *thou* and *doth, 'mid* and *ere, sate* and *spake* and *palfrey* on every page, and find it difficult to accept and forget them as a mere inevitable convention of the hoop-skirt period. And I pass rapidly over much droning and moralizing, pages of fond advice like this:

> Moderate tasks and moderate leisure,
> Quiet living, strict-kept measure
> Both in suffering and in pleasure—
> 'Tis for this thy nature yearns.

Even the more famous meditative utterances sound a little thin and obvious, seem levelled at the Rugby schoolboy rather than adult minds—things like *Self-dependence, Progress*—yes, and *Morality,* which begins with this fine-spirited, much-quoted stanza:

> We cannot kindle when we will
> The fire which in the heart resides;
> The spirit floweth and is still.
> In mystery our soul abides.

[ 192 ]

> But tasks in hours of insight willed
> Can be through hours of gloom fulfilled.

True enough, all these articles of a skeptic's faith; all these creed-utterances of a soul which had been stirred out of Church-of-England security by Darwin, Huxley and other heretics. It was a rude world—the winds of doubt were blowing through the academic corner wherein this poet was born and reared; and he met them with stern heroism, buttoning up his fleece-lined overcoat. But contrast these outpourings of a spirit somewhat over-clad, with the naked fire of William Blake or Emily Brontë or Emily Dickinson, and we see at once the difference between the first and the second orders of human minds.

So in the narrative and the more-or-less dramatic and lyric poems. We have a gentle sauvity, a reasoned wisdom, an ordered fineness which is almost beauty; but we have never a flash of deep intuition or a line of intolerably magic music. *Sohrab and Rustum* is Victorian classic—controlled and scholarly, delicately and correctly carved; shapely too, a well proportioned, carefully built design. But the smell of the library is in it—it remains an admirable literary essay in the abbreviated epic form.

It is in such retelling of old legends, however, that Arnold is at his best. Some inquirers have wondered what he would have accomplished if his training had been less academic, but probably his achievement would have been less fortunate. No university can either make or unmake an original mind—the academic quality in Arnold must have been inborn, inherent, and the training was necessary to his art. In *Tristram and Iseult* there is a certain persistent loveliness, in spite of languors and repetitions. We see the lovers through a patterned veil as they go through the traditional motions of passion; and and the lines flow gently, with a quiet and authentic music. And in *The Scholar-gipsy, The Forsaken Merman* and other poems we wander in a poetized world, quite free from the cruelties of wind and weather.

It was natural that a mind imaginative of the past should accuse its own time. The poet cries to the scholar-gipsy:

> O born in days when wits were fresh and clear,
> And life ran gaily as the sparkling Thames;
> Before this strange disease of modern life
> With its sick hurry, its divided aims,
> Its heads o'ertaxed, its palsied hearts, was rife—
> Fly hence, our contact fear!
> Still fly, plunge deeper in the bowering wood!
> Averse, as Dido did, with gesture stern,
> From her false friend's approach in Hades turn,
> Wave us away, and keep thy solitude.

"This strange disease of modern life" was more directly the underlying subject of Arnold's prose essays, and his plea for "sweetness and light" was an accusation politely levelled against his time. What would he think about our time, I wonder?

WALT WHITMAN'S simple, self-sufficient life is a record of unhurried cumulative power, which waited until mid-career before setting itself to address the world. Though he lived seventy-two years, his complete works of verse and prose are easily contained in two volumes.

Rereading the *Leaves* consecutively, instead of repeating my favorites over and over, I have been reminded of a visit—in 1910—to the Rembrandt galleries at the Hermitage in Petrograd, where, in two hundred or more canvases good, bad and indifferent, one could study the great painter in all his moods, search his genius through days of faltering or excess as well as days of triumph.

Even so with Whitman, though he was less prolific than Rembrandt, his spiritual kinsman. His *Leaves* show his genius entire—the times when it lagged into prosy moralizing or leaped into bombast, as well as those proud hours of the Lincoln elegy, or *Out of the Cradle Endlessly Rocking,* or the *Whispers of Heavenly Death.* They show—again like Rembrandt—his power as a colorist, as a draughtsman of immense and revolutionary rhythms, as a democrat and lover of men, and as a serious-minded thinker; also his limitations of perspective and range, caused by lack of humor and certain disabilities in self-criticism.

Almost everything has been said about Whitman, from

the sneers of his detractors to the large praise of present-day enthusiasts—as when a recent article in the *Mercure de France* mentioned him, quite casually and as a matter of course, with Dante, Homer, Shakespeare and a few other greatest masters. His centenary found his fame established and his mockers rebuked; already his bearded figure had grown and simplified into colossal monumental granite, as indestructible as a mountain, a place of pilgrimage for the imaginations of men. There he is, as Henry James might say; and there, whether we like it or not, his spirit may have the power of the *vates* to bring These States to his feet, and mold ideals for the democratization of the world.

It may be our province to mention with special emphasis certain details of Whitman's service to poetic art. Even that noble shelf-monument, *The Cambridge History of American Literature,* by closing one period with Lowell and opening another with Whitman, shows how two exactly contemporary poets may live in different ages and be ruled by contrary stars. Whitman began a new era, and the finis which he uttered to the old was heard by "foreign nations and the next age."

Of course his first and most obvious service to poetic art was his insistence on freedom of form—his rejection of the usually accepted English metrics, and his success in writing great poems without their aid. Not that he misprized Chaucer, Shakespeare, Shelley and the rest; but he must find for himself a rhythm as personal as theirs. His second service was corollary to the first—the rejection of clichés, including archaic diction and so-called "poetic" phrasing. That this rejection was not wholly instinctive, but enforced by conscious labor, is proved by a sentence from *Specimen Days:*

Commenced putting *Leaves of Grass* to press for good, . . . . after many manuscript doings and undoings. I had great trouble in leaving out the stock "poetical" touches, but succeeded at last.

Such authority as he had for these rejections of the long-accepted, the worn, was derived rather from Asiatic than European classics—"the Hebrew Bible, the mighty Hindu epics, and a hundred lesser but typical works." And this brings us to his third service to the art, a service larger than the others, and purely spiritual—his reassertion of the ancient conception of the poet as prophet, and of poetry as religion, as an ecstatic expression of faith. He says:

All the poems of Orientalism, with the Old and New Testaments at the centre, tend to deep and wide psychological development—with little, or nothing at all, of the mere aesthetic, the principal verse requirement of our day.

To biblical poetry especially he ascribes:

Faith limitless, its immense sensuousness immensely spiritual— an incredible, all-inclusive non-worldliness and dew-scented illiteracy (the antipodes of our nineteenth-century business absorption and morbid refinement)—no hair-splitting doubts, no sickly sulking and sniffling.

And he asks:

Will there ever be a time or place—ever a student, however modern, of the grand art, to whom those compositions will not afford profounder lessons than all else of their kind in the garnerage of the past? Could there be any more opportune suggestion of what the office of poet was in primeval times— and is yet capable of being, anew, adjusted entirely to the modern?

Thus his effort as a poet was to free the art of conventions of form and phrase, and to kindle in it the old

[ 197 ]

sacred fire. Poetry was to be no longer an ornament of the libraries—it was to get out-of-doors and sing the large faiths—faith in life and death, in love and war, in mountains and trees and rivers, in the sun and sky and the good hard flesh of the earth; and it was to sing these large faiths in large rhythms, rhythms that follow the beat of winds and waves, rather than in man-made metrics.

He was but one of many—there would be armies of poets to follow him! "The personnel, in any race," he insists, "can never be really superior without superior poems!" And in *Blue Ontario's Shore* he cries:

Of all races and eras, These States, with veins full of poetical
    stuff, most need poets, and are to have the greatest, and use
    them the greatest.
Their Presidents shall not be their common referee so much as
    their poets shall.
Soul of love, and tongue of fire!
Eye to pierce the deepest deeps, and sweep the world!

Indeed, at this point enthusiasm begets his one besetting sin—the poet is lost in the rhapsodist, and we have turgid pages describing this bard of the future, "west-bred" and "of the common stock." Such turgidity, such excess, should hardly be mentioned, however—only the lesser masters are impeccable artists. Let us pause rather over certain poems in which spirit and art are in complete accord.

I find this—on the whole, and in spite of lapses which are carried in triumph, as it were—in the poem *Walt Whitman,* which (if I am not mistaken) opened the first edition of *Leaves of Grass.* This poem was a declaration of spiritual and artistic independence; and technically it established his rhythmic system, which follows the diversified regularity of waves sweeping the shore, or of hills curving along the horizon, rather than the exactness of closer intervals. The poem has magnificent passages, from the much quoted—

I loaf and invite my soul;
I lean and loaf at my ease, observing a spear of summer grass—

to that trumpet-note near the end:

I too am not a bit tamed—I too am untranslatable;
I sound my barbaric yawp over the roofs of the world.

This poem was also the poet's declaration of faith, a faith fundamental, universal:

Waiting responses from oracles, honoring the Gods, saluting the sun;
Making a fetish of the first rock or stump, pow-wowing with sticks in the circle of obis;
Helping the lama or brahmin as he trims the lamps of the idols;
Dancing yet through the streets in a phallic procession, rapt and austere in the woods.

*Children of Adam* also contains magnificent passages, but as a poem it moves less surely than the other; as if the poet, in asserting the nobility of sex, were more conscious of fighting a battle, and therefore less spontaneous. In most of *Calamus, Salut au Monde,* and *Song of the Broad-axe,* the poet is lost in the rhapsodist. In the *Song of the Open Road* we find him again, and follow him through the gates of the West; and *Out of the Cradle Endlessly Rocking,* with that song of the sea-bird to its lost mate, is a perfect and prodigious masterpiece.

In many of the *Drum-taps* we hear, as in no other modern songs of war, the gathering and mighty tramp of armies; also the rush of city crowds at the call, the "spirit of dreadful hours," and the ultimate spirit of reconciliation:

Beautiful that War, and all its deeds of carnage, must in time
    be utterly lost;
That the hands of the sisters Death and Night, incessantly
    softly wash again, and ever again, this soiled world.

Superb also are certain of the *Marches Now that the
War is Over;* and most glorious of all, of course, is that
grandest, most serene of elegies, *President Lincoln's Burial Hymn,* "When lilacs last in the door-yard bloomed."
In all his songs of death—"heavenly death," "delicate
death"—some of them beautiful beyond praise, is the same
high serenity.

"I hear America singing," he cried, and it is for us and
those who follow us to fulfil the prophecy. The *London
Times* has pointed out how accurately, in *Years of the
Modern,* he foresaw the present situation of the world—
the "tremendous exits and entrances," the "new combinations," "the solidarity of races," the "issuing forth
against the idea of caste," the "marching and counter-
marching by swift millions." Perhaps, at this period of
epic climax in the affairs of this nation and all nations,
we may close with his word of warning:

To The States, or any one of them, or any city of The States,
*Resist much, obey little.*
Once unquestioning obedience, once fully enslaved—
Once fully enslaved—no nation, state, city of this earth ever
    afterward resumes its liberty.

## COMMENTS AND QUERIES

LITERATURE, like life, is a revelation of human souls, and the soul of the author is the reader's most fascinating quest.

This sententious utterance may have been uttered before in a large variety of other words, and would not need to be uttered again save to refute the advice of those who find in literature a prodigious array of cut flowers and would have us disregard leaf, stalk and soil. "You find all the world in Shakespeare," they say, "except the poet himself"; or, "Byron was a rotter in a rotten age, but sing to yourself *There be none of Beauty's daughters* and forget the author"; or, "Genius is a miracle straight from heaven—environment, encouragement, family, friends, enemies, what have these to do with it?"

But in spite of the absolutist who lays down such laws, one goes happily back to the search for Shakespeare himself in his plays—that enigmatic lover and doubter, "serenely sly," who hides, but never completely, his inactive ineffectual self, and its despair and rapture, behind the grand gear and gusto of his plays. Or back to Byron, flaunting melodramatic sins in a thousand "poems for women," but keeping his common sense and rebel's humor for *Don Juan,* and his ecstasy for a few imperishable songs. And one wonders how many times genius has been trampled or frosted in the bud, for once that soil and sun and rain, and maybe skilful nurture, have brought its perfect flower to bloom.

Even so, reading modern poetry is primarily a quest for the poets themselves—a quest, that is, for friends of the spirit among keen observant imaginative contemporary minds musically attuned to the rhythms of life. It is an alluring quest, yielding at times rich rewards; and the friends it makes have signed an unequal contract— their bounty endures whether the reader continues to accept it or not.

It is a procession of widely differing human types which the reader of modern poetry may choose his friends from —could any other art or profession match its variety, I wonder? There is Vachel Lindsay, imaginative evangelist of Beauty, crusading through the country with her trophy on his sleeve, chanting her hymns to new tunes as he quixotically charges her enemies on his winged and fiery-hearted steed. There is Robert Frost, shrewd, kind, observant, like the New England farmers he loves to talk with and about; neighborly but still a bit secretive, with eyes and ears that watch and listen for a richer color and deeper rhythm than appear on the surface, and a mind that guards its reserves, that tells not quite all the tale. There is Conrad Aiken, debonair, well groomed, polite, as he looks under the bed and in the closet for shadowy secrets of discontent, and tunes his plaintive lyre to tell a sorry tale. There is Edgar Lee Masters, huge, careless, profound; laughing loud, suffering beyond reason, plunging deep into life and giving out liberally, fiercely, with a gusto of humor and passion, whatever he finds of beauty or ugliness, glory or shame. There is T. S. Eliot, delicate-fingered, sensitive-minded, afraid of draughts; looking at the world through windows, through books, through proud old gateways; feeling its unreality as it dissolves before his protected eyes in a chaos of foolish loves and witless wars.

Ah, they come crowding! Edwin Arlington Robinson, icily clear, scrupulously brave, seeking the iron truth and the crystal beauty as he studies the world from a peak of isolation and somehow sees it well. Carl Sandburg, common man among common people, big man among the great, with a fist like Samson's, a heart like a woman's; an ear for the ground-swell rhythms of the laboring earth and a voice like soft winds and deep waters. Maxwell Bodenheim, picturesquely perverse, working off his inferiority complex on his would-be friends so that his would-be enemies may stare. William Carlos Williams, the Puritan *malgré-lui,* good citizen, good doctor, *bon père-de-famille,* but as naughty on paper as a graduate imagist should be while he fits his rebellious moods to elusive rhythms.

Have you enough to choose from? But the procession is not half over, even if one disregards the young things who are getting into marching form. West and East are represented, town and country and the wilds. Behold Lew Sarett, bold hunter and forester, kin of Indians and mountain lions, who hangs his harp in the wind and wrestles with the angel—or demon—for his poems. And by way of contrast comes George Sterling, lavish, wasteful of life and art, throwing himself away on an easy-going muse. And then William Rose Benét, child-hearted for joy, wistfully romantic in a world gone daft with facts and theories. And Alfred Kreymborg, blithe troubadour of the streets, singing his cheerful way through the sprightly rhythms of this fascinating world. Padraic Colum, wandering Celtic bard, friend of fairies, whom America is making over into a respectable citizen, but without taking the edge off his lyric flare. Ezra Pound, bold singer, great teacher, deep delver for buried treasure, autocrat of the study-table, attorney for the prosecution against modern civilization—or barbarism. John Gould Fletcher, Mississippi-born cosmopolite, color-symphonist, in word-rhythms, of London, Arizona, Japan. D. H. Lawrence, orchid-minded, rooted in dank glooms and sprouting a scarlet flower—"the most brilliantly lost man I can imagine," a poet says of him, "fleeing always with a violent grace from his own shadow." And Wallace Stevens, rich as a bee with the honey of beauty, splendid as a butterfly with her colors, flaunting his serene delight in the face of the heedless world, quizzing the universe with solemn laughter; yet hiding always his deepest secret, hushing his wisdom to the tune of ineffable music, guarding under his coat the round and indivisible whole against all of life's frustrations.

And the women!—not so numerous as the men, nor so different each from each; but true to their sex and not imitative of the other. The most masculine-minded of them of course was Amy Lowell, whom the Lord made a great executive and the muse seduced into poetry; brilliant, able, magnetic, commanding—what muse, having aroused her with a whisper in the ear, would have dared to disobey her slightest behest! In contrast with her strenuous power comes the airy figure of Edna St. Vincent Millay, springing like a gold-petalled lily out of life's rich soil, and shining in the sun. And Sara Teasdale, shy, inviolate in her delicate womanliness, singing fine songs in a pure mezzo-soprano voice. Then Marjorie Seiffert, sophisticated, intellectually daring; lover of life and laugher at it, keen to its varied music. Helen Hoyt, splashing rhapsodist, spontaneously lyric, in love with love. Elinor Wylie, smooth and proud, carving her poems precisely, out of hard wood. And Agnes Lee, observant, imaginative, peering along highways and by-ways for things no one else would see. Lola Ridge, sternly impassioned protagonist; Leonora Speyer the magnificent; H. D., strict in perfect line like a Greek statue. And many more—ah, many more!

Surely among so many, and so different, we may all find friends. Who are yours?—perhaps, in all this catalogue I have not mentioned the two or three with whom, of all modern poets, you feel the closest sympathy.

[*The above essay, which remains unchanged from the first publication, reminds one of the ravages of death. Since it was written, the following poets have passed into the ultimate silence:*
*Amy Lowell, April, 1925; George Sterling, November, 1926; Elinor Wylie, December, 1928; D. H. Lawrence, March, 1930; and Vachel Lindsay, December, 1931.*]

PROPHECY is always reckless, but therefore all the
more alluring. And if one's mood is for projection
rather than reminiscence, only the wise future can contradict one's errors. So we may perhaps venture an inquiry as to what is coming in this art of poetry—this
persistent and imperishable art which the human race,
at certain seasons, for certain periods, tries in vain to
forget.

To begin with the technique, we suspect that more,
rather than less, freedom of form is coming. It seems
a quaint reaction that certain sages should be shouting,
"Free verse is dead!" The sculptor might as well say
that marble is dead, or the painter that oil colors are in
their grave; bronze for the one and tempera for the
other to be hereafter the only wear.

One is moved often to wonder at the narrowness of
the field still generally accorded to poets as compared
with the ample kingdoms reigned over by the other arts.
A musical composer may choose between song, sonata,
symphony, étude, rhapsody; between violin, piano, harp,
drum, saxaphone, jazz band or the whole grand orchestra;
between soprano, contralto, tenor, bass, or combinations
of these in duet, quartette, chorus or opera. The painter,
from thumb-sketch to the decoration of a palace; the
sculptor, from an ivory netsuke to a granite quadriga; the
architect, from a log-cabin to a state-house: all these have

space to dream in and the choice of a thousand modes. But the poet!—his domain was rigidly bounded by the ancients, and therein must he follow appointed paths. Epic, tragedy, comedy; ode, ballad, lyric: these he must serve up in proper blank verse or rhyme according to established forms and measures. And woe be to him if he break through hedges and try to sprint for the wilds!

No, as men release themselves from materialism and demand more and more from the arts, the arts must become more immediately responsive, their forms more fluid. Poetry especially can not wear the corsets, or even the chlamys, of an elder fashion. As Burton Roscoe put it in one of his newspaper articles:

> Poetry is a succession of revitalizations, the introduction of novelty in an effort to escape anæmia: from the odic modifications of Horace, to the invention of rhyme, to the displacement of Pope's couplets, to the breaking of the tenuous and unwieldy alexandrine by Hugo, to its further splintering by Verlaine, to the eruption of Whitman, and to the forms of the present day.
>
> Granted that much of the new poetry is bad, that it is unmusical, that it is graced neither by emotion nor by beauty, that it will perish in the oblivion that claims all bad stuff—and even much that is good. What of it? The same is quite as true of poetry in the older established forms.

Shall we, who listen eagerly to Prokofieff, refuse to Wallace Stevens a hearing for his subtle and haunting compositions, as if with wood-wind instruments?—rhythms as heavy with tragic beauty as a bee with the honey of purple roses. Shall we disdain Emanuel Carnevali's splashing rhapsody, *The Day of Summer,* because it isn't a sonata, nor yet a proper Miltonic ode? Shall not Vachel Lindsay play the organ, or even a jazz band, at his pleasure?—and is it for us to prescribe for him the harp or the flute? Hadn't Amy Lowell as much right

[ 209 ]

as Bach to write a fugue of tumbling rhymes and elaborate interwoven harmonies? And shall Ezra Pound, composing nocturnes and fantasias as delicate as Chopin's, be reminded that the public prefers Strauss waltzes? Should Carl Sandburg, with a modern piano under his fingers, be restricted to Mozart's spinnet? May not Cloyd Head assail the Shakespearian tradition, even as Debussy assailed the Beethoven tradition, with modern tragedies as close in texture, and as mystically expressive of our innermost feeling and dream, as the Frenchman's *L'après-midi d'un Faune?* And shall Edgar Lee Masters, who, of all our modern poets, has the most epic vision—shall he be denied free symphonic range within his large horizon, because staccato poets and careful critics object to his smashing paces?

One might pursue the analogy further. Is it a violin of finest quality that H. D. plays? Is Richard Aldington's *Choricos* sung from some high place to the thrilling notes of a harp? Does Carlos Williams prefer piccolo solos with whimsical twists and turns of half-humorous melody? Does H. L. Davis breathe through the woodwinds music of a mournful mysterious Brahms-like beauty? If Edna Millay sings to the lyre, and Sara Teasdale to the lute, must we be deaf to the delicately emotional lyric solos played on a reed by such younglings as Mark Turbyfill or A. Y. Winters—tunes of thistledown texture? And shall the full poetic orchestra of the future be confined to the instruments, and the melodic methods, of Elizabeth's time, or Queen Anne's, or Victoria's, or even of all three?

Yes, we might pursue the analogy into wearisome detail, but enough has been said to present our point, which is, that the poetry of the future must have more freedom instead of less; and that, if the public is less tolerant of new methods in poetry than in music, painting or sculpture, it is because it is less educated in modern poetry than in the other modern arts—less educated and more obstinately prejudiced. When Stravinsky plays at a modern symphony concert, he confronts an audience which has been carefully led up to his iconoclasms through years of the most expert music both classical and modern. He gets intelligent sympathy from a large proportion of that audience, and the praise or dispraise they give him is based on knowledge. But when Wallace Stevens or Cloyd Head or H. L. Davis faces a modern poetry audience, most of his readers are as full of the past as the *Quarterly Review* was in the time of Keats, as firm for long-accepted canons and sanctities.

The public, we protest, should educate itself in this art and be less cock-sure in its verdicts. "To have read *Hiawatha* is the eighth grade" does not make a competent connoisseur, and one may not turn down the imagists because one can't scan them in finger-counted iambics. Poetry may be on the way toward as great variety as modern music enjoys, whether in the number, length and placing of notes (syllables) in the bar (the foot); in variety of rhythmic phrasing; in tempo—from *andante* to *scherzo;* in movement—from *staccato* to *legato;* in tone-color, timbre, and the countless other refinements which should make poetry, like music, infinitely expressive of the emotional life of our age. Music is a much younger art than poetry, yet in a few centuries it has gone far beyond poetry in the development and recording of rhythms. Music has had the two advantages of a universal language and a scientific system of putting on paper tune, pitch, rhythm, tempo, and all other details required for complete presentation; whereas poetry has been hampered by language-isolation, and by an antiquated system of metrics—a mediaeval survival in this scientific age, as empirical and misleading as astrology. Professor Patterson of Columbia is almost the first investigator to make a scientific study of speech-rhythms; and it may be reasonably hoped that such work as his will aid the poet of the future to study the past with more knowledge, to rid himself of hampering and artificial restrictions, and to discover new possibilities of beauty in his art.

Indeed, we may look forward with some confidence to a widening of its range. Poetry is like to be recognized more generally as a vocal art, and to be used much more than formerly in connection with music and the dance, both lyrically and dramatically. In spite of postponements and disappointments, one may hope for a proud future, perhaps an almost immediate future, for the poetic drama. And this, if it comes, will bring poetry into close connection with the sister arts of color—whether in scenery, lights or costumes; and modelling—whether of sculpturesque or architectural forms; as well as the dance and music. It is more than probable that some poetic plays of the future will be produced with more or less static mimes, or even with puppets; for the pitiful incongruities of life, whether for tragedy or comedy, may be very appealingly suggested through such a conventionalization of the actor.

Thus there would seem to be good reason to hope for a richer period in the not distant future of poetic art in America. If much has been gained during the last ten or fifteen years, we have reached merely a new viewpoint toward wider horizons. No art is static—it must go on or retreat. The poets must make the art more necessary to the people, a more immediate and spontaneous expression of their life, their dream. A people imaginatively creative enough to invent a telephone, an airplane, to build great bridges and skyscraper towers, is full of the spirit of poetry—the poets have only to set it free.

EVEN chemistry, I am told, is not so exact a science as to exclude mystery. Does it not teach that certain widely different compounds are products, in the last analysis, of the same elements, combined in the same proportions? The process of combination—the electric affinities of atoms—there is the riddle!

I was reminded of these strange contradictions by reading, in a recent *Atlantic,* a review of certain books of verse; or, rather, by reading certain generalizations to which the critic's subject leads him. With all the world's masterpieces of poetry to work with, that reviewer's mind evolves a conclusion which satisfies him as logical and just; and here is mine producing, with exactly the same materials, a diametrically opposite result.

He has been dealing with certain "contrasting experiments in poetic drama." The theme of one of these dramas, he says, "has the inestimable advantage of possessing already a hold upon the imagination of the general; an advantage which great dramatic poets from Æschylus to Shakespeare have sedulously pursued, and which the best of their successors down to Mr. Stephen Phillips have continued to pursue"; whereas the author of the other play "is actually trying to interpret the present moment in verse"—an effort which compels the bewildered critic "to think there is a real incongruity between their substance and their form." And at last we find him laying down the law thus:

No great dramatic poetry, no great epical poetry, has ever dealt with contemporary conditions. Only the austere processes of time can precipitate the multitude of immediate facts into the priceless residuum of universal truth. The great dramatists have turned to the past for their materials, not of choice, but of necessity. Here and there in the dark backward and abysm of time, some human figure, some human episode, is seen to have weathered the years, and to have taken on certain mysterious attributes of truth; and upon this foundation the massive structure of heroic poetry is builded.

But surely the contemporaneousness of all great art is a truth too important to be at the mercy of anyone's experiments. The masterpieces of every art—I venture to generalize even more broadly than the reviewer— have been the complete, the ultimate expression of the age which produced them, never in any sense an echo of any other. They express the universal truth through the medium of the thought, the feeling of their own time, and they owe nothing to the past except the basic materials—the stones and mortar, the words and the singing voice, the vast background of nature and human nature, the dreams, the faith, the aspirations, which belong to all the ages, though they take widely varying forms in their progress through the centuries.

Of course, his protest is obvious: "However expressive of its age the masterpiece may be," he will say, "it turns to the past for its themes." I answer that in a restricted and superficial sense it does sometimes, and sometimes not, but that in a larger and deeper sense it never does. He will confront me then with instances: What of Hamlet, Macbeth, Lear? What of Œdipus, the Prometheus Bound, Faust? What of Paradise Lost, yea, of the Iliad itself, whose heroes lived and fought centuries before Homer sang?

[ 215 ]

But in every one of these instances, I contend, the theme was strictly contemporaneous, and the characters were the imaginative embodiments of the feeling of the poet's time. Milton's theme was the Puritan faith, and his God, Satan, Adam and Eve were most wonderfully his neighbors. Homer was the creator of Achilles, Agamemnon, Hector—yes, of the Trojan war itself; he made the whole epic history out of a contest less poetically promising than a Mexican revolution, and in doing it he made use of all the religious imagery and significance with which his high-reaching imagination, and that of his compatriots, enriched the bareness of the theme; in short, he "dealt with contemporary conditions." Would the reviewer contend that Shakespeare found in Hamlet or in Lear a human figure which had "weathered the years and taken on certain mysterious attributes of truth"? If he would, let him strip his mind completely of these great tragedies, and look up the childish old wives' tales which served as the poet's point of departure. Shakespeare took a hint from some foolish ditty; from that point he changed plot and characters to suit the convenience of his strictly modern purpose, to make his work express his own feeling, his own time.

I might ask him about certain other masterpieces of art in which the materials, as well as the general theme and spirit, are of the most absolute contemporaneousness. What, for example, of the Book of Job and the Hebrew prophecies? What of the Parthenon, of the Hermes of Praxiteles? What of the Gothic cathedrals, of Don Quixote, of Molière's comedies, of Velasquez' portraits? What of Dante, whose Beatrice and Francesca he did not find in that "dark backward and abysm of time" where our critic—and so many others, alas!—would locate the treasury of art? For us, but not for the mighty Florentine, these ladies, and other people his contemporaries, have "weathered the years and taken on certain mysterious attributes of truth." But it was Dante who gave them to time and men's hearts, and all that has been said about them since has been but echoes of echoes.

Never, with any great poet, was his theme "remote" and "aloof" from his own time. Never has he dealt with anything else but "contemporary conditions." It is only the minor poet who declares himself "the idle singer of an empty day," who finds his age prosaic, and delves forever in the past of old romance, and so necessarily becomes more and more remote, more and more attenuated, in his art. Many a clever and promising poet has gone that way.

The academic temperament which speaks in this reviewer and in many another critic strikes at the vitality of modern art. True, such strokes cannot quite be fatal, because no great poet will stop for any critic. But the poet may be cruelly hampered, heavily impeded, by such misdirected efforts of his contemporaries; he may be compelled to spend much of his time and energy in warding off blows. His joyousness may be baffled and whipped into melancholy; his clear vision may be clouded with bitterness. It is much easier for an artist to pluck flowers along the wayside than to labor in the vineyard, especially when a thousand voices are pleading for the flowers. But the flowers wither in his hands, and only the grapes produce the wine of life. Where should our poets be?

THE immense reach of modern causes and issues, the interdependence of all the peoples of the earth, may well assure us that we live in a great age, an age which gives more scope than any in past history for the vision and conquest of great minds and the free action of little ones. Immersed in immediate pessimisms—war's horrors, the treaty's imperfections, the difficulty of attaining peace or any other spiritual achievement of the people, the over-loaded opulence of our time crowding out significant living and thinking, the over-strident near noises and far cries discordantly clamoring—discouraged with all this seeming chaos, we are too prone to forget the epic immensity of its challenge. It is for the individual soul, now as always before in the history of the race, to master all this, to see through the chaos of his time, and resolve it into forms of power and beauty.

In other words, it is our job—the job of the poets, artists, scientists of our age—to mold the future of the world. The scientists are doing their part with sublime audacity—are the poets and other artists doing theirs?

It may be wise to search our consciences for an answer to certain accusations which I find summarized by one of the greatest constructive scientists of our era, the late Charles P. Steinmetz, who, until his death in 1923, was chief consulting engineer of the General Electric Company, whose demoniacal—no, god-like—turbines deal out light and power all over the world. Dr. Steinmetz contributed an introduction to a book by Charles M. Ripley, E. E., entitled *Romance of a Great Factory* and privately printed at Schenectady, New York. The introduction opens with the following quotation from some tritely palavering academician:

We are living in an unromantic age. Before the shriek of the locomotive the wood-nymphs have fled, and the factory whistle has driven away the romance of the old times. Art and poetry cannot flourish in our cold engineering age.

Dr. Steinmetz comments as follows:

Thus says the professor of literature, dissecting the masterworks of by-gone ages from Homer to Goethe, and telling us what literary art is.

Why do our literary men of today write "best sellers"—books whose only redeeming feature is that they are forgotten as quickly as sold? They fail to see the wonders of our day, the greatest in the world's history; they find nothing worthy of their literary skill, in our "cold engineering age"! But, over and again, they repeat the story of erotic sentimentalism, running up and down the scale from hysteria to pathological degeneration. Hopelessly out of touch with the world of today, they see nothing in it except sensual erotics of the more hysterical types. . . .

When Homer wrote the *Iliad* and the *Odyssey* he told us of the adventures of *his* age; the conquest of Troy; the wanderings of the navigator through the terrors of the ocean at the dawn of history. Three thousand years later, in his autobiography, *Faust,* Goethe tells us the adventures and aspirations of *his* age; from the youthful efforts to conceive the absolute—groping after the ideal of the true and beautiful—up to the satisfaction of sedate manhood, helping mankind to conquer Nature and make the earth a better place in which to live.

The great writers of the past wrote of the age in which they lived, but the writers of today are out of touch with the twentieth century. . . . .

Is there no poetry in this world of ours? Do we really lack romance in this scientific and engineering twentieth century? Or is it not rather that the ignorance of the average literary man disables him to see the romance of our age!

There is more poetry, more romance, in the advances which we have seen in our life-time than ever Homer described.

We navigate not only the surface of the Mediterranean, but its very depths by submarine. We fly to the higher altitudes of the skies by aeroplane. We fling the human voice over thousands of miles, across continents and oceans, by telephone. Unborn generations will hear the living voice of our musicians, bequeathed to them by the phonograph. Our great-great-grand-children will see in action our prominent men of today, recorded and everlastingly perpetuated by the cinematoscope, that new historian of these great times.

There is romance in the life of the vigilant mariner who listens to the wireless message from distant shores. There is tragedy in the fate of the giant battle cruiser. . . . . There is romance in that mighty spinning top, the steam turbine, fed by the stored sunlight of prehistoric ages; ages when ferns were giant trees, and our ancestors were crawling things in the slime on the shores of the lagoon—not very long ago, as time is counted in the universe. . . . .

In the modern factory there is far more romance and poetry than there has ever been in the history of the past; but we must be living with it to see and understand it. That is, we must be living with the men of our century, and not sheltered in the dust of past ages.

All this one has no desire to contradict. It is evident that the man of science is the romanticist of our age—the poet is a hard and cold seeker of truth in comparison with the modern fire-bringer. But I should like to project one inquiry a little further than Dr. Steinmetz, in his challenge, has gone. The inquiry is essentially this: Is not the truth one and indivisible, whether of science, art, philosophy, or anything else? Do we not analyze too narrowly in differentiating the creation of the artist from that of the scientist, calling the one a contribution to aesthetics and the other to material invention? In short, does not all power spring from the spirit—call it of man or of God?

The poet is almost invariably unmathematical, unscientific. On that side his mind, too often, is a blank, and he easily assumes that the forces thus let loose in the world are not spiritual but material. Yet the poet (let me use this word generically, as representing all artists, especially all literary artists)—the poet virtually monopolizes men's ears: what he says goes, because the scientist can merely build his truth—he cannot utter it. And may it not be true that by his blindness to "the soul of the machine," to the spiritual power inherent in its creation, the modern poet establishes a dissonance between the energy of our age and its art?

Just here may be the source of the vague discomfort felt by the average imaginative mind (please note that I say the average *imaginative* mind—and there are a few imaginative minds in every vocation, from the cobbler to the statesman) in its effort to get into sympathetic relation with modern literature and art. And here may be the reason why modern life and modern art are not one undivided unity, one complete well-rounded circle, as they were in the world's great ages—such periods of transcendent human expressiveness as those of Pericles, of the Gothic cathedrals, of the Sung emperors, of Queen Elizabeth. This vague discomfort is perhaps a just arraignment; and it may be up to the poet, rather than the scientist, to get in tune with his age.

Once in tune with it, once in sympathetic union with the forces now at work in the world, it is quite possible that the poet, and after him the people, will find the confusion of our age resolving into harmony, that he will begin a rounding of the circle which may make the next age as divinely complete and expressive as those others.

This will not be through writing eloquent praise of the super-locomotive or the giant airplane; but through feeling to the very depths, and expressing to the very heights, the spiritual adventures of the human soul in its use of, and conquest over, whatever powers and agencies the searchers and discoverers of the time have revealed. He will round the circle of beauty in his own way, but it must be the way of knowledge and sympathy—it cannot be the way of ignorance and scorn.

Even so enlightened an observer as Waldo Frank misses this point in *Our America,* which is nevertheless a luminous book of fundamental criticism of our present-day American world. If Mr. Frank could have seen that the pioneer—and the pioneer and the scientific inventor are essentially one type—if he could have realized that his "pioneer" was pursuing a dream rather than mere material riches, he would not have had to call Lincoln a "miracle"—a miracle of spiritual power arising out of a crassly material environment. Lincoln was a son of the pioneers not only physically and intellectually, but above all spiritually. In him the brooding melancholy of their endless quest, the power that paused for neither hope nor despair, that accepted no fulfilment but pressed on ever to the next goal—in him their heroic imaginings flowered into symmetrical beauty and grandeur. And the men of Lincoln's breed today are men like Dr. Steinmetz, pushing on from knowledge to knowledge through the encompassing darkness of our fate.

The fact that their discoveries are misused by meaner men for material gain has nothing whatever to do with the case. It is no more true today than in Homer's time or Elizabeth's—there are always grafters to suck the blood of heroes.   But the poet should see beyond the grafter to the hero: if he confuses the two, or neglects both, he is no true interpreter of his age, or prophet of the next.

## FLAMBOYANCE

" AMERICA needs the flamboyant to save her soul"
—so said Vachel Lindsay at one of those Glacier
Park camp-fires where he and Stephen Graham talked of
art and life to the indifferent mountains.

He might have added that America tries to satisfy this
need in strange and often uncatalogued ways. America,
living an exemplary three-meals-a-day-and-bed-time life
in a wall-papered home, goes now and then *en masse* to
the circus to see men, women and animals perform exquisite and impossible feats of grace and daring. What
could be more flamboyant than the trapeze-performer
hurtling through the air, the tiger leaping through man-
made hoops, or the elephant poising his mighty bulk on
his two forelegs lifted to the top of bottles? What more
flamboyant than the painted clown, timeless type of the
race, laughing that he may not weep, grinning through
a thousand tragic jests while little human beings perform
their miraculous tricks around him?

And America, sitting respectably at home with its
newspaper; America, suppressing its feelings and cen-
soring its artists; America, fearing emotion as the gate-
way to perdition—America finds the flamboyant in the
courts, and listens to every passion-molded word uttered
to judge and jury in Reno or New Brunswick or South
Bend.

Jazz, the Follies, the flapper in orange-and-green gown

and war-paint of rouge, the skyscraper lighting its thousand windows, the airplane skimming the clouds, the freshman shouting his college yell—these are all extravagant, impossible frenzies of color in a world that refuses to be drab. Even the movies, devoid as they are of color in the physical sense, are gaudy in the imaginations of the people who watch them; gaudy with exaggerated romance, exaggerated comedy, exaggerated splendor or grotesqueness or passion. Human souls who are not living impassioned lives, not creating romance and splendor and grotesqueness—phases of beauty's infinite variety —such people wistfully try to find these things outside themselves; a futile, often a destructive quest.

The imagination will not down. If it is not a dance, a song, it becomes an outcry, a protest. If it is not flamboyance it becomes deformity; if it is not art, it becomes crime. Men and women can not be content, any more than children, with the mere facts of a humdrum life— the imagination must adorn and exaggerate life, must give it splendor and grotesqueness, beauty and infinite depth. And the mere acceptance of these things from without is not enough—it is not enough to agree and assert when the imagination demands for satisfaction creative energy. Flamboyance expresses faith in that energy—it is a shout of delight, a declaration of richness. It is at least the beginning of art.

IF writers of verse could sit even a single month beside the editor of almost any magazine devoted to the art, if they could read the letters and manuscripts which come from all over the habitable world, and share the talk with visitors from far and near, no doubt the dramatic little procession would answer some of their doubts and questions. It would show them also how many bitter lessons in humility the editor of such a magazine receives, how remote his standpoint must be from that Olympian attitude of which he is sometimes accused, how he is saved by severe discipline from any pretense of infallibility.

Often one is asked, "How could you have refused So-and-so's poems!"—and is informed that Professor A., or the illustrious Mr. B., or the super-enlightened Mrs. C., had read them with great admiration, and advised the poet to submit them. Now, granting that the admiration and advice were sincere, and not merely an amiable and quite permissible "passing-the-buck," in ninety-nine cases out of one hundred the friendly admirer himself would refuse the poems on discovering that every week at least fifty manuscripts quite as good pass into the editor's office and out again. In other words, he would find that he had not been able to resist the intimate appeal of an isolated manuscript, sent to him with some touching story or some friendly recommendation: he had read the poem with more favor than it deserved, or than he himself would have felt if he had seen it in print.

Indeed, it is difficult to resist this intimate appeal. Even editors, hardened as they are, sometimes "fall for it." "In this office you deal with naked souls," said one of *Poetry's* observant visitors; and his remark is more poignantly true of the general ruck of impossibles which flood its mails than it is of even the best poems received from trained artists whose business it is to reveal their innermost truth. "The barber's wife of the Middle West" will confide to paper and send on, with a fluttering heart, to a magazine emotional secrets which she would conceal from her best friend, and bury in the sands of oblivion from her tonsorial husband; and the half-baked grocer's clerk of Philadelphia, or farmer's son of the Kansas plains, will hopefully string rhymes for an editor which he would not dare expose to the gibes of his baseball co-teamers, or even to the awe of his best girl.

The most comically-pathetically bad verse that we receive as editors of *Poetry* belongs to this class of intimate self-revelations; also much of the merely commonplace palaver which is neither comical-pathetic nor anything else. And often its return is as much of a shock to the author as the *Quarterly's* review was to Keats. Here, for example, is the haughty reaction of one of these self-confident dreamers:

The editors of *Poetry* either do not know what real poetry is, or else they have reasons of their own for declining such manuscripts as I have sent them. . . . . Pray tell me, where will an unknown poet look for appreciation if not to a journal devoted to poetry?

Such over-confidence in one's own genius, while neither the rule nor the exception among the impossibles, is quite common; and by no means confined to the uneducated. Usually it springs from artistic isolation and secretiveness —lack of will or opportunity to get competent outside criticism. The poet who writes in secret, and broods over his unappreciated manuscripts, almost invariably exaggerates their importance; indeed, fifteen years' intercourse with poets has led me to the conviction that self-training in solitude is the worst training in the world. "Look into thy heart and write!" is good advice, but not if interpreted to mean, "Look nowhere else!" The poet should know his world; and, so far as his art is concerned, any kind of battering from his world is better than his own self-indulgent brooding. Let him join, or organize, a poetry club in his school, college or neighborhood, where good poetry, old and new, may be read and discussed, and his own verse slashed to pieces. Let him try his poems on editors, and see what happens. If he is a poet, he will get some necessary training; the bigger he is, the more the self within him will harden into shape under the discipline. If he is not a poet, he will find it out sooner in the world than in the closet.

A Byronic figure rises before me as I write, a war-time visitor. A packet containing his diary and poems had arrived through the mail, together with a letter asking the editor to keep the packet for the author, as he would soon be going to the war. A touching faith that the poems were masterpieces was revealed between the lines of the letter, and the editor was permitted—nay, invited—to be the first to read and be convinced.

With a sinking heart I unfolded the poems: a few

were enough—they were, beyond all possibility of error, hopelessly, abysmally commonplace. Not wishing to be responsible, against the hazards of life and death, for a packet so precious to its owner and of no possible value to the world; and feeling, moreover, that the young man needed a hint of disillusion, I wrote appreciating his confidence and asking him to call and talk the poems over.

It happened that three poets were present the afternoon he called: Carl Sandburg—mellow, massive and human; a young journalist from Wisconsin, witty, clever and up-to-date; and Max Michelson, always kind, wise and sympathetic. The visitor was presented, and invited to join in the touch-and-go talk on poetry and poets. Did he do so?—not he! He didn't even hear it as he sat in the remotest corner gazing at the ceiling—a darkly melancholy and handsome figure of haughty youth; and not until the others had gone would he come to life.

Well, I went through a few poems with him, trying to lead him to some perception of their paleness, and urging him against his intellectual isolation. "But Keats —" he protested, and paused. "Keats was not a solitary," I replied; "he published his first book at twenty-one, and two or three others before he died at twenty-five—and he had excellent friends and critics, Leigh Hunt and Shelley among them."

The young man carried his packet away, silenced but not convinced.

Many tales might be told to illustrate the would-be poetic temperament. Not all such candidates for the laurel are self-deceived; one, for example, wrote, after two or three rejection slips:

If my poems are no good, won't you tell me? It won't take long to say so, will it? I don't want to go on wasting time if I can't turn the trick.

And another, a distinguished-looking gray-haired far-western lady with a bunch of newspaper clippings, exclaimed, with keen exactness:

My friends in my town are crazy over my verses, and this editor keeps begging for more of them; but I don't want to make a fool of myself—I feel sure they are just silly little things!

The other side of the picture—the editor's adventures among real poets—would be more difficult to reveal, because well-known personalities are involved whose biographies are not yet for all the world. But it is a thrilling tale, full of rainbow colors and episodes both lyric and dramatic.

IN the *Literary Review* of the New York *Evening Post* Lawrence Mason tells whimsically of the tortures he has endured in hearing poetry read aloud. Listing "several different methods," he says:

Some chant or intone it in a dulcet sing-song that woos reluctant slumber from her lair. Some attack it with athletic vigor, and pride themselves upon the sheer speed of their delivery. Others find the *summum bonum* in emphasizing the beat with the deadly regularity of a metronome. Still others coldly isolate and anatomize each line till there is no more savor in it than in a dried prune. Others, again, so boggle and halt and garble and apologize and re-read that the hearer is driven to madness, despair, or violent revolt.

And he refers to a cousin "whose method is none of these—his sole and sufficient guiding principle is to conceal from his unfortunate hearers every evidence of versification."

Mr. Mason's suffering reminds me of my own experience with a certain "eminent dramatic revelator" (so advertised) who, in programs ranging from *Othello* to *Deburau*, followed the method of Mr. Mason's cousin, but enriched it with a kind of vocal gymnastics inherited from the elocutionary school of the eighteen-seventies.

It would seem to be a rare gift—the beautiful reading of poetry. Even the poets themselves are often disappointing, though there is usually a degree of beauty and illumination to be gained from a poet's reading of his own verse. The poet instinctively emphasizes rhythm,

[ 231 ]

sometimes even to the point of intoning or chanting it; indeed, he rarely carries this too far. But not all poets have good voices, an accent neither too local nor too studiedly correct, and a simple effective delivery.

Certain poets, of course, it is a privilege to hear—their reading is as much a work of art as the poem, and the two fit together in indissoluble unity. I used to feel this of Lindsay, whose first reading of *The Congo* at *Poetry's* first banquet—in March, 1914—was a triumph in the double art. But of late Lindsay has acquired bad habits —his reading has become too loud and melodramatic. John Masefield's very simple reading of his poems is beautiful beyond words, because of that marvellous bass voice of his, rich with all the sorrows of the world. Carl Sandburg also has a deep-toned organ in his throat which he uses with subtle simplicity in the proof of his delicate rhythms. The fine voice of William Butler Yeats is of higher pitch than these; his quiet intoning of poetry nobly illustrates its beauty. Lew Sarett's presentation of his Indian poems is their perfect and almost necessary completion. Robert Frost's personality and voice also fulfil and emphasize the quality of his poems. Witter Bynner has a rich voice and graceful delivery, but an over-precise utterance mars the effect of his reading for me. Alfred Kreymborg, Carlos Williams, Maxwell Bodenheim—each of these complements his very personal rhythm in the utterance of his poems. And Padraic Colum brings to us the authentic Celtic tune—he is even more of an Irishman than Mr. Yeats.

I wish I could say as much for the women. Amy Lowell was one of the most accomplished of them, and Lola Ridge, Helen Hoyt, Marjorie Seiffert, Florence

Frank, Jean Untermeyer all read well, some of them excellently—all simply, and in rhythmic fulfilment of their poems; but none with quite the artistic beauty which some of the men have attained.

On the stage one rarely hears beautiful utterance of poetry. In all my unusual experience of theatricalized Shakespeare, which, beginning with Edwin Booth in my sixth year, includes almost every distinguished interpreter since his time, I have heard only one whose reading of the lines—no, not reading, not anything remembered and recited—whose spontaneous utterance of the lines—seems to me of such perfection, such strange and consummate beauty, as to be forever memorable and—alas—incomparable. This was Ada Rehan: to hear her as Viola or Rosalind was to be moved by a voice, deep and rich like falling waters, which turned English words into speech-music of transcendent quality, music that moved one like Kubelik's violin or Pavlova's dancing.

Among women, Ellen Terry was perhaps Miss Rehan's closest rival; but her voice was not quite so bitter-sweet, and there was a slight jerkiness in her delivery which gave it vitality and picturesqueness but detracted from absolute music. Mary Anderson had a voice like a cello, of extraordinary richness and range, and a fine sense of poetic cadence; but her delivery, though beautiful, to be remembered always with joy, was more deliberate and studied, leaning more to the old rhetorical school.

Booth was wonderful, of course—my youth shone with the romantic glamour of him. But it must be admitted that Booth mouthed his lines by overstressing his consonants, and that his delivery was not the spontaneous utterance of perfect art but the brilliant recital of speeches learned. He was a great artist of his Victorian time and his somewhat rhetorical school; but he was not an originator, not one of the genius-illumined who strike out new times, new methods.

Henry Irving had a more far-seeing mind, but his gift was for the spectacular. His speech was gusty and storm-ridden, his cadences churned and broken like a bold skiff outriding a gale. It was an adventure to listen to the lines of his Shylock—the poetry was so often in danger and so unexpectedly triumphant. He ranted early and often, but his ranting was always in the picture, always in the service of a deliberate conventionalization, a planned and achieved pattern. The modern poetic drama has scrapped his particular convention; but we may still envy him his skill, for we cannot yet claim to have established our own convention.

If Booth and Irving ranted sometimes, Lawrence Barrett ranted always; and John McCullough was seldom above the temptation, although his robust blank verse had always a certain beauty of cadence. Richard Mansfield came in a time of more simple Thespian manners, but he broke up the lines, he had no sense of rhythm; whether in *Henry Fifth* or *Beau Brummel,* he spoke always prose. Of all the male actors I have heard, Forbes-Robertson is the most assured master of poetic cadence; but his reading of Shakespeare, though beautiful, is sophisticated and deliberate—it lacks the spontaneity, and also the variety, which made Ada Rehan's, and even Ellen Terry's, a continual flaring of new fires.

The Irish Players were rhythmically endowed beyond any other company of my remembrance; which is not strange, since Irish speech is musical with poetic cadence, and these players were trained by Synge and Yeats and Lady Gregory, the three poets who have used it to the highest poetic purpose. This beautiful rhythmic speech was the secret of their charm, the one most potent reason for the effect of artistic unity and beauty in their rendition of the great plays of the Celtic renaissance.

The subject has led me to reminiscence when inquiry was intended—we have lingered with the masters instead of seeking examples in common life. If few actors read poetry with due regard for the rhythm, still fewer public readers have any conception of the primary principles of the art they profess, even when they have freed themselves of the hideous old elocutionary tradition which deliberately destroyed poetic cadence, broke up the lines, and turned poetry into agonizing prose.

This tradition is chiefly to blame for banishing from modern life an art which should be at least as common and friendly a pleasure and solace as music. A good voice, a sense of rhythm, simple unexaggerated utterance, all showing respect for the line and revealing the larger cadences which overlie the basic pattern—such a combination may make the reading-aloud of poetry, in any household or group of friends, a joy as fine as the excellent playing of a musical instrument.

More encouragement of this art might reveal and develop exceptional talent in persons scarcely aware of it. I remember an exquisite out-door presentation of Ernest Dowson's *Pierrot of the Minute* by two young sisters who had never realized their rare gift for the most delicate musical subtleties of poetic dialogue. And in the history department of the University of Chicago hides a certain modest professor whose reading of the

[ 235 ]

*Ode to a Nightingale* gives his friends an experience as magnificent as Muratore ever offered with his proudest solo, or Paderewski in his palmiest days.

The reading of poetry should be an easily accessible delight instead of the bore which it usually is. The defect chiefly to be avoided is a certain high-sounding rotundity which most people assume like a toga when they start to read poetry aloud. Most voices need training, to be sure, to develop the latent beauty in them; every school should teach the proper use of this delicate musical instrument within us. Given a good voice properly controlled, an ear for poetic rhythm, and the simplest possible observance of the pitches and tones of poetically enhanced speech, and you have the beginning of good reading of poetry—a beginning which practice, and the stimulus of emotional and imaginative intensity, may develop into high artistic beauty.

## THE POET AND THE COMPOSER

THERE should be a closer affiliation between poetry and the allied arts of music and the drama—perhaps also the dance. If the movies, and the scarcely less photographic commercial plays, are banishing poetry from one end of the stage, it must needs go around to the other door, and re-enter hand in hand with the opera and lyric song, with the ballet, and perhaps, paradoxically, symbolic pantomime. Times are changing, and the arts with them—the poet, the composer, the dancer should prove their pliancy, their mobility. They should not—indeed, they cannot—stay apart; they must get together and co-operate, and accept each other's influence. At present our poets and composers move in different orbits, have scarcely a bowing acquaintance with each other either personally or professionally.

Not long ago *Musical America* published an article by Charles Albert Case, a well-known tenor, entitled *The Quest of the American Song,* and sub-titled *A Challenge to Poets rather than Composers.* Mr. Case thinks that the American public wants American songs, and that the singers are eager for this change from the usual polyglot programs, but that it is impossible to make up a sufficiently interesting and varied recital without foreign aid. And for this condition he thinks our poets are more to blame than our musicians. He contrasts our meagreness with German and French richness, and reminds us that

[ 237 ]

a good song must unite two arts—a fundamental truth which both singers and auditors too often forget. He inquires, "What constitutes a good song?" and answers his query thus:

*A good poem adequately set to music.* There is the whole matter in a nutshell.

The many bad American songs are bad either because the text was trivial to begin with, or else was carelessly read and consequently inadequately interpreted in music. In some cases the text was even "adapted"—distorted, pinched and pulled into the approximate shape of a ready-made melody. Ready-made melodies are like ready-made clothes. They fit nobody because they were made to fit everybody.

Schubert read Mueller, Goethe, Heine, Rueckert, Uhland, Shakespeare. Schumann read Rueckert, Geibel, Uhland, Eichendorff, Moerike. Chausson read DeLisle and Gautier. These men read the best poetry of their time, and they read it with true understanding and genuine respect. What greatness there was in them lay largely in their power to discriminate, to select fine poetry from the mediocre, and then to bend to the task of making worthy musical settings. Too often our young Americans write as though they thought the lyrics of which they try to make songs were not good enough for them. . . . .

I have frequently been asked by young aspiring composers to help them find words to set to music. They say: "You know—something you consider singable. I haven't time to read." This is rank impudence. I never offer such people much sympathy. I do not think they should be encouraged. It seems to me that one must read much poetry to understand a little. Reading, and reading with unusual intelligence, is part of a song-writer's job.

Thus far Mr. Case's indictment accuses the composers, but he concludes with a fling at the poets:

I have real sympathy for the trained, educated, honest-intentioned American composer who reads native poets and finds so little to inspire him to exercise his genius. Surely his material is limited. Eventually we shall have truly noble American songs. But first there must be noble American poetry. We have many Americans who have the taste to choose and the ability adequately to set beautiful poetry to music. But American song-writing is at the same stage of development as American poetry.

Now, with all due deference to Mr. Case and his "trained, educated, honest-intentioned American composer," we doubt whether either one of them has sympathetically investigated the extraordinary range and variety of modern American poetry. We doubt whether either one of them, having discovered a poet suggestive for his purpose, has ever tried to get acquainted with him, even if he was a neighbor, and discuss this highly interesting esthetic problem on which the future of American song depends.

There is, among American artists—poets, musicians, and all the others—a curious professional aloofness which fights against co-operation. The architect makes his design, the sculptor models his isolated figure, the painter paints his easel picture, all separate and alone; they do not get together, as in the Phidian or the Gothic age, or the Renaissance, to pool their energies and make a grand, complete and monumental building. In the same infertile way the poet writes his poem apart in his traditional garret; and the musician, seeking a song poem, or a ballet motive, or an opera libretto, reads in his library uncharted seas of poetry, history and romance instead of going where modern poetry is created and swinging into its current, so that the two arts may move along together and mutually inspire each other.

Among themselves, poets—and doubtless musicians, painters, and the rest—are free-and-easy enough in intercourse and criticism. But this professional aloofness, this shyness, comes in the way of attempts at co-operation. A distinguished Chicago composer says he is "very familiar" with the work of certain equally distinguished Illinois poets, though, to his regret, he has never succeeded in harnessing up their poetry to his music; but we doubt if he has ever attempted to work *together with* any modern poet, in the frank give-and-take of such a partnership, toward the production of a wholly modern and American work of art. When I protest against his going back to the nineties for a pseudo-romantic motive for a ballet, when I suggest Stevens or Kreymborg, H. D. or Edna Millay, he answers by what might be called a flank attack:

> I am very grateful to you for the copies of *Poetry* which you sent to me containing the Stevens and Kreymborg pieces. I like particularly the *Three Travelers,* although I doubt whether I could improve it any with music.
>
> It seems to me that the thing we must all remember, in talking about an opera libretto, is the fact that we must depend for our effect on the poetry or the drama of the *action* rather than on the poetry or drama of the *words*. Therefore, the *ideal opera* librettist would be the poet gone dumb who, by his simple gesture, could make us jump through any hoop he pleases.

But even if this composer and others are turning toward pantomime and ballet rather than opera, preferring the orchestra to the human voice, even so they cannot eliminate the poet; for though no word be said, no song sung, the imaginative invention of some poet, dead or living, must furnish the motive, the story, the plot. And no doubt the ballet of the future will include the poem either as an introductory recitative or a series of lyric, perhaps choral, interludes; as in Rimsky-Korsakov's ballet-opera, *The Golden Cockerel*. Thus it is for the composer to choose whether he will be true to his own age and race by linking up with modern poets and deriving his stimulus from imaginations now actively functioning; or go back to dead poets for his motive, and thereby run the risk of endangering the vitality of his own art, in not connecting it up with either the present or the past.

But however important ballet and pantomime may prove as motives for modern music, it is safe to predict that the human voice will not lose its prestige. And it must be safe to predict that the sooner our composers look to their poet-neighbors for the texts of opera, oratorio, cantata, song-cycle, ballad, madrigal, song, instead of searching all ages, myths and languages of the past, the sooner will our musical art become up-to-date and racially expressive.

SUBJECTS for reflection are always numerous, but perhaps two will be sufficient for one article, and even these two may be essentially one—the general American attitude toward our poets and their poetry. The first division of this subject might be entitled *Frugality,* the second *Deprecation.*

In government lists and other official catalogues, *Poetry* is classed as a "trade paper," along with the *Breeders' Gazette, Bakers' News, Barrel and Box, The Billiards Magazine,* and hundreds more from A to Z. Of all the many lines of human activity represented in those closely printed columns, probably the poet's trade has the fewest organs, and surely no other trade supports its organs with such severe and chastening discipline of frugality.

But if poets enforce this iron discipline of frugality, matched in the spiritual sphere by that of critical austerity, so the great American public enforces the same discipline on its poets. In these days of leaping expenses the paltry rates paid to them have not been raised, the few prizes given them in this rich country show little increase in number or size, and no scholarships are as yet endowed—for the Amy Lowell Traveling Scholarships await the death of her chief heir. The millionaire collector who pays twenty thousand dollars for a first edition of Poe's *Tamerlaine,* would not hand over five hundred to keep some other starving poet alive, or print a book for him which may some day, in its turn, be a prize of collectors. One comes across cases of poignant necessity and suffering, the failure to relieve which, and thereby release brilliant talent for its true work, is an absurdity of our civilization. As the New York *Nation* said in an editorial entitled *A Broker in Books:*

The pitiful amount of public or private assistance given to American artists, men of letters, scientists, is one of the scandals of our civilization. Even England, by the pensions of her Civil List, has done infinitely more than we. And in countries where Anglo-Saxon neglect of the arts is not a tradition, literature has for a hundred years been encouraged as we have not even dreamed of encouraging it. We are the richest people in the world, and we are importing the rarest books as fast as we can find them and dislodge them. Yet we have practically no pensions or prizes for literature, and almost no endowment of research.

Our scholars spend exhausting and prohibitive hours at teaching or editing to keep themselves dustily alive. Our poets, even our successful poets, paid less for years of admirable work than a successful painter may receive for the work of a few weeks or even days, must live on the very margin of subsistence or else devote the greatest part of their strength to trivial work. If the state will not pay as much attention to such matters as it pays to experiments on hog cholera or the eradication of poultry pests, our men of great wealth might be expected to take a hand. Yet every day brings tales of amounts paid for books of merely eccentric or fashionable value, the income from which would sustain some precious career of poetry or learning.

From this iron discipline of frugality enforced on our poets by their fellow-countrymen, let us pass to the second division of our subject—shall we call it the brazen discipline of deprecatory skepticism?

We are accused of being a boastful race—or agglomeration of races; and in certain crude and obvious commercial specialties perhaps we have earned the impeachment;

but we have never boasted enough of our men and women of original creative genius, never believed enough in the distinction of their achievement, or sufficiently impressed upon them our sense of its value. We have waited for Europe to remind us of them—the cases of Poe and Whitman, of Wilbur Wright and Willard Gibbs, are only too typical—and we have withheld due recognition and reward until the foreign wreath was sent over to decorate their brows, or more often their graves.

What might not be said for American poetry of the past eight years if our Kultur were energized with as militant a national consciousness as that of our late antagonist? Listen to this rounding-up of the new German poets, sent from Berlin to the London *New Age* by our former naturalized compatriot Herman George Scheffauer, who returned to his native Prussia in 1915:

In Germany a new voice is rising out of the discordance—perhaps one that will dominate it. In this voice there is a note of eternity—it is tidal. . . . .

Whole choirs of poets have arisen, following a new star and burning with a new message to men. Let the Englishman who reads German procure, for example, Dr. Kurt Pinthus' anthology *Menschheits-Dämmerung*. Let him read Theodor Däubler, Franz Werfel, Johannes Becher, Ludwig Rubiner, Walter Hasenclever, August Stramm, René Schickele, Georg Heym, Oskar Loerke—and scores of others. Let him give ear to the sonorous symphonic note of the artisan poets of the *Werkleute* (*"Nyland"*) movement—Jacob Kneip, Wilhelm Vershofen, Josef Winckler. The book-shops swarm with books the titles, the very bindings of which cry out that they have arisen new-fledged out of ruins. A new age is climbing out of the Past.

Today more vital poetry is being published and read in Germany than ever before, and—this is again characteristically German—probably more "enemy" poetry than in enemy lands themselves. The price of paper and printing has reached ruinous heights; yet so intense is the thirst for books that more are being published than in war-time or in peace-time, when Germany's production reached (1912) 34,800 volumes, England's 12,100, France's 9,600, or 51, 25 and 24 per head of population respectively.

Now I have never listened to those "choirs of poets" whose names Mr. Scheffauer rolls off with such enthusiasm—my German is insufficient, even if their books had crossed the ocean. But I have read the Deutsch-Yarmolinsky anthology and a few other translations, so perhaps I have some right to confess a private skepticism in regard to the brilliancy of their "new star" and the potency of their "new message." My point, however, is simply to contrast the enthusiasm of their audience with the deprecatory skepticism of ours; and to urge upon our countrymen a little of that loyalty to one's own which is perhaps over-developed in Germany.

Of course, I should be willing to pit our present-day poets, man for man or choir for choir, against those of any country in Christendom; because I believe, aided by such small linguistics as I possess and fortified by such information as I can gather, that no other group is doing work so vital and various and beautiful, so true to the locale and to modern life. So let us assume Mr. Scheffauer's attitude, and capture his eloquence for the service of our own poets—perhaps even improve upon it, as follows:

In America a new voice is rising out of the clamor and tumult—perhaps one that will dominate the storm. In this voice there is a note of eternity—it is tidal.

Whole choirs of poets have arisen, following a new star and burning with a new message to men. Let the European who reads American procure, for example, Dr. Monroe's anthology, *The New Poetry*, as well as the files of her magazine. Let him read Carl Sandburg, Edgar Lee Masters, Vachel Lindsay, Ezra

Pound, John Gould Fletcher, Amy Lowell, Robert Frost, Edwin Arlington Robinson, Wallace Stevens—and scores of others. Let him give ear to the sonorous symphonic note of the socialist poets of the labor movement—James Oppenheim, Arturo Giovannitti, C. E. S. Wood, and many more. Let him listen to the clear singing of women—sopranos like Sara Teasdale and Edna Millay, mezzos and contraltos like Helen Hoyt, Alice Corbin, Louise Bogan and Agnes Lee. Let him be amazed at the variety of mood and manner displayed: from the romantic rhyming balladry of William Rose Benét, to the imagist's delicate discoveries of new beauty, set forth in new measures; from Vachel Lindsay's rich orchestrations of the white pioneer, the Negro and the Chinaman, to the aboriginal tunes of Dr. Gordon and Miss Skinner; from the high aesthetic aloofness of Wallace Stevens, to the democratic loving-tenderness of Carl Sandburg, and the searching, almost surgical realism of Edgar Lee Masters. The book-shops swarm with books the titles, the very bindings of which cry out that they have arisen new-fledged out of the spiritual need of a thinking, imaginative people. A new age is climbing out of the Past.

Today more vital poetry is being published and read in the United States than ever before. The price of paper and printing has reached ruinous heights, yet more books are being published than in war-time or in peace-time, when the production reached (will some statistician supply figures?).

How does it sound—this German eloquence applied to our own poets? If, as is certain, this is not over-praise, why should it not be uttered? Why should we always smile and deprecate and question, with a niggardliness disguised as scrupulous intellectuality? Such an attitude conceals our most precious spiritual treasures, and deceives the rest of the world. It lays us open to such charges as Mr. Scheffauer hurls at us from the capital of his "land of poets and thinkers," whose "latent creative energies have gone forth to conquer a new empire." From that lofty Prussian vantage-ground we and our former Allies are "Brute Might armed to the tusks," and Germany is molding the "New Renaissance of

Humanity . . . content to leave the offal and rubbish of a doomed mechanized and mammonized epoch to those to whom these things are still Baal."

The people of America should learn that their poets cannot do their work alone. An artist must feel his neighbors behind him, pushing, urging, arousing him, if he is to achieve his utmost. The great epochs, in any department of human activity, come only when a strong creative impulse in the minds of the few meets an equal impulse of sympathy in the hearts of the many. A masterpiece is no isolated miracle, but a conspiracy between a man of genius and his epoch.

IT is instructive, in art as in politics, to watch the workings of the public mind. I think it was John Quincy Adams who, nearly a century ago, considered proficiency in the arts unworthy of free and enlightened citizens. Probably the numerical majority of his race, on both sides of the ocean, are still of his opinion, but they no longer utter it with his confidence. Their security has been imperiled, not so much by the effrontery of artists in producing masterpieces, as by the endless talk, the noisy wig-wagging of solemn tongues and pens, which these masterpieces, and their train of lesser works, have excited.

To such a degree has the good citizen's contempt of art been shaken, that he has begun to encourage certain of its manifestations. The arts of painting, sculpture, music and architecture are now heavily endowed in many of our cities. So many prizes, traveling scholarships, rich purchases, and other rewards now await the aspiring painter or sculptor that it is scarcely possible for him to maintain any longer that modesty of fortune and demeanor which once seemed necessary to his development. Indeed, the public seems at last quite willing to admit that starvation and other forms of avoidable suffering do not assist a man of genius to paint or carve.

Not yet, however, does the public admit this of the poet. Large prizes and high prices may not injure the painter, million-dollar orders may develop the architect, but any such substantial evidence of favor would undermine the precarious vitality of the poet. He is lucky if he gets a mere pittance from editors, insufficient to support him on bread and water in a hermit's cave. He competes for no scholarships, and for few prizes. For him no American Academy at Rome opens its richly gilded doors—though why a poet should not require cosmopolitan experience as much as any other artist is a mystery deeper than Lord Dundreary's.

In the *Contributors' Club* of *The Atlantic* a few years ago were some anonymous reflections upon *Poets' Hard Times,* reflections which sum up a familiar point of view about poets and poetry with convenient compactness. A few excerpts will present the gist of the argument:

These are hard times for the honest minor poet: not because, as Mr. George Moore adventurously asserts, art is dead under the curse of universal locomotion, nor because the singer is denied a just hearing by the public. . . . . The honest minor poet wakes up in these days to find himself a child in a world of energetic serious maturity. Even the daily headlines bring home to him that no one needs his songs of hills and leaves and clouds, of elfin things and gypsy feet, even of love and death, touched as they are in his music with the kind deceiving shimmer of dreams. . . . .

With the nations reeling like drunken regiments, . . . . it is no wonder that the little singer finds himself beaten into humble silence. It he is honest, he knows that the world needs the burning insight and power of a prophet, or the simplicity of eternal childlike Truth. If he is not great enough in complexity to attain the one, nor great enough in simplicity for the other, he has nothing to say. . . . .

He is like a young person in a house of tumult and sorrow. He yearns to help, but he is dumb before the terrible or noble facts about him. If he utters himself, he is aware of inadequacy, and expects to be brushed aside. Even if sometimes he feels sure that his dream-knowledge sees deeper than the darkened

[ 249 ]

eyes of his friends, he dares not insist till Time has given him the right to be heard. He must grow up before he can speak. . . . . Or, to put it more plainly, he must be great to be worth hearing. When he can never be great, nothing is left for him but silence, and wonder. He may always keep the wonder. . . .

His courageous silence will leave more sky-room for the great songs sure to come. His wonder will open to him some private port of Paradise, gleaming with the proud light of Truth.

This kind of talk is still heard in more or less authoritative places, although, like the phrase "minor poet," it is somewhat out of fashion. I am not convinced of the heroism of that self-abnegating might-be bard, who is "beaten into humble silence," struck "dumb before the terrible and noble facts about him." Were Coleridge, Keats, Shelley—many others—struck dumb by the terrible and noble facts of the Napoleonic wars?—yet these singers of "clouds and leaves and elfin things" were minor poets to their contemporaries. Did any one of them hush his "sweet-chiming words" to "leave more room for the great songs sure to come?" No, for he knew that the great song, the great work of art, is merely the highest tree of a forest, rarely an isolated miracle; and that even the highest tree must grow from a sapling.

This being a strenuous age of universal locomotion, war and other bedevilments, the world has no use, we are told, for the poet unless he is an Isaiah or a Hans Christian Anderson. One might as well say the world has no use for gardens, or dwellings, or symphonies, for sculptured friezes and monuments, for portraits and landscapes, for Venetian glass or Chinese rugs, for jewels and laces, for club-houses and art museums. Because my favorite painter is not moved to depict cosmic horrors like Verestchagin, shall I bid him burn his brushes and take to

brooding in a corner? Because the world is madly busy
and furiously rushing to and fro, shall no one play the
piano, or plan a fair house, or dream by a brook under the
tree? Or, Mr. Essayist, "because thou art virtuous, shall
there be no more cakes and ale?"

The poet, in any primitive society or any well-organ-
ized civilization, should be as much a matter-of-course
as the carpenter. No tribe, no city, is complete without
one, and the better he is the more effectually does he
complete it. But for any community to demand the
ultimate perfection of its poet, to expect him to be silent
unless he can speak, like Moses, from Mount Sinai, is
as absurd as it would be to forbid to a carpenter his
tools unless he can at once, though unpracticed and unappreciated, turn out Chippendale chairs.

Some reader may retort with another familiar senti-
ment—"the true poet can't be silenced." But the trouble
is, he *can* be silenced—by starvation of body or soul,
song-deafness of his generation, or other obstructions; and
there is nothing more dangerous, more bitter and per-
verted perhaps, than a silenced poet. If "no one needs
his songs," his "wonder," far from leading him to "some
private port of Paradise," usually ends in toxic decay or
some violent explosion, like other suppressed forces.

The poet alone is continually reminded that lack of
food and sympathy are good for him. Listen to this
luminous exposition of the world's duty toward its poets,
from a writer in one of our most respected weeklies:

Even if he (the poet) shared the limited assistance which
endowments give to scientists and scholars, it would sap
society's sense of duty toward the arts . . . . And he may find
various sweet uses in his adversity—a close acquaintance with

life, a call to perseverance, and the protection of his art from the soiling hand of money-grubbing.

The fearsome critic need not complain that society has not done its full duty by the poet; teaching him "the sweet uses of adversity" not only by protecting him from the soiling hand of money-grubbing, but by turning upon him the deaf ear and lifting against him the stone wall. Is there any third-rate painter in America or Europe who has never received two hundred dollars for a picture? Yet when *Poetry* first offered this amount as an annual prize the world was agape with amazement that a poem could earn so much money. Mr. Sargent was no more famous as a painter than Mr. Yeats is as a poet; yet the labor of a week or two would be repaid, in the one case, by from five to ten thousand dollars, in the other by little of nothing.

But let us continue with our illuminating advisor:

We are not, however, without consolation in watching the discomfort of men like Moody and Thompson, counterparts of many other poets. The necessities of occupation in an unkind environment seldom rob us of anything of the highest value. The commanding figure, under modern conditions that make a Chatterton's fate almost impossible, will be discovered ere the shades of the counting-house close around him. Or if, like Browning, he remains undiscovered, some appreciation lets his generous spirit still work along the plan that pleased his boyish thought.

The beauty of this reasoning is beyond the reach of criticism. Put Shakespeare under "the necessity of occupation in an unkind environment;" in other words, set him to pegging Elizabethan shoes for a living: *Hamlet* is never written, and the above writer is not robbed of anything of the highest value because even so divinatory a mind can not conceive of *Hamlet's* being possible until it *has been written*.   In the same way he finds a Chatterton's fate impossible under modern conditions: alas, the modern Chatterton is not only possible but numerous; but when his genius is snuffed out by death, poverty, public apathy, or the compulsion to waste his time and brains earning a living, he is lucky if he gets a brief paragraph in a newspaper instead of immortal fame.

How can the most discerning observer hear in his heart the unsung songs?   How can he tell what the world has lost by silencing its poets and crucifying its prophets?   A masterpiece of art is not a miracle of individual genius so much as the expression of a reciprocal relation between the artist and his public.   He who must butt his head against a stone wall of apathy cannot long produce his best work.

But in a more profound sense these essayists' point of view is piteously wrong-headed, and piteously typical of much wrong-headedness at the present hour.   In such platitudes indeed, such tawdry thinking, lies the cause of the hideous futility of war; and every poet who sings of brooks and clouds, of elfin beauty, of love and death, thereby utters his heroic protest, helps to remind us of essential truth.   Are we to believe, forsooth, that this is "a world of energetic serious maturity"—because men are riding in steamers and motor-cars, and building skyscrapers, and killing each other at intervals by millions at the call of rotten dynasties and ideas?   Rather is it a world of overgrown children playing with expensive and explosive toys.

If this world ever grows up into "energetic serious maturity," it will be because the common feeling of the crowd arrives at wisdom. And wisdom is now, as it ever has been, insight into the eternal verities of truth and beauty. Every artist who helps the world to see truth and beauty—be it merely by a pastel landscape, or a carved kitten, or a song to a butterfly's wing—"does his bit" toward reminding us of eternal verities, and thereby bringing the world nearer to "serious maturity." He is an advance agent of civilization, that higher civilization which means wisdom, forbearance, humor, joy in life and magnanimity in death.

"WHAT are the women's clubs doing?" said a critical observer somewhere in Iowa. "Here is the richest—*per capita*—state in the Union, with more colleges to the square mile than it knows what to do with, and all the women organized into clubs which are fiddle-faddling with every subject from Homer to garbage. Yet we can't get anything done which requires a little tight-fist loosening—even the roads that our rich farmers drive their Fords through are made of mud! Why don't the women's clubs wake people up—start something—instead of holding good-clothes meetings and lionizing the latest celebrity?"

I looked around—it was the same familiar crowd of women—yes, and a few men—somewhat too well dressed and well fed for a tempered human weapon in this democratic age; the same rather wistful crowd of housed and guarded souls, holding resolutely to the material goods they felt sure of, and casting about doubtfully and frugally for half-suspected spiritual joys. What *were* they doing? Anything beyond the satisfaction of personal ambition and curiosity?—beyond a kind of intellectual bargain-hunting involving emotions of triumph almost as keen as the under-price purchase of a fur coat?

The dryness, the drabness, the thinness of life in this land where generous nature invites to richness and beauty —that is the danger which has come with the waning of the Puritan ideal.   The original Puritan lived an intense religious life; his faith was narrow, perhaps, but it struck deep.   He walked in the light of it; he lived with his stern exacting God.   He was frugal, no doubt, but saving money was not his chief problem—he had to save his soul.   His religion fed his imagination with visions of heaven and hell; under the impulse of it spiritual life— embryonic or more developed—was possible.

But as time went on, bringing new generations and scientific revelations, this heavenly manna turned to dust and ashes.   The village-bounded Puritan ideal could not reach out with modern science and grow with inter- national experience.   Though it may still survive with some vitality in little strangely islanded and isolated church-groups here and there, it has been swept away as a spiritual motive from minds aware of their world.

When mediaeval Christianity was swept away as a spiritual motive by the deluge of the Renaissance, its long and sedulous cultivation of the creative instinct of beauty left the arts as a refuge for human souls.   Roman Catholicism had become merely a symbolic social system, perhaps, for men caught in the new current; but in the ever-creative arts they could live, vitally and imagina- tively, the life of the spirit.   But to the Puritan the arts were a temptation of Satan; even the creative instinct of beauty was suspect.   So when his fenced-in religion withered, his spirit had nothing left to feed on; grasping at material desires—mere food-and-shelter splendors— the spirit in man, starving but undying, found these, as it must always find them, the gilded husks of death.

We have come a long way from women's clubs, per- haps, but not too far to get back.   The women's clubs were one response to this spiritual need—a wistful search for living grain instead of husks. And they have done much—they have ploughed up the ground, perhaps fertilized it, for a new harvest. The only trouble is, they don't know what to plant; they lack insight and direction. They get too much blind satisfaction out of good works —useful material benefits—and fail to realize that their planting should be of food for the spirit, that the one indispensable need of this country is for an enriched spiritual life.

Now an enriched spiritual life, in any community, is possible only through development of the imagination— the creative instinct of beauty. Religion does that whenever and wherever it springs, in each individual soul, from a real and vital faith. The arts do it whenever and wherever they spring, in each individual soul, from a real and vital faith. No human being was ever created who had not, somewhere within him, the instinct to create beauty. The zealot creates God, the supreme beauty. The lover creates his ideal mistress, the mother creates the child—both love-shaped into living beauty. The statesman, the philosopher, create beauty in orderly societies and abstract unities, the carpenter in his panelled wall, the farmer in his evenly planted field. The too common suppression of this universal instinct—through misuse of the machine, through the marshalling of "hands" (without brains) to monotonous labor, through the idle pleasures and accumulations of the rich, through other time-consuming, soul-destroying abuses of modern "civilization"—is chiefly responsible for social unrest; and the perversion of this instinct is chiefly responsible for crime.

[ 257 ]

To develop and direct this instinct for the creation of beauty, to resist the tendency toward sterilization of the mind in our educative and industrial processes—in short, to enrich the imaginative life of the people—this should be the primal aim of our women's clubs and all our cultural organizations. In admitting, for example, as any frank observer is compelled to, that clothes are the only form of artistic self-expression of which nine-tenths of our young girls are keenly aware, is to draw up an indictment against their parents and teachers, and the whole system which has brought them up to such sterility of the imagination. Joy in clothes is better than no creative joys at all, but why shouldn't these girls have been led to sing, dance, rhyme, carve, make toys or furniture, textiles or garments, or even delicious dishes—to create something of their own? And this not by the imposition of laws and examples from the past, but by the exercise of that personal impulse toward artistic expression which animates the little dancing, picture-drawing child?

Every woman's club should be an agency through which its members, their children and their community in general, may advance to more complete self-expression in beauty. It should aim at the discovery and encouragement of each person's imaginative impulse or artistic aptitude—of each person's special dream; and not be discouraged if the response is often crude or trivial.

But perhaps this would mean a reversal of systems of education and schools of thought beside which the Russian revolution is as a molehill to a mountain!

ALL the movements of the day—all the isms and schools and drives—fade into insignificance compared with the movement to get rid of war. This movement is not out of place in these pages—in fact, it is immediately the poet's business.

For poets have made more wars than kings, and war will not cease until they remove its glamour from the imaginations of men.

What is the fundamental, the essential and psychological cause of war? The feeling in men's hearts that it is beautiful. And who have created this feeling? Partly, it is true, kings and their "armies with banners"; but, far more, poets with their war-songs and epics, sculptors with their statues—the assembled arts which have taken their orders from kings, their inspiration from battles. Kings and artists have united to give to war its glamour, to transmute into sounds and colors and forms of beauty its savagery and horror, to give heroic appeal to its unreason, a heroic excuse to its rage and lust.

All this is of the past. The race is beginning to suspect those old ideals, to give valor a wider range than war affords, to seek danger not at the cannon's mouth but in less noisy labors and adventures. When Nicholas of Russia and William of Germany, in solemn state the other day, invoked the blessing of God upon their armies, the emotion that went round the world was not the old thrill, but a new sardonic laughter.

As Cervantes smiled Spain's chivalry away, so some poet of the new era may strip the glamour from war. Tolstoi's *War and Peace* and many lesser books are chapters of the new revelation, and modern science, modern invention, have aided the race in its half-conscious effort to unveil the bitter hideousness of the war-god's visage. But the final word has not been said; the feeling that war is beautiful still lingers in men's hearts, a feeling founded on world-old savageries—love of power, of torture, of murder, love of big stakes in a big game. This feeling must be destroyed, as it was created, through the imagination. It is work for a poet.

There will be a new poetry of war, and the time for that poetry is now. It must be written in peace, for when war begins there is nothing to do but fight. War is no more inevitable between nations than between individuals: as duelling was outlawed long ago in all civilized states, and its elaborate and long-accepted code of honor relegated to the scrap-heap, so shall war be outlawed by the assembled nations of the world, and its elaborate and long-accepted code of international law become a dusty byword of history. War is an absurd anachronism in this closely connected talking and trading world; and modern science has made it an anachronism poisonous and murderous beyond the maddest dreams of the darkest devils of hell. It must end if the white race is to preserve its numbers, its supremacy, its creative energy and power, and the proud fabrics of its civilization.

We face a war to the death on war, and none can afford to be a slacker in it. In this ultimate war the deadliest weapon is the germ of thought in human brains. Only the poet can spawn that germ, and send it flying forth by invisible millions to mature in the minds of men. Cervantes wrote *Don Quixote,* and suddenly a rotten thing, long ready for death, was dead. Let some poet— or perhaps a number of poets in a number of arts—stab with laughter or scorch with tears the rotten hulk of war, and suddenly the world will know that war is dead.

ELSEWHERE in this volume I have offered a study of Amy Lowell's work as a poet. But her so recent death makes her, so to speak, a historic character whose personality should be recorded before one's impressions fade. Hence it may be in order to recall a few details of incidents which make her live in a friend's memory.

Before *Poetry* began, its editor-to-be read all the verse in the previous five years of the principal American magazines, and sent notices of the adventurous project to those poets who seemed worth while. Among these was Amy Lowell, who had had a sonnet or two in the *Atlantic*. The first letter of a long series was a cordial answer to that appeal, sent from her summer place in Dublin, N. H., on September 7th, 1912. "It is a most excellent undertaking," she wrote, "and ought to do much to foster poetry, which has a hard time to get itself published now." And she promised to send some poems later, after her first book should have appeared; and enclosed a check "for a subscription and a little more," our first present from a poet.

At that time Miss Lowell's name was merely a name to me, and Boston genealogies had not impressed their proud authority on my imagination. But during the following winter I was enlightened. The president of Harvard was being dined by alumni in Chicago, and at the same moment his wife was the guest of honor at a feminine banquet where I occupied an inconspicuous place. As we were beginning the dessert, an imposing figure appeared in the remote distance at the top of a half-flight of steps, and "Oh, there's Amy!" said Mrs. Lowell, in a voice which accepted resignedly anything that Amy might do. Even then I did not connect this "Amy" with my correspondent, two of whose poems we had by that time accepted; absorbed, I listened to her melodious words of greeting and watched the ponderous and regal figure slowly descend the steps.

She took possession of the occasion and the company— no one else was of any account. Our hostess presented her to each of the dozen or so women at the table as we all made room, and my mind was still wool-gathering when, on hearing my name, the newcomer turned a powerfully reproachful eye upon me with the query, "Well, since you've taken 'em, why don't you print 'em?"

So this mighty personage of august physique and fortune and lineage, sister of the president of Harvard, cousin of James Russell Lowell, was my correspondent, my poet-contributor, she of the beautiful handwriting and the meticulous precisions of taste in words and phrasing! I was not only duly impressed, I yielded gladly to the spell of her half-magnificent, half-humorous personality— for there was always a laugh in her to confuse the magnificence. She literally sank into a chair, spreading herself comfortably and quizzing the crowd; doing not more than her share of talk, perhaps, but monopolizing much more than her share of attention.

The next time I saw her was nearly a year later, when she came to "place" with us her second group of poems, among them *A Lady, Music, The Gift,* and others lyrics now well known. I remember feeling that the star of literary empire was turning westward when this Bostonian daughter of the Lowells brought her poems to a Chicago mart. The April number of 1914, which opened with them, was our first to be set up in linotype (since discarded), and somehow a line was dropped out from the final proof in such a way as to slant the meaning of the sentence very disagreeably. I shall never forget how the wires hummed because of this error. The poet's voice over the long-distance telephone was not angry—she kept her temper and did not blame the poor editor—but it was filled with anguish unutterable and not to be consoled. From that time I realized to the utmost certain exactitudes in Amy Lowell's taste and temperament which all her friends and business associates had to live up to. She might never arrive on time at a dinner and rarely even at one of her own lectures, she might take it lightly when one of her beloved sheep-dogs chewed a poet-visitor's trousers and narrowly missed his flesh, she might revise at will certain other social formulae, but let an editor change a comma in one of her poems, or differ from her on a question of phrasing or rhythm, and said editor would be jammed down very effectively into a mood of proper deference.

It was during the early summer of 1913 that she went to England, met Ezra Pound and the other imagists, and dined and wined and motored them with a lavishness unheard-of among poets. The acquaintance led to pleasant friendships with Fletcher, H. D. and Aldington, and to a pleasant enmity with Ezra Pound—for two such dominant personalities could not get on in the same boat. So a note of discord strained the imagist harmonies as the tocsin sounded for battle between the vers-librists and their foes.

She did her part in this and other literary conflicts, both with her pen and on the platform. Before an audience her magnetic personality always commanded the crowd, and she was one of the few lecturers I have ever heard who could read a written address as effectively as if it were an extempore speech. She seemed to like lecturing, and the contacts with youth and new energies which it gave her; and she felt a quiet pleasure in shocking some of the conservatives she came from by embracing adventurous causes and ideas. She took her work very seriously, however; and to be wholly sincere in what she wrote, and ambitious of excellence in her art, was inevitable in a character like hers.

As the years went on we became better acquainted, and I visited her once or twice in her big ancestral mansion in Brookline. I remember with special delight the great library, whither she used to descend before dinner-time from her private domain on the third floor. Here, after the stately repast, she would sit enthroned in a corner of the lounge, and here she loved to linger and talk until at least three o'clock in the morning—for she always inverted day and night, and felt pathetically aggrieved if her visitor's spirit did not rise to her hours. She was an eager and delightful talker, indulging a discursive and experimental mind—a mind with much shrewdness and commonsense and whimsical humor under its more decorative impulses. And in that richly rusty old beautiful room, book-filled to the ceiling, she seemed completely at home with the forbears of her blood who had lived

there, and of her intellect whom she could invoke from
ten thousand volumes.

At one end of this spacious and comfortable library
was the small room containing her treasure-vault of
manuscripts—the precious collection of papers in the
handwriting of Keats and many other poets, autographed
volumes in fine bindings, etc., which now enriches the
Harvard Library.

One might tell many stories of Miss Lowell's kindness,
of her solicitous appreciation of exceptional people and
their difficulties. A number of poets known and unknown were aided by her at critical moments in ways that
may never be revealed. I remember her intense admiration for Eleanora Duse, and her persistent effort to soften
the fatigues of the great artist's fatal American journey,
and contribute to the luxury and ease of her too-brief
life among us.

It was the day before Duse's funeral, in May of 1924,
that I talked with Amy Lowell for the last time. The
poet and actress had become, through correspondence,
devoted friends, and Miss Lowell had traveled to New
York to pay the final tribute. She seemed as vital as
ever—I little thought that she would follow to the
grave within a year. She was then deep in the Keats
book, which had grown in her hands much beyond the
limits she had originally intended. I could see how
oppressive the immensity of this labor had become, how
she longed to be through with it. "I came home to face
a simply terrific summer," she wrote to me afterwards,
on October twenty-fifth; "to tell the truth I am simply
worn out." And she enumerated some of the incredible
exactitudes of detail which trip an author up in com-

pleting and getting through the press a work of that character and magnitude.

In the last letter I ever received from her, written a month later, she said: "I am still drowned in proof. *Volume I* is on the presses, *Volume II* marches to completion slowly but inevitably, and some day I shall be a free woman again." And she looked forward to a few weeks of rest before her projected lecture-tour in England.

But it was not to be. She had overstrained her strength and the weeks of rest turned into weeks of suffering. All of a sudden she lay still, at rest indeed. Her share of our little earthly life was over.

She was a great woman, a true and loyal friend, and, in the finest sense of the phrase, a good sport. She was the first to go of the poets conspicuous in the "new movement" which began in 1912. It seems impossible that a spirit so vivid and vital has left the place she loved, and will speak to us in the flesh no more.

*November 10th, 1879-December 5th, 1931*

VACHEL LINDSAY is dead. A voice which thrilled us is suddenly silent. A strong life in mid-career, erect for another score or two of years on earth, falls prostrate, and the dust which held it together for marching, thinking, singing, dissolves into the earth it came from, collapses, decays. But out of this perishable mass of cells came something which lives, something whose imperishability may be not only a fact but a symbol. Words set in patterns intricate and beautiful survive as the rhythmic breath of a spirit demanding immortality.

Memories come crowding as I try to realize that there will be no more incidents of friendship to remember. They began nearly twenty years ago, for before *General Booth* led off *Poetry's* fourth number in January, 1913, its author had appeared in the old office in Cass Street, and had recited his poem in the big round chanting voice which has stimulated so many audiences. By that time other young poets were wandering into the sanctum, and we used to have long confabs there, or over spaghetti and red wine at an Italian restaurant around the corner. Those were the days!—Lindsay has often spoken of the inspiration he received out of those discussions, those trade talks of poets seeking and giving light.

A year or more later came the great moment of the Yeats banquet, which Lindsay had come up from Springfield to attend; when the famous Irish poet publicly addressed the obscure American with a compliment for *General Booth,* which by that time had initiated our Guarantor's Prize, although its author was still regarded by the public with some suspicion. Mr. Yeats said:

This poem is stripped bare of ornament. It has an earnest simplicity, a strange beauty; and you know Bacon said, "There is no excellent beauty without strangeness."

And it was another great moment when the young American, so honored, responded by reciting *The Congo* for the first time, startling the Irish bard and the rest of us with the rhythmic roll of his dramatic chant.

From that time, as I rejoice to remember, *Poetry* honored itself by presenting some of Lindsay's now-most-famous poems. Not *The Congo*—because for that, before we heard of it, the poet had received seventy-five good dollars from an eastern magazine, which after all never dared print so eccentric a manifestation of poetic genius! But the group of thirteen moon poems ran like a gay fantastic dance in our tenth number; a year later we offered that delicate viol solo, *Aladdin and the Jinn,* and the leaping roaring blare of *The Firemen's Ball* and *The Santa Fé Trail*—two poems played by a brass band. And in 1915 *The Chinese Nightingale* was ours to crown with the Levinson Prize and pass on to undying fame—a masterpiece of wavering rhythms and exotic colors, of spiritual grace and beauty. In 1916 came *The Booker Washington Trilogy,* with the grandly heroic *John Brown* for its second number, celebrating the half-mythical figure of a nation's history and dream:

> Old John Brown,
> Old John Brown.
> And there he sits
> To judge the world.
> His hunting-dogs
> At his feet are curled.
> His eyes half-closed,
> But John Brown sees
> The ends of the earth,
> The Day of Doom.
> And his shot-gun lies
> Across his knees—
> Old John Brown,
> Old John Brown.

So it went on, with poems gay or serious, whimsical or tragic. In 1928 the staff of *Poetry* decreed to Lindsay an Award of Honor of five hundred dollars, the largest prize in our long list of awards. This was given "for the high distinction of his best work, which, in the opinion of the committee, shows original genius, deriving, to an extraordinary degree, from nobody but himself."

The lively sequence, *Every Soul Is a Circus,* printed in October of that year, was the last of our many entries over his familiar name. From its final poem these lines may be quoted as a word of farewell to his fellow-craftsmen:

> For every soul is a circus,
> And every mind is a tent.
> And every heart is a sawdust ring
> Where the circling race is spent.
>
> . . . . . . . . . . .
> . . . . . . . . . .
>
> So come, let us be bold with our songs, brothers,
> Come, let us be bold with our songs.

These poem-entries were punctuated by visits. The poet would appear in person to emphasize his art with talk of tramps over prairie roads and mountain trails, of

books he had read about Buddha or Confucius or the
Virgin Mary, of *Paradise Lost* or *The Divine Comedy,* of
Mary Pickford or some jazz artist of the newest make.
We learned that here was a man of wide and varied
learning, and of an iridescent and glamorous imagination
which, like a fairy's wand, could turn familiar things to
splendor. And we felt dimly, in spite of his robust voice
and other realistic details of personality, that here perhaps, in our very presence, sitting in the battered old
arm-chair of the *Poetry* office, might be one of the im-
mortals.

But this is not the moment for exact appraisal of Lindsay's genius. In the essay on page 21 of this volume I
have tried to study his art, to estimate its values and its
hope of permanence. Today, in the first shock of our
great loss, I can add little to that review—it is not the
moment nor yet the place. For I am writing at the
poet's own desk, in the little second-floor study of the
roomy Victorian house where he was born, overlooking
the Governor's mansion and yard in his beloved little
capital city of Springfield. Yesterday, after a fine service
in the crowded church, we saw his coffin lowered into his
native soil, beside the graves of his parents and grand-
parents, along the slope of a ravine in the lovely woodsy
cemetery which holds the ashes of Lincoln. Already a
place of pilgrimage for all the world, this historic graveyard has now another shrine, where future visitors, in
increasing numbers as the years go by, will lay their
wreaths of tribute.

It is fitting that the town which Lindsay so loyally
loved had come to recognize the honor of his citizenship.
It is fitting that his last public reading was given there, in

the very church where a week later we bade him goodbye
—given before an audience so large and enthusiastic as to
make the poet feel that at last he had "won Springfield."
To convince one's neighbors is perhaps the last and most
difficult proof of genius. From the spring of 1929, when
he came home with his family after five years of being a
"guest of Spokane," the city he loved had lifted him on
its shoulders, so to speak, in a loyal tribute of admiration
and affection. In his funeral sermon the Rev. Clark
Cummings asked us to "accept him as our prophet," thus
recognizing in this poet the spirit of the *vates* who must
preach "the gospel of beauty" and lead his people while
he sang. And among the poems read to prove his
apostleship, and show how profoundly, in this difficult
age, he grieved for his countrymen, was this brief invocation, *The Leaden-eyed:*

> Let not young souls be smothered out before
> They do quaint deeds and fully flaunt their pride.
> It is the world's one crime its babes grow dull,
> Its poor are ox-like, limp and leaden-eyed.
> Not that they starve, but starve so dreamlessly;
> Not that they sow, but that they seldom reap;
> Not that they serve, but have no gods to serve;
> Not that they die, but that they die like sheep.

Like his neighbors of Springfield, it may be that Lindsay's contemporary fellow-countrymen have been slow to
admit the full stature of his genius. It may be that the
final verdict will have to wait for "foreign nations and
the next age." One has detected now and then a mood
of patronage in notices of "the jazz poet," "the troubadour poet"; and the material rewards accorded him
have been pitifully small and few. But time has its own
wilful way of bringing in its revenges, and under that

[ 272 ]

protecting aegis one may feel that the fame of this poet is secure. As the years pass, his slighter work will be forgotten, and the poems which survive will rank at last among the most vital and beautiful interpretations in art of the spirit of man as it moves and works in our time and place.

So I thought yesterday morning when I looked for the last time upon his face, and found it strangely luminous with a beauty beyond the beauty of life. Here indeed was perfect peace; here was a hint of the ultimate wisdom. For the brief moment before dissolution little of earth was left in this powerful and noble mask—all the lines of care which had troubled us were obliterated, smoothed away. To gaze upon this poet's face in death was to admit his greatness, and commune with a spirit far loftier than the loftiest dream life had granted him on earth.

OF all the so-called civilized peoples, at least in the Occident, Americans have been credited with the greatest love of wild nature. The people of "these states" instinctively take to the woods for a holiday—the woods or the waters or the mountains—to a greater degree than any Europeans; or, it has been averred, than any Central or Southern Americans. Our ancestors, coming here from crowded Europe, gradually discovered the wilderness and became infected with its lure. The magnificence of Nature in our ever-growing West—its infinite variety of beauty and grandeur—was a perpetual invitation to the pioneer. And now that those days have well-nigh passed, the children of pioneers feel the same call, and obey it as they can by camping and mountaineering under primitive conditions, and by setting aside vast areas of wild scenery as people's playgrounds for all time to come.

Mr. Henry Seidel Canby, discussing in the *Yale Review* this "survival of the pioneering instinct," said:

Since our writing ceased being colonial English and began to reflect a race in the making, the note of woods-longing has been so insistent that one wonders whether here is not to be found at last the characteristic "trait" that we have all been patriotically seeking. . . . . It represents a search for a tradition, and its capture.

We commemorate annually the first Thanksgiving day of the pilgrim fathers, who decreed a feast because they had so nearly starved before the gathering of their first harvest. I had always read the story with solemn sympathy for the pilgrims until that hardy woodsman, Hamlin Garland, pointed out how absurd it was to starve in those forests filled with game. "The fools," he said, "they hadn't sense enough to learn of the Indians—they couldn't eat until they had cleared some land and grown grain! But their sons learned," he added reflectively.

And their sons have been learning ever since. The early settlers, who hadn't much art, had to go to nature for beauty; and their children, whose art has been largely derived—not a spontaneous self-expression but an inheritance or the imitation of an inheritance—their children still go back to nature for the most simple and direct communion with beauty. Confused and wearied by bad art—(for poor design in architecture, poor color and form in house interiors, furnishings, dress, etc., poor literature in books and newspapers, poor music in clattering rhythms of vicious noise, are all bad art, and therefore infinitely confusing and wearying)—their children throw on civilization the blame for ugliness, and go to the wilds to satisfy their unconquerable need of beauty. And out of this refreshment, this re-creation in nature, may indeed spring, as Mr. Canby suggests, an art more indigenous and original, more truly our own, than all the feudal operas we sing or the Doric-temple railway stations we build.

I sometimes think that the race will be saved through love of nature, saved at last from the collective rapacity of greed and the collective violence of war. Such anachronisms can not long survive among people who continually test their living and thinking by immediate

contacts with wild beauty and primitive simplicity. Our
own inheritance of vast areas of mountain and desert,
forest, lake and sea-coast—areas which can never be
civilized—may be regarded as our most precious possession, an ever-flowing fountain of youth for the nation.

And what will our poets do with this inheritance? At
the beginning of the nineteenth century, after two hundred years of pioneering, they had learned less from the
Indian than those early Mayflower pilgrims, and so
strong was the colonial instinct that it took another half-
century to "get the lark out of American song." Even
when the poets began to be aware of the out-of-doors, it
was rural nature, not the wilderness, which appealed to
them, as in these home-bound lines from the hymn which
we all sing to a foreign air:

> I love thy rocks and rills,
> Thy woods and templed hills.

Here the poet's vision was limited by a gentle village
slope with granite out-cropping by the stream and a
church half hidden among the trees.

The Anglo-Saxon voyagers of six to eight centuries
ago knew and loved and hated the sea, and in their sea-
songs is the power and grandeur of the wilderness beyond
anything since attained in English poetry. Who that has
read Mr. Pound's marvelous translation of *The Sea-
farer* has not felt in it a deep and bitter sense of nature,
missed since then by even the masters of English song?
Shakespeare has some wonderful lines about the sea; he
felt it as England's protector and possession. Byron
hurled some magnificent rhetoric at not only the sea but
the mountains—the first English poet to be intimately

[ 276 ]

moved by mountains, which is not strange since there are no mountains in England. And Swinburne loved the sea as well as a landsman can, gave it long odes of rhythmic praise. But the unknown author of *The Sea-farer* knew and sang the sea as his lover and enemy, slave and master, as the vastness immeasurable out of which he was born and into which at last he would sink like a spent seagull in a storm.

From the formation of the English language this note of wildness is rarely heard. A few of the old ballads have it, but rarely the great English masters. We get the tang of it from Ireland—from Synge especially, from Yeats and Colum somewhat less—with a special Celtic flavor, but coming, as it were, from dells and clearings, not from great spaces.

It is almost a platitude to repeat that Mother Earth is the great renewer of the race, both physically and spiritually. But it would be well if we were to search the platitude more deeply, and realize that she is also the great renewer of the arts, and that it is from her, rather than from schools and precedents of the past, that our artists, our poets, will draw the nectar of the gods. Since men began to build houses and gather together in villages and towns, they have been too prone to accept roofs and walls as a normal condition of human existence, and to confine their interests more and more to the small efforts and small talk incident to small and confined areas. Thus artistic traditions which began generously, with a free out-of-door range, become narrowed down as the generations pass, become fixed in the walls and roofs of precedent and law, acquiring a definiteness and sanctity to which they are not entitled. The arts, like groups and races of men, inherit too much from the super-civilized past; even more than super-civilized human beings do they need the great renewal from Mother Earth who bore them.

In this country we have been, on the whole, too content with those walls and roofs of precedent built by the arts of the past. Yet in spite of this handicap our best work in the various arts rides free more or less, and carries a message from the wilderness. We hear a hint of it in the finest poems of Emerson and Bryant, Whittier and Longfellow. We detect a sentimentalized version of it in the landscapes of the Hudson River School and in the out-of-door yearnings of colonial houses. We feel its freedom more strongly in the simple porch-winged villas, and in certain frankly expressive sky-scrapers, which are developing architectural style without much aid from historic design. It became a dominant motive in such painters of land and sea as Inness, Wyant and Martin; and some of their successors are carrying on the proud tradition. Cooper of course handed it over in chunks; in Hawthorne it was a longing and an agony; and Thoreau subdued it to a scholar's use and nobly philosophized it. Poe was lyric with its passion and color—a caged mocking-bird beating his wings; and in another art Albert Pinkham Ryder was a somewhat more fortunate parallel. Even in Whistler, who carried the war into Europe, we feel the flavor through all the sophistication. Mark Twain preserved its epic bigness through all his social and literary adventures. And in Whitman it was the breath of life, the force which enabled him to over-ride all confining barriers. In the future, as we become more self-confident, less colonial

our art should inevitably get more and more free of walls
and roofs. Its triumphs will come from those who knock
down, not those who prop up, such erections; or perhaps
rather from those who, enriched by the discipline of their
somewhat imprisoning beauty, are strong enough to pass
through and beyond it and go free.

Edgar Lee Masters gave us *Spoon River* in this spirit;
and Vachel Lindsay and Carl Sandburg as well are,
artistically considered, the educated sons of pioneers.
Indeed, besides these, we feel it today in many varying
voices: in the poems from Indian motives of Lew Sarett,
Dr. Gordon, Miss Skinner, Mrs. Austin, Alice Corbin
and others, as well as in direct translations by Natalie
Curtis and other students; in John Gould Fletcher's
poems of Arizona and other wild places; in C. E. S.
Wood's *Poet in the Desert;* in Edith Wyatt's praises of
the Great Lakes and the western heights; in the spacious
Oregon pastorals of H. L. Davis; in the *Cowboy* and
*Rainbow* anthologies, with their rich stores of folk-lore.
And the spirit of it, though not precisely the locale, one
finds in such a poem as Mr. Frost's *Snow;* and in H. D.,
who, however preoccupied with Greek symbols, is essentially a poet of wild nature.

Our poets must face the issue. As with their confrères
in the other arts Europe has hitherto been their place of
pilgrimage, and those who stay there almost inevitably
become wandering cosmopolites who, fascinated by the
extremes of a sophisticated culture, become more adept in
expressing these extremes than the natives themselves.
Mr. Pound and Mr. Eliot are cases in point: born under
the flag, they do not lose their love of freedom—in fact,
it gives a special edge, a tang, to their observations and

interpretations of a life too long cribbed, cabined and confined; but practically they become limited to these aspects of life, and lose touch with, and faith in, bigger spaces and larger realities.

A young New York poet, who recently went west for the first time, wrote from Taos, New Mexico, of "the influence of the beautiful maternal West upon my jaded sense"; and added:

> I shall like the West when I get used to its generosity. The East is so small and I have been lessened in its presence far beyond my wishes.

There we have a truly enlightened acknowledgment of what our south-western wonderland may do for and with the soul of man: a wonderland in which Nature herself has conceived and developed the vast pre-Adamite architecture of the Grand Cañon and of those strange terraced fortresses in the Painted Desert; and in which old barbaric tribes have taken Nature's hint in mesa-pueblos that grow out of the desert as expressively as the cactus or the mesquite. This magic wonderland is destined to a strong influence over the future of American art— the only question is, how soon will this influence begin as a recognizable force?

In the education of the spirit wild Nature is the supreme teacher. The artist who remains in towns, or in suburban parks and gardens, or even he who takes summers out-of-doors in cultivated farm-lands, misses the spiritual discipline of freedom, the supreme renewal. He may be unaware of this loss; super-sophisticated worldling, clinging to the skirts of civilization, he may be content to repeat and elaborate—to build French chateaus in

North Carolina or Ionic-colonnaded sky-scrapers in New York, to plant Italian gardens on the sand-dune bluffs of Lake Michigan, to carve out archaic-Greek rhythms in sculpture and Miltonic or Swinburnian rhythms in poetry. Meantime our vast western wonderland is waiting for him; Nature, the ultimate modernist, is ready to broaden his vision and enormously increase his range, ready to give him, not more learning but power over all his learning, not man-made facts and monuments but God-made grandeur with its lesson of spiritual energy and control.

Twenty years ago I travelled from Italy to Arizona, and to my profound surprise found Arizona the bigger thing of the two. Europe or the wilderness?—the choice will become more and more urgent for our seers of visions.

Search not in cities for the Pierian spring!

# POETIC RHYTHMS

*A Word about Prosody*
*Rhythms of English Verse*
*Dr. Patterson's Researches*
*The Free Verse Movement*

RHYTHM is of course a universal principle, the very pulse-beat of life and of all the arts. From the amoeba to man, from the atom to the star, rhythm, or power moving regularly in time-beats, is a recognizable law which all creation must obey. The more closely modern science studies the universe—through microscope, telescope, or the naked eye and brain of man—the more astonishing and magnificent becomes this infinite harmony: an intricate weaving of small patterns within great ones, a march of ordered melody, outreaching human eyes and ears, outracing even the human imagination. The arts are an effort to join in, to weave little imitation patterns, sound little imitation tunes. Even the static arts must respond with balanced form and color in painting, sculpture, architecture—else their manifestations are temporary and incongruous, part of the perishable scum and waste.

Music and poetry seem to have been among the earliest and most direct human manifestations of the universal rhythmic impulse. At first they were united—lyric rapture instinctively fitted words to melody, as it does still in certain forms of spontaneous folk-song, like keening over the dead, or other primitive rhapsodies of prayer and praise. But as life became more complex, the two arts separated, developed each its own imaginative and technical expression of the rhythmic instinct. Literature began in the creation of poems too beautiful to be left to chance memories and tongues, and therefore committed to writing. After the passing centuries had heaped up an accumulation of these masterpieces, the analysts took hold of them; and out of the practice of dead poets grammarians began to make rules for poets yet to come. Thus prosody was born. And thus gradually it developed into a rigid system of verse-structure.

Poetry is an art. Prosody is, or should be, a science. The art has always preceded the science—that is, men have sung, built, carved, drawn pictures on walls or rocks, long before any rules were laid down for their guidance in any of these performances. Not that the artist was lawless, but law with him was an instinct, not a formula: an instinct for rhythm, color-values, sound-values, mathematical purity of line, and for the balance, proportion, harmony in all these. After the artist had done his work, creating beauty through following his instinct for her immutable laws, the scientific thinkers came along and made laws definitely founded upon his product and definitely limited by his achievement. They decreed that as the artists of the past had done, even so must the artists of the future proceed: and why?—the artists of the past had produced masterpieces; therefore, how otherwise could masterpieces be produced?

All this may be a repetition of the obvious; but when inherited and accumulated rules become a constraint and an encumbrance one needs to be reminded now and then that they were made originally not by an infallible and omniscient God but by very fallible and half-ignorant men; indeed, not even by creative artists, but by critics and classifiers who studied them. When Aristoxenus of Tarentum, a contemporary of Alexander the Great and therefore much later than the golden age of Greek poetry —when this grammarian "first laid down definite laws for prosody as a department of musical art," he founded what was at the time a good workable science for the guidance of Greek poets; and if few Greek poets came after him to reward his labors and those of other grammarians who gradually built up the science to their complete satisfaction, yet the poets of conquering Rome accepted the doctrine and adapted their measures to its principles.

How far the Roman poets benefited by this acceptance of laws made for another language, whether their poems would have been better or worse if they had never heard of Greek prosody, is a question for more accomplished linguists than the present writer. However, it is certain that the harmonics of the two great classic languages are in closer accord than they are with those of any modern language, especially those languages more or less derived from the speech of the barbarians whom Caesar fought.

When Hephaestion's manual of Greek meters, written in the second century of our era, was finally printed in 1526, its influence was carried into modern times. The classic nomenclature—the dactyls, anapaests, spondees, iambs, etc., of Greek and Latin, languages whose syllabic quantities were fairly rigid—became the accepted terms in modern tongues of much more changeable quantities and emphatic stresses. Naturally the system proves a misfit; especially in English it is inaccurate and misleading— a mediaeval remainder oddly anachronistic in this age of scientific research. Even Edmund Gosse, by no means a radical, reminds us of its limitations:

[ 287 ]

It must not be forgotten that the prosodical terminology of the Greeks, which is often treated by non-poetical writers as something scientific and even sacrosanct, dates from a time when ancient literature had lost all its freshness and impulse, and was exclusively the study of analysts and grammarians.

Thus our inheritance of classic prosody has been as out of place as a renaissance altar in a Gothic cathedral. The trouble is, it was a superficial and partial affair to begin with, an analysis of appearances rather than fundamentals. Classic prosody was as scientific, no doubt, as classic chemistry, geography, physiology, or even astronomy; but it is no more satisfactory to a modern student than would be one of those dusty curios of the groping and unscientific past. That any remnant of this pseudo-science should have survived to trouble the poets of the very differently constructed English language is an anomaly which results merely in confusion and controversy. Prosody as the English grammarians have handed it to us, with its inherited Greek terms, its artificial scansion, its false grouping of measures, and its numerous other constrictions, should be swept away altogether, to make room for the building up of a true science of speech-rhythms, a science which may prove as useful to the poet of the future as the science of counterpoint is to the composer, of color and light to the painter, of proportion and stress to the architect, and of mathematics to all.

A beginning has been made, but progress is extremely slow, as this branch of scientific research offers pioneer hardships and few rewards. Sidney Lanier's *Science of English Verse* asked a few challenging questions, and pointed out that music-rhythms and verse-rhythms are essentially the same thing and follow the same fundamental laws; philologists, chiefly German, have written articles on speech-rhythms and verse-rhythms; and perhaps the most revolutionary contribution of all is Dr. W. M. Patterson's book on *The Rhythm of Prose,* with the phonographic researches which led up to it. Later than these, we have also the masterly treatise of E. A. Sonnenschein of the University of Birmingham, *What is Rhythm?* which should relegate all the old confusing errors to the dusty past. A beginning has been made in a true and universal science of prosody; but it has not penetrated far enough to be of much assistance to the poet, who, alone among artists, has been compelled to find out everything for himself.

MISCONCEPTION of this subject is still so general that it may be useful to clear the ground by some consideration of its elements. Not only many school rhetorics, but certain textbooks of prosody insist that the rhythm of English verse is, as they put it, "accentual," in contradistinction to the rhythm of classic verse, which they pronounce "quantitive." Even George Saintsbury, in his ponderous three-volume *History of English Prosody,* refuses to take sides "in the battle of Accent versus Quantity," which is as if one should preface a treatise on astronomy with a refusal to decide whether the earth goes around the sun or the sun around the earth.

Since Sidney Lanier, musician and analyst as well as poet, wrote his *Science of English Verse,* there is no longer any excuse for persistence in the old error. Rhythm is rhythm, and its laws are unchangeable, in poetry, in music, in the motion of tides and stars, in the vibration of sound-waves, light-waves, or the still more minute waves of molecular action. Always and everywhere rhythm is measured movement, a regular succession of time-intervals more or less marked off by stresses. English verse is as quantitive as Greek verse, because its primary rhythms depend quite as essentially upon the time-values of its syllables, upon its marshalling of long and short syllables in feet of a given length; while its secondary rhythms, its phrase-movements, mark off with larger curves longer rhythmic intervals. The fact that in English the syllabic "quantities" are more changeable than in Greek and Latin makes no difference with this essential truth; our verse also is quantitive, even though the Greek ear may have demanded more exactness in length of syllables, while the English ear permits our poets greater liberty in making many syllables long or short at will. Nor does our use of accent, rhyme and other devices, some of them unnecessary to the Greek poet, make any difference. Accent is universal in human speech, though slight in certain languages; while rhyme, alliteration, etc., also mark off and emphasize rhythmic intervals.

The best way of clearing our minds of error is to think of verse in terms of music. We have been told so persistently that an English foot consists of a given succession of "accented and unaccented syllables" that it becomes less confusing to discard the word foot altogether and use instead the musical term bar. It would be a good thing if we could also discard the old terms—iambic, trochaic, anapaestic, dactylic, etc.—and classify poetic measures merely as three-time or four-time. For this is the fundamental difference, and a recognition of it would make us free to analyze as many varieties of movement in each as there are in music. In modern poetry, as in modern music, the tendency is toward increasing freedom and variety of movement in both the bar and the phrase, involving closer and more extended intervals and subtler cadences. The music of Messrs. Debussy and d'Indy is paralleled by the poetry of Messrs. Vildrac, Romains and other young Parisians, and in English by that of the Imagists and others. But at present we are analyzing, not the new measures, but the old, as the iambic should be studied before *vers libre*. Nor can the secondary rhythm, the grouping of bars together in phrases, be considered until the movement within the bar is clearly understood.

All English poetry is in either three-time or four-time—that is, each bar counts three beats or four; for the language does not admit of the five-beat measure found infrequently in oriental poetry. If we continue using the old terms, the three-time measures are: the iambic, each typical foot or bar consisting of a short and a long syllable, to be indicated by an eighth and a quarter note; the trochaic, the trochee reversing the iambus; and the tribrach, consisting of three short syllables, represented by three eighth-notes. The four-time measures are: the anapaestic, each anapaest being two short syllables and one long; the dactylic, one long and two short; both these measures being varied by the spondee, a foot of two long syllables. The long syllable consumes in utterance twice as much time as the short, and in English usually, though not always, it carries a slight stress or accent. All the above measures are varied by rests, inversions, etc., exactly as in music; and modern free verse is showing us how great a variety is possible within the bar, especially in four-time, in the number and length of syllables and rests.

In a poem, as in a piece of music, the first technical point to be noted is the time: is the piece written in three-time or four-time? Does each bar count three beats or four? The musician is always informed, for the kindly composer states his time at the beginning of his opus as openly as he states his key; but the reader of poetry has to find out for himself whether a given poem is in three-time, thus belonging usually to the great iambic class, which includes probably ninety-nine hundredths of all English verse; or in four-time, so belonging usually to the much smaller anapaestic class.

Having discerned the measure of the poem, one may analyze the poet's lines exactly as the composer analyzes and writes down in notes the air which floats through his mind. One will need most of the musician's materials—that is, one will need quarter-notes and eighth-notes, and sometimes half-notes and sixteenth-notes; quarter-rests and eighth-rests, dots, ties and triplets—almost every device, in short, used by the musician for expressing time. The expression of tune is not attempted here.

Let us select for analysis one of the most beautiful strains of music in English verse, Shakespeare's seventy-first sonnet. The typical bar is an iambus; for example the bar *for me,* in which the first syllable counts one beat and the second two. The voice discovers in each line five bars followed by a pause of one bar; the first two lines showing no variation from the iambic type, while others vary widely, as follows:

No long - er mourn for me when I am dead

Than you shall hear the sur - ly sul - len bell

Give warn - ing to the world that I am fled

From this vile world, with vil - est worms to dwell.

[ 293 ]

Nay, if you read this line re-mem-ber not

The hand that writ it, for I love you so

That I in your sweet tho'ts would be for-got

If think-ing on me then should make you woe.

Oh if (I say) you look up-on this verse

When I per-haps com-pound-ed am with clay

Do not so much as my poor name re-hearse

But let your love even with my life de-cay:

Lest the wise world should look in-to your moan

And mock you with me aft-er I am gone.

The fourteen lines of this beautiful sonnet show almost all the variations of which iambic pentameter is capable. A few others may be found in the first three lines of Hamlet's most famous soliloquy:

To be or not to be— that is the ques-tion

Wheth-er 'tis no - bler in the mind to suf - fer

The slings and ar - rows of out - rag - eous fort-une

In these examples the voice pauses for the length of a bar at the end of each line; but this circumstance, though incidental in a large majority of lines, is by no means a rule for all. Blank verse, both epic and dramatic, often sweeps down line-boundaries, as in the following examples from Shakespeare and Milton:

> Besides, this Duncan
> Hath borne his faculties so meek, hath been
> So clear in his great office, that his virtues
> Will plead like angels, trumpet-tongued, against
> The deep damnation of his taking off.
>
> Of man's first disobedience, and the fruit
> Of that forbidden tree, whose mortal taste
> Brought death into the world and all our woe,
> With loss of Eden, till one greater man
> Restores us, etc.

In the common hymn measure, with lines of four and three feet, or bars, alternating, the voice always lengthens the short lines by a pause of one bar, as in *To the Cuckoo*, by Wordsworth:

Oh blithe new - com - er ! I have heard

I hear thee and re - joice

Oh cuck - oo ! shall I call thee bird,
Or but a wan - der - ing voice ?

Readers will vary slightly from these formulae, of
course, in minor details—for example, in the length of
certain syllables; but in general they will follow them
rather closely. Study of them will show that each bar,
like a bar of music, takes the same amount of time for
utterance as every other bar, except that the reader, like
the musician, varies the tempo in phrasing; it will show
that the succession of long and short syllables in these
bars, and also the position of the stress, or accent, varies
almost as widely in poetry as in music; that rests or
pauses of varying lengths occur frequently, sometimes
even at the point of usual stress, and more often than
not, to the length of an entire bar, at the end of each line;
that a long syllable sometimes bridges two bars, counting
one beat in each; and many other points—too many to
be mentioned.

Thus far we have studied only the iambic measure,
which is so dear, so natural to the English ear that until
the time of Shelley and Coleridge other measures were
rare in English verse, being found only, I think, in early
poems of the *Piers Ploughman* type, in certain ballads
and Elizabethan songs, and in Dryden's two musical odes.

Coleridge's *Christabel* is in the main iambic, but it is
richly varied by a free use of tribrachs and rests. It is
in tetrameter lines, three of which, typical of all, may
be analyzed as follows:

Trochaic verse is rare in English, but Shelley handled the measure with exquisite delicacy in this beautiful song from *Prometheus Unbound*. Strict accuracy would require, perhaps, a 6-8 measure for the notation of most trochaic verse, its alternate stresses being stronger than the others:

*The Skylark* is much less consistently trochaic, though on the whole it may be so classed. Longfellow's *Hiawatha* is a heavier example.

Longfellow's *Evangeline* is another three-time measure, one still rarer in English, which may account for the confusion of the commentators over this poem. Even Prof. Genung makes the usual mistake of saying that it is written in the dactylic hexameters of antiquity. But instead of the majestic four-time combination of dactyls and spondees which produced "the mighty thunder-roll of Homer's verse," Longfellow achieved only a light and lilting three-time measure, as follows:

[ 297 ]

This is the forest prim - e-val; the murmuring pines and the hemlocks–

Nothing could be more misleading than to call this measure dactylic. True dactyls are rare in English, being so difficult of achievement as to be impossible for a long poem. Mr. Charles G. D. Roberts has written a few fine classic hexameters, and George Meredith gives a hint of the true Homeric measure in his few fragments from the *Iliad*. For example:

Nay, nor is ev - er the roar of the fierce fire's rush so a-rous-ing

As rose then stu - pen-dous the Tro-jan's cry and A - chai -ans.

For English hexameters these are very good, though even our loose laws of quantity resent the poet's making the first syllable of *ever* long. The slow succession of long syllables in the second line produces an effect very rare in English verse. Spondees were common in Greek and Latin, but our poets have rarely used four-time measures. In our three-time iambic measures spondees are often used to vary the rhythm, but only by extending the length of one syllable into the next bar, as in the following lines from *The Tempest:*

Wound the loud winds, or with be-mock'd at stabs

Kill the still clos - ing wa - ters, as di - min - ish

[ 298 ]

Here *loud winds* and *still clos* are all long syllables, and the poet gains his spondaic effect by shortening the syllables which follow them.

George Meredith's *Love in a Valley,* which has many true spondees, is a charming experiment in four-time, of a movement much lighter than the classic hexameters:

Un - der yon - der beech-tree stand-ing on the green sward

Couched with her arms be - hind her lit - tle head—

Four-time measure of a still lighter movement, with a swift succession of short syllables and many rests, is much used nowadays in comic verse, especially in the librettos of comic operas. A familiar example is Bunthorne's song in Gilbert and Sullivan's *Patience:*

If you're anx-ious for to shine in the high aesthet-ic line

As a man of cult - ure rare—

All the above examples of four-time measures may be roughly called dactylic in type, since the long syllable and the stress usually begin the bar. But in English most four-time verse is anapaestic in type, with the long syllable and the stress at the end. Usually English poets treat their anapaestic verses very freely, not only using spondees, which are allowed, but often forcing short syllables to do the work of long ones—an irregularity which is not, however, so offensive to the English ear as it would have been to the Greek. Two masterpieces

of English anapaestic verse, Shelley's *Cloud* and Coleridge's *Ancient Mariner,* show all possible variations.
Here are the first two lines of the former poem:

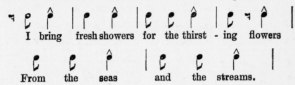

*The Ancient Mariner* has been a puzzle to the analysts,
because usually they have tried to scan it as iambic
verse, therefore in three-time, and so have quite missed
the secret of its slow and pounding four-time movement.
Many feet have only two syllables, it is true, but they
are either spondees or else the first syllable has one beat
of the bar and the second three. Two famous lines, for
example, read as follows, and therefore they are not in
the least iambic, even though each bar has but two syllables:

*The Ancient Mariner* has a magic music, but its
rhythm is perhaps the least bound by ancient rules of
all familiar English poems. A child feels it, but few of
the elders who sit in judgment have seemed to understand it. In the first stanza the slow fall of the long
syllables is very stately and beautiful. And the poem
holds this pace to the end:

It is | an an - cient mar - i - ner

And he stop-peth | one | of three

By thy long | gray beard | and glit - ter - ing eye

Now where - fore stoppst | thou me ?

The bride - groom's doors | are o - pened wide

And I | am next | of kin.

The guests | are met, | the feast | is set—

Mayst hear | the mer - ry | din.

Thus the four-time measure of this poem is richly varied, its typical foot being of two syllables, the second three times as long as the first. Spondees are common, the following line being almost entirely spondaic:

Hold off— | un - hand | me, gray - beard loon !

The poem may be roughly called anapaestic, if that term may be enlarged to include all four-time measures

which usually have the long syllable and the stress at the
end of each bar. The following line is all anapaestic:

For the sky  and the sea   and the sea   and the sky

Swinburne, of course, has sung in anapaests more than
any other poet, and held with more regularity to the
type. In certain poems of his the measure is perhaps
too regular and the music therefore monotonous. *Ata-
lanta in Calydon* has a number of anapaestic songs, for
example:

We have seen thee, O love, thou art fair, thou art good - ly, O Love!

Thy wings make light  in  the  air  as the wings  of  a dove.

Here is another anapaestic measure which he loves:

When the might  of  the  sum - mer

Is  most  on  the  sea:

When the days  o - ver - come  her

With  joy  but  to  be,

With rapt - ure of roy - al en-chant - ment, and sor -

cer - y that sets her not free—

Poe's *Raven* moves to a four-time measure, and therefore it is not in the least trochaic, as it used to be classed:

Once up-on a mid-night drear-y, as I pon-dered weak and wear-y

O-ver ma-ny a quaint and cu-ri-ous vol-ume of for - got-ten lore—

Shakespeare and one or two of his lyric contemporaries produced now and then a quite magical effect by a swift change of measure from three-time to four-time, or the reverse, as in every stanza of this song:

Come a - way, come a - way, Death,

And in sad cy - press let me be laid.

Fly a - way, fly a - way, breath—

I am slain by a fair cru - el maid.

My shroud of white, stuck all with yew—

Oh pre - pare it!

My part of death no one so true

Did share it.

Tennyson tries the same experiment in this song, with a success somewhat less exquisite:

The splen-dor falls on cast - le walls

And snow - y sum-mits old in sto - ry

The long light shakes a - cross the lakes

And the wild cat - a - ract leaps in glo - ry

Blow, bu - gle, blow! set the wild ech-oes fly - ing!

Blow, bu - gle, an-swer ech-oes— dy - ing, dy - ing, dy - ing!

These analyses cover almost all the variations usual in English metrics. Certain measures, common in Greek and Latin, alter their rhythms when English poets experiment with them. A classic choriambic foot, for example, consists of four syllables—a long, two shorts, and a long, and counts six beats; whereas in the hands of Swinburne and others it becomes a charming thing, but very different. Horace's choriambic lines run thus:

Ex - e - gi mon - u - ment' ae - re per-en - ni - us

In English the attempt to write such a line results as follows:

Come, love, o - ver the fields, green with the spring's first kiss.

The Latin measure is stately, the English is a delicate dance-time.

*Vers libre,* whose rhythmic subtleties may be only at the beginning of their development, is a demand for greater freedom of movement within the bar and the line. In the following examples, quoted by Charles Vildrac in his *Notes sur la Technique Poétique,* the four bars, or feet, in each are of the same length, while the number of syllables varies from two to six:

*Cette rose | à ton corsage |*
*Cette fleur rouge | à ton col entr'ouvert | . . . |*
—*André Salmon*
*Oh elles existent, | elles attendent, |*
*Ils n'auraient qu'à choisir, | ils n'auraient qu'à prendre. |*
—*Charles Vildrac*

The above analysis is, I repeat, elementary, and perhaps too conservative in attempting to use the familiar terms of the old unscientific classification and nomenclature.

[ 305 ]

The analysis of poetic rhythm on the basis of musical notation seems so obvious as to make it incredible that Sidney Lanier should have been the first to apply it to English verse. Poets usually think too little about the elements and laws of that verse-music which must be an instinct with them. A closer study would enrich their own rhythms, and greater zeal in acquainting the public with the technique of poetry would increase the general understanding of the art. More scientific knowledge of this subject is necessary in order to remove English poetic theory from the rack of "accentual" prosody, and restore it to the great universal laws of rhythm, to which all music and the poetry of all languages must consciously or unconsciously conform.

RHYTHM—the universality of the principle, its scientific basis, its application in the arts, especially in the speech arts—has always fascinated me. Of course it is an element of unalterable law: from the electron to the most enormous sun in space, every object moves rhythmically, in vibrations or pulsations or orbits, hastened or retarded between incredible extremes of slow or swift. All life is governed by heart-beats, and the arts are man's effort to respond to the universal impulse, his effort to create movement in time, or to mark off color-rhythms and space rhythms in patterns which suggest that movement.

From childhood I have groped among rhythms strongly felt but difficult to analyze. Many of them are beyond the scope of this inquiry—they would lead us far afield; but among them I have speculated long and often on the rhythmic laws that govern verse, prose, and speech—laws which these phenomena of human utterance can not escape. It has seemed to me obvious that not verse alone is rhythmical, but that prose also, whether on the page or the tongue, is bound to follow the universal law, is set to a pattern of time-intervals which it must unconsciously fulfil. And it has seemed to me strange that whereas musical notation is, in effect, a scientific analysis—a kind of picturing—of the rhythms of music, neither verse nor prose has been scientifically presented in any exact system of notation. Science, which has been speculating during the past century in almost every other direction, has apparently neglected to investigate language-rhythms— for of course the puerile systems of verse-scansion inherited from our ancestors are as unscientific and out of date as pre-Galileo astronomy.

So it is like going home after a long journey to read *The Rhythm of Prose,* by Dr. William Morrison Patterson, published by the Columbia University Press. Science has been invading at last my favorite field; indeed, she has been building up, during the last twenty years, quite a bibliography on the subject, while I, ignorant of the German language and of journals of psychology and philology, have been groping along with only Lanier's *Science of English Verse* for a basis—a book which began the discussion in 1880. Dr. Patterson, fully informed in all this literature, possesses also a scientific mind, and scientific instruments for making photographic and phonographic records of the human voice in its utterance of both verse and prose.

I am quite out of sympathy with those sensitive poetic souls who resent this intrusion of science. The truth can do no harm, and in this case it must do incalculable good in the enrichment of our sense of rhythmic values. The poet of the future, discarding the wilful empiricism of the past and proceeding upon exact knowledge, will greatly develop and enrich our language-rhythms just as music-rhythms are being developed and enriched by composers fully educated in their art, who add knowledge and training to that primal impulse of heart and mind which we call genius. The poet hitherto has worked in the dark, or at least in a shadow-land illumined only by his own intuition. Henceforth science will lend her lamp; she will hand him the laws of rhythm just as she hands to the painter the laws of light and color, or to the architect the laws of proportion and stress.

Dr. Patterson has made a good beginning, and I read his book with complete sympathy and accord except when he tries to draw with more or less definiteness a line between the rhythms of prose and verse, calling the former "syncopated" and the latter "coincident"; or, as he puts it:

> Language is regarded as rhythmically "prose" so long as syncopation and substitution predominate over coincidence between the accented syllables and an under-unit series of subjective time-intervals. When coincidence predominates, language is rhythmically "verse."

This seems to me an effort to explain a difference which does not exist. I wish he would throw all such distinctions into the scrap-heap, where the old metrical distinctions—iambic, trochaic, dactyllic, anapaestic, etc.— must be thrown by every modern mind, not because they are entirely false but because they are inexact, and are moreover inextricably associated with false usage, so that the subject of poetic rhythms requires a new notation and nomenclature.

I find syncopated rhythms in verse—metrical as well as free—and coincident rhythms in prose; and a somewhat prolonged and diversified study of the subject inclines me to say that no absolute line can be drawn between the rhythms of verse and prose. They fade into each other by gradations so slight as to be indistinguishable. If we confine our inquiry to English, and begin, let us say, with the sharply defined iambics and systematized caesuras of Pope, we glide unconsciously, through numerous stages, into the "freer" larger rhythms of Shakespearean or Miltonic blank verse. From these it is but a step to the varied rhythms of the best free verse; from these but another step to the finest poetic prose (the Gettysburg speech, for example). The next rhythmic step from this brings us to more conscious oratory (Webster's reply to Hayne is an example), and from this we could pass gradually toward the pitter-patter rhythms of common journalese, then the tum-te-tum of cheap verse, and before long complete the circle back to Pope again.

The anapaests of Shelley and Swinburne, the carefully weighed spondaic-dactyllics of Meredith, would fall into the circle as four-time variations of a pattern usually three-time in English verse but accepting four-time more readily in prose. And the various lyric forms are but the weaving of closer patterns.

I maintain that each step in the above process marks a difference of degree merely. The commonest talk of journalese falls inevitably, as Sievers says, into *"sprech-takte,* or speech-bars, with a tendency to equal duration." And in the greatest poetry ever written we have merely this same assembling of time-units, only they are more adroitly assembled and grouped, with a more conscious measuring of syllables and weighing of stresses. The underlying rhythmic principle is the same, I repeat, in both prose and verse.

The rhythmic difference, scientifically speaking, between verse and prose is rather, I should say, in the *grouping* of time-units (let us call them by the musical term bars)—rather in the *grouping* of bars, which is cadence, than in syncopation or coincidence within the bar itself. In verse, and more or less in poetic prose, the cadence tends to return upon itself, to effect what Miss Lowell calls a "curve." It is the sweep of this secondary rhythm which counts, which makes the distinction between poetic and prose rhythms. And this secondary rhythm is no more "occult" in good free verse than it is in good metrical verse.

Dr. Patterson talks a little wildly, I think, in his chapter headed *Vers Libre.* Either *vers libre* has been badly read into his instruments—which is all too probable —or he accepts as *vers libre* some of its hopelessly prosy modern manifestations. In a later article which he contributed to the *North American Review,* we find his mind cleared of its misconceptions. Here he classifies English rhythms as follows, linking up modern free verse with the ancient Anglo-Saxon rhythms; and he concludes by urging the poets toward fuller and still freer experiments:

Unitary verse, the elastic swing of which furnishes a key both to Miss Lowell's *Painter on Silk* and to the disputed rhythm of *Beowulf,* our most ancient epic; metrical verse, in which our later poets did their singing and conjuring; spaced prose, the oratorical and "embroidering" form of syncopating experience that characterizes so much current *vers libre;* and, finally, fluid or normal prose, such as we find, for example, in Addison, in Macaulay, and, with singular perfection, in Newman—these are the four major *genres.* Mosaics and blends, polyphonic prose and polyphonic verse—these are their permutations and combinations. It is the discussion of *vers libre,* however, that has led us to our attempts at an analysis which we hope possesses some practical value for literary artists. Our heart is with all poets—metrical and free; but we are particularly indebted just now to those of our contemporaries who have instinctively composed in these *genres* and thus helped us so materially to hear, or to think we hear, not only the music of

[ 311 ]

everyday language—the rhythm of its prose—but also its ancestral cadence, the forgotten swing of "unitary verse."

This lost child of our House of Rhythm, after so long wandering unrecognized through the "mosaic" paths of the King James Version, of William Blake, of Walt Whitman, of Synge, and of Tagore's translations, is worth being rescued and presented in proper integrity. The final word as to this lies with the poets, not the critics. You have our affection—however we may glare at you in the precincts of our dungeon-laboratories. Your generation is proving its gift of fire. . . . . We believe in you younger poets particularly, and in your future; for, apart from our impressions of your vigor and sincerity, surely it is a significant thing if, in your newest songs, we hear, quite suddenly, the harp of our ancestors!

It is hardly necessary to say that Prof. Patterson's book, and the above remarks on the subject, concern rhythms alone, and that none of the other elements—emotion, imagination, tone-color, sound-quality, etc.,—are considered, elements which unite with rhythm to make up poetic beauty, and to assert the distinction between poetry and prose.

A FRENCHMAN of my acquaintance, becoming aware recently of the emergence of the United States from barbarism, uttered a lament which gave me a new sensation: "So great a people," he exclaimed, "and no language of their own!"

I confess it had never occurred to me that a nation needed a separate and individual language of its own to sustain or prove its greatness, or that our inheritance of English speech and literature was anything but an advantage. There is a sense, however, in which my friend's lament was not unjustified, for an inherited language means inherited racial traditions and loyalties, inherited literary forms and practices. It means acceptance instead of creation, acquiescence instead of a fresh adventure. And acceptance, acquiescence, may easily go too far and become a fixed habit.

With the English language and literature we inherited the classic prosody, and followed its laws as a matter of course in all our earlier attempts at poetry. Now the classic prosody is a formidable affair. With Greece for its sire and Rome for its dam, it had ruled the mediaeval family of languages, and held their aspiring lyric offspring within strict and proper metric bounds. The run-away Anglo-Saxon son and heir, far off in his isolated island, had at first shown a rebellious disregard of family rules and precepts; but a great poet named Chaucer had taken him in hand at just the right formative moment,

[ 313 ]

and impressed upon him the superiority of the iambic Gallic paces over the heavy lumbering hoof-beats of song which his saga-singing mother had been crooning to him from her northern memories.

Thus the three-time iambic measure became the accepted rule in English poetry. And a very good rule it has been on the whole, bringing out the flexibility, the musical variety, of the somewhat Normanized Anglo-Saxon tongue of our forefathers. Until the closing decade of the eighteenth century there were few exceptions, certain Elizabethan songs and Dryden's two musical odes offering almost the only experiments in four-time rhythms attempted in English since Langland wrote *Piers Ploughman*.

Elsewhere in this volume I have criticized our modern acceptance of the pseudo-science of prosody, which we have inherited from the unscientific past and from languages of different structure. For the purpose of this inquiry, let the old terms be forgotten, and let us study verse-rhythms as marking either three or four beats to the bar. And let us remember that in verse, as in music, a three-time bar has been made up in various ways in the work of our greatest poets. In Shakespeare's seventy-first sonnet, for example, I find usually the typical iambic bar; that is, a short syllable and a stressed long one, whose time may be expressed by an eighth-note and a quarter-note. But I also find the following variations: short, rest, short; three shorts; short syllable and long rest; rest and two shorts; two very shorts and a long, etc.

In other words, the English poets have by no means made up their bars on the *ti-túm ti-túm ti-túm* principle of a pure iambic succession, but have varied this succession to the limit of their power. And when Shelley, Coleridge, occasionally Burns and Byron, afterward Hood, Swinburne, and many others, tried experiments with four-time measures, they found possible a still greater variety of syllabic movement within the bar.

Thus we find that English poets have usually defied the grammarians and been more "free" than the laws allowed. When they departed from this course, when they made and obeyed strict metrical rules, as in the Queen Anne period, they merely prepared the way for a revolution. Shelley and Coleridge rebelled against Pope, Whitman and the modern vers-librists against the Victorians. No man, least of all a poet, can afford to walk in fetters; and each rebellion has widened his range.

The modern vers-librists, then—I use the word in the English-American, not the French sense—have fought for elbow-room, for greater freedom of movement in the bar, the line, the cadence, the strophe. In so far as they have written poetry, and not what Howells wittily called "shredded prose," their fight has availed to break down the grammarians' smug barriers and enrich the language with beautiful poems in a new, or at least newly recovered, mode.

Whitman was a self-sufficient personality, the rare type of man who, isolated and alone, moves on in his own way quite unconscious that other ways have been hitherto preferred, and untempted by their comparative ease and smoothness. The exact metrics of the prosodists might never have been invented so far as he was concerned; what D. H. Lawrence calls his "lovely, lovely form and rhythm" was his own personal achievement, "the perfect utterance of a concentrated spontaneous soul." Its influence moved fitfully, and in unexpected ways. His neighbors knew him not, but in attics across the sea lesser instruments tuned in with his orchestra, and his sweeping clouds of sound became delicate nuances. Paris grew aware of him, and Paris transmuted and passed on his rhythmic influence. And the little group of young poets in London who called themselves Imagists received the gospel of freedom from Mallarmé and the rest, written cloistrally, as it were, on fine parchment with decorated and illuminated lettering.

They proceeded, with religious fervor, to put in practice the new ideas and impose them on an art which had stiffened and prettified under the old formulae. Rhythms, whether three-time or four-time, were to be more varied through a freer action of syllables and rests within the bar, a more individual grouping of bars in lines, and a larger, more musical sweep of the rhythmic phrase across the barriers of bar and line. Poetry, in the opinion of these experimenters, could no more rest on the rhythmic laurels won by the great poets of the past than the sister-art of music could be content forever within harmonic boundaries set by the masterpieces of Beethoven, Mozart, or Brahms. If modern music could make room for Debussy and Stravinsky and even jazz, modern poetry should be able to listen with an open mind to Ezra Pound and H. D. and Richard Aldington, and whatever "Others" might try still more adventurous experiments, even though they should ride roughshod over long-accepted precepts and prejudices.

At the head of this group, in 1912 earlier and later, was Ezra Pound, a man who, whatever one may think of his poetry, was born a great teacher, born to be a leader of a school. An inquiring and provocative mind is his, never content with the conventionally accepted thing, always searching beneath surfaces and appearances, always violently rejecting the lifeless, the over-ornate, the stilted, the merely formal. An inspiring influence this poet has been, unfailing in the courage of his convictions; leading others, not necessarily to agree with him, but to examine their own foundations and standards.

When the poets of this small group, foregathering in London though mostly Americans, began to send their poems to Chicago and print them in the first numbers of *Poetry* during 1912 and 1913, "Imagism," though a wee small voice, was very upsetting to those who heard it. Many were the "Is-this-poetry?" protests received by the editors during that first exciting year. Yet changes have moved along so rapidly during the past decade that these first poems of the revolution seem hardly revolutionary as one reads them today.

Richard Aldington's *Choricos,* in the second number of *Poetry,* was the first Imagist poem ever printed. As it holds its own, in my opinion, not only as one of the finest poems of the group, but as one of the finest of this century, it may be well to pause long enough for a slight analysis.

Except for its use of *"thou,"* permissible in a poem solemnly addressing Death in a Greek guise, the diction is the English of modern speech. The words are chosen for tonal quality and beauty of sound—rich full syllables that move slowly in tribute to the majesty of the subject, a hymn in praise of Death. The measure is a slowly marching four-time, singularly free and varied in detail; showing a frequent use of long syllables, sometimes in spondaic succession, sometimes with rests. One might diagram the basic rhythm of this poem about as follows, the bars being (theoretically as in music) of equal length, and each quarter- or eighth-note representing a long or short syllable:

The an - cient songs

Pass death - ward mourn - ful - ly.

Cold lips that sing no more, and with-ered wreaths,

Re - gret - ful eyes, and droop-ing breasts and wings—

Sym - bols of an - cient songs

Mourn - ful - ly pass - ing

Down to the great white sur - ges,

Watched of none

[ 318 ]

I doubt if the most conventional prosodist would deny the rhythmic beauty of this majestically marching poem. Yet, though in four-time, it is neither anapaestic nor dactylic. The rhythmic pattern, while absolute and authoritative, shows much more variety than had been customary in English verse.

In the notes of this early number of *Poetry,* Mr. Aldington is described as "a young English poet, one of the 'Imagists,' a group of ardent Hellenists who are pursuing interesting experiments in *vers libre,* trying to attain in English certain subtleties of cadence of the kind which Mallarmé and his followers have studied in French." The name which these poets had chosen, then printed for the first time, became part of the signature under their second group in *Poetry,* which were by "H. D., Imagiste," a poet who has been called the most imagistic of the school. The almost staccato movement of her three-time poems was very different from the legato of *Choricos.* An analysis of one of her shorter poems, *Oread,* published later and famous as typical of the school, may be of service:

The above diagrams, one in four-time and the other in three-time, offer merely a hint of basic rhythms; but they show that free verse is metrical in the sense that it divides into time-unit bars, and they suggest the variety of movement attainable in measures less confining than the statutory iambic, than Shelley's four-time anapaestic-spondaic in *The Cloud,* or even the strictly schooled experiments of Swinburne. On the basic rhythmic pattern, whatever it be, of any poem the poet weaves his larger cadences, the rhythmic phrase carrying the metric bars as a great wave carries ripples. Free verse has been called by Amy Lowell "cadence verse," but all poetry is

[ 320 ]

cadence verse in this sense, that all poetry has a double rhythm, an overlay of sweeping cadences on the smaller patterns of time-unit bars. Miss Lowell powerfully sponsored the movement through those *Some Imagists* anthologies of 1915-16-17, which, with her explanatory prefaces, aroused widespread interest and discussion.

The Imagists strove not only for a freer prosody, newer and more personal rhythms, and the language of modern speech, but also for the integrity of the image, for a hard clear style, and for a rigid concentration which should discard every unnecessary word, every unstructural ornament. It is hardly too much to say that they have imposed these conditions on their contemporaries, that no poet today can disregard them with impunity. The old lavish diffuseness, the sentimental softness, the rhetorical eloquence, the "poetic" diction, theme and ornament, so common a half-century ago, are not the modern wear. I don't mean that the Imagists have been the only influence in this direction: the Irish group, headed by Yeats and Synge, were earlier in the field with similar ideas, certain translations from the Orient and from Roumanian and other folklore had exemplified them, and the poetry of Emily Dickinson and Edwin Arlington Robinson had stripped the art bare of eloquence and furbelows. But the Imagists came at the psychological moment when these influences were ripening to a climax, and their formulated and announced doctrine clinched the ban upon the old excesses and made the "revolution" an accomplished fact.

The free-verse movement has been essentially a plea for a personal rhythm, for the poet's independence in working out his most expressive form and using it without prejudice. It has called typography to its aid as a legitimate emphasis—an aid which countless mere pretenders have invoked to make their "shredded prose" look like poetry, thereby confusing a too casual public. Besides triumphing in the many serious poems of great beauty which have enriched our literature of this period, the form has proved a delightfully variable medium for experiments in the whimsical, the grotesque—moods too rare in English verse. Alfred Kreymborg's gay monthly *Others,* running through 1916-17 and perpetuating its entries in anthologies, enlivened us with all discoverable audacities, some of them as successful examples of the grotesque as were ever achieved by the cleverest cartoonist or carver of netsukes. Free verse, in short, may fit any mood with a masterpiece, if only the poet be a great enough master.

Most of the poets considered in the first section of this volume have followed this method either wholly or in an important part of their work. Carl Sandburg uses free verse entirely, Edgar Lee Masters turned to it for *Spoon River* and many other poems. Wallace Stevens has invoked it for his plays and many of his finest lyrics. Maxwell Bodenheim has done his best work with it. Amy Lowell, Marjorie Seiffert, Marianne Moore, Helen Hoyt, have all sounded its harmonies to very different effects. Lew Sarett, Constance Skinner and others have matched aboriginal tunes to its cadences. Alfred Kreymborg, Orrick Johns, Carlos Williams, have found it expressive of both whimsicalities and dreams. Indeed, it would be impossible even to mention the names of the poets who have used free forms with high distinction during the past ten or twelve years. For free verse has a wider range of expressiveness than the exact metrics so long in vogue, and probably, in the hands of masters, an equal range of beauty.

## THE END